THE MYSTIC QUEST

David S. Ariel

The Mystic Quest

An Introduction to Jewish Mysticism

Schocken Books New York

The author gratefully acknowledges permission to reprint excerpts from the following material: *The Varieties of Religious Experience* by William James. Reprinted by permission of William Collins Sons & Co. Ltd., Glasgow, Scotland. • *Zohar: The Book of Splendor* by Gershom Scholem. Reprinted by permission of Schocken Books, published by Pantheon Books, a division of Random House, Inc., New York. Copyright 1949, renewed 1977, by Schocken Books Inc. • *The Sages: Their Beliefs and Opinions* by Efraim Urbach. English edition, 1975, vol. 1. Reprinted by permission of The Magnes Press, Jerusalem. • *Mishnat ha-Zohar* by Isaiah Tishby, Hebrew edition, vols. 1 and 2. Reprinted by permission of The Bialik Institute, Jerusalem. • *Zohar: The Book of Enlightenment* translated by Daniel Matt, Copyright © 1983 by Daniel Matt. From the Classics of Western Spirituality Series. Used by permission of Paulist Press, Ramsey, New Jersey.

Library of Congress Cataloging-in-Publication Data

Ariel, David S.
    The mystic quest : an introduction to Jewish mysticism / David Ariel.
      p.   cm.
    Originally published: Northvale, N.J. : J. Aronson, c1988.
    Includes bibliographical references and index.
    ISBN 0-8052-1003-2 (pbk.)
    1. Mysticism—Judaism—History.   2. Cabala—History.
    I. Title.
[BM723.A69   1992]
296.7′12′09—dc20   91-50861

To Kay

CONTENTS

ACKNOWLEDGMENTS

This work is the product of a fifteen-year study of *Kabbalah* to which I was introduced by Prof. Asher Finkel at New York University. My studies continued at The Hebrew University of Jerusalem under the guidance of Profs. Rivka Schatz-Uffenheimer, Isaiah Tishby, Yosef Dan, and Efraim Gottlieb and, later, at Brandeis University under the direction of Prof. Alexander Altmann. Prof. Marvin Fox of Brandeis University introduced me to a conceptual and philosophical approach to Jewish mysticism, which formed the underlying method of this book. Prof. Gershom Scholem, the pioneer in the modern study of Jewish mysticism, whom I served as a teaching assistant at Boston University, helped me immeasurably in my studies.

My colleagues and friends at Wesleyan University, particularly Profs. Jeremy Zwelling and Paul Schwaber, introduced me to fresh conceptual approaches to the study of religion drawn from the fields of religious studies and psychology. Dr. Rosemary Balsam introduced me to innovative ways of thinking about kabbalistic symbolism drawn from her perspective as a psychoanalyst. Other close friends, including Prof. Joel Rosenberg and Dr. David Paradise, contributed new ways of thinking about issues of deep concern to me.

The Jewish community of Cleveland has provided me with the opportunity and motivation to write this book. The students at the Cleveland College of Jewish Studies, a center of higher Jewish learning for adults and educators, have inspired me to write a book that introduces and explains Jewish mysticism. My close colleagues and friends at the College, Profs. Moshe Berger, Ori Z. Soltes, Bernard Steinberg, and Lifsa Schachter have offered valuable suggestions and criticisms in the course of writing this book. Good friends and colleagues, especially Profs. Rachel Elior and Lawrence Fine, and Linda Tobin-Pepper, challenged me with their questions and suggestions along the way. Joshua Rubenstein served as my model and mentor in all matters literary.

This book could not have been written had it not been for the support and encouragement of the Board of Governors of the College, particularly its Chairman, Dan Aaron Polster. The staff of the College, especially Dr. Deborah Polster, enabled me to devote precious and undisturbed time to this book. My able and amiable assistant, Jan Vrh, provided valuable technical assistance and support. Jacqueline Stern prepared the bibliography. Jean Loeb Lettofsky, Director of the Library, assisted by providing many difficult-to-locate books. The professional leadership of the Jewish community, especially Steve Hoffman, Barry Shrage, and David Kleinman, have helped broaden my own intellectual horizons beyond the scholarly world to the Jewish community in countless ways.

Through his deep personal interest and knowledge of the subject, Arthur Kurzweil, Acquisitions Editor of Jason Aronson Inc., has supported me throughout the project with his comments and questions. Elena Le Pera, Production Editor, has patiently guided this book and the author through the labyrinth of production with able assistance from Muriel Jorgensen, Editorial Director, and Becky Amster, Copy Editor. To all of these, I owe a debt of gratitude.

I am grateful to Bonny Fetterman, senior editor of Schocken Books, for her consistent support and devotion to this book, and I am pleased that this paperback edition is published by Schocken, whose list always represented to me the greatest tradition of modern Jewish writing.

My wife, Kay, and our children, Judah, Micah, and Aviva, have lived with this book for several years. Kay is the ideal reader for whom I write, and for that reason this book is dedicated to her.

David S. Ariel

INTRODUCTION

In the last two centuries Jews have often discounted the presence of a persistent mystical tradition in their midst. Although there have been powerful mystical movements in Judaism since antiquity, modern Jews living in Western countries found these parts of the Jewish tradition to be among the most cumbersome baggage they carried into modernity.

Mysticism and Judaism have been inextricably linked together since antiquity. During the second century mystical practices were common among the most learned and respected rabbis and perhaps among people on the periphery of normative Judaism. Since then mysticism has assumed a prominent place in Judaism and has exercised an important influence upon Jewish history. It is, therefore, surprising that so little is commonly understood today about the mystical tradition in Judaism.

Some of the most important prayers in Judaism, such as *Lekhah Dodi* (Come, My Beloved), which is recited each Friday evening, involve mystical interpretations of Judaism unfamiliar to most people today. This prayer, surprisingly, is a hymn to the feminine dimension of God and involves an attempt to unify the supposedly masculine and feminine aspects of the hidden God. Similarly, Martin Buber's retelling of Hasidic legends is incomprehensible without some knowledge of the Jewish mystical tradition that has all but disappeared in the last two hundred years. Yet even today, the mystical tradition breathes in the fiction of Isaac Bashevis Singer and the graphic art of Yaacov Agam.

This book introduces the reader to the breadth and depth of Jewish mysticism. It is intended to make the meaning of Jewish mysticism accessible to a general audience in two ways. First, I have explained the underlying meaning of Jewish mysticism in language that can be understood by an uninitiated reader. Jewish mystics speak in a rich, symbolic language that is incomprehensible without a guide and explanation. Second, I have translated many passages from Jewish mystical literature originally written in Hebrew and Aramaic. I have also drawn upon the growing volume of scholarly literature on the subject, much of which has been written in Hebrew and German. Most works written in English about Jewish mysticism are either too scholarly or too inaccurate to faithfully represent the subject. The task of this author, therefore, has been to serve as a translator in a dual capacity.

The Mystic Quest is concerned primarily with the development and meaning of the *Kabbalah*. *Kabbalah* (pronounced *kab-ba-lah'*), literally the Hebrew word for *tradition,* is the name of the Jewish mystical movement that began in southern France and Spain around 1200 and was joined by many adherents during the eighteenth and nineteenth centuries. Although at times *Kabbalah* was the dominant religious movement in Judaism, it was largely abandoned by Jews living in Europe and other Western lands after the French Revolution.

Beginning in the late eighteenth century, Jews were allowed out of the ghettos and were admitted, many for the first time in history, into European society. But the price of admission into modern society often was the surrender of those characteristics that set the Jews apart, such as their styles of dress and eating, their language, their unique observances, and even their religious beliefs. In order to prove that they were as modern as anyone else, many Jews dispensed with those teachings that stressed the uniqueness of Judaism, the divine character of the Torah, the special relationship between the Jews and God, and the belief in the messiah in favor of more universal, rational, and modern ideas. In the process of proving their worthiness as citizens, many Jews abandoned the most unique elements of their religion and suppressed much of the powerful tradition and folklore of Judaism.

Although the *Kabbalah* is a unified tradition of Jewish mysticism, there are many different schools of thought within the *Kabbalah*. I have presented the main outlines of the *Kabbalah* without attempting to take into account the entire range and variety of beliefs within the movement. I have presented what I believe to be the main elements of Jewish mysticism in an understandable fashion even if it has meant some loss of accuracy in areas where scholars might wish for more precision.

The *Kabbalah* contains many Jewish traditions and spiritual teachings that reflect the popular imagination of the Jews throughout history. This mystical tradition has been a perennial aspect of the Jewish religion. In the modern age, however, the mystic quest in Judaism has been relegated to the discarded past. Jews today often search in vain for spiritual depth. Some have turned away from Judaism and even look to other religions to find their spiritual sustenance. Few are aware that Judaism contains a rich and complex mystical dimension waiting to be uncovered. This book was written in part to make this aspect of Jewish culture accessible to people in search of their cultural and religious roots.

David S. Ariel

A NOTE TO THE READER

I have employed certain conventions that may be unfamiliar to many readers. Dates according to the Gregorian calendar are usually indicated by B.C. (*Before Christ*) and A.D. (*Anno Domini,* Latin for *in the year of our Lord*). Since these conventions reflect a Christian concept of history, they are generally regarded as inappropriate among historians of Judaism. The terms B.C.E. (*Before the Common Era*) and C.E. (*Common Era*) are used when writing Jewish history. I have employed these terms throughout this book in reference to dates according to the Gregorian calendar.

There are several common systems employed in transliterating Hebrew terms. The most popular form is the phonetic system that is in standard usage in popular books, magazines, and newspapers. The disadvantage of this system is that it does not accurately correlate with the original Hebrew. I have adopted the less familiar system of transliteration employed in modern scholarly literature. It is a modified version of the transliteration rules of the *Encyclopedia Judaica*. Certain common spellings have been maintained, such as "Kabbalah," for terms that have generally entered common English usage.

All translations in this work are my own, except where otherwise noted as quoted from another source.

All passages from the Hebrew Bible have been cited in the translation of the Jewish Publication Society.

TRANSLITERATION RULES

א	–		ל	l
בּ	b		מ	m
ב	v		נ	n
ג	g		ס	s
ד	d		ע	–
ה	h		פּ	p
ו	v		פ	f
ז	z		צ	tz
ח	h		ק	k
ט	t		ר	r
י	y, i at the end of a word		שׁ	sh
כּ	k		שׂ	s
כ	kh		ת	t

1

Seekers of Unity:

The Nature of Mysticism

What is mysticism? The *Oxford English Dictionary* defines *mysticism* as follows:

> The opinions, mental tendencies, or habits of thought and feeling, characteristic of mystics; mystical doctrines or spirit; belief in the possibility of union with the Divine nature by means of ecstatic contemplation; reliance on spiritual intuition or exalted feeling as the means of acquiring knowledge of mysteries inaccessible to intellectual apprehension.

The earliest usage of the root word *myein,* from which the term mysticism derives, occurs among the ancient Greeks who coined the term *mystikos* to describe a ritual in which one shuts one's eyes in order to close off the world and experience other realities.[1] In the seventh century B.C.E., for example, practitioners (*mystes*) of the mystery cult at Eleusis would detach themselves from mundane stimuli during the festivals celebrating the sowing, sprouting, and reaping of grain harvests. The *mystes* would participate in secret rituals that dramatized the myth of the mother goddess, Demeter, the goddess of grain, and her daughter, Persephone, who was captured by Hades, god of the dead. Although no account of the actual practices exists, some records indicate that

1

the rituals of the Eleusinian cults involved elaborate initiation ceremonies consisting of eating, drinking, singing, ritual bathing, and meditative trances that culminated in symbolic marriages with the gods.[2]

Mysticism today has come to mean something other than the technique of initiation into mystery cults. William James (1842–1910), brother of novelist Henry James, describes some of the characteristics of mysticism in his book *The Varieties of Religious Experience: A Study in Human Nature*. When he wrote this book in 1902, he was an American pioneer exploring the psychology of religion, a field that had not yet been touched by the theories of Sigmund Freud. James attempted to understand the psychology of religious experiences, feelings, and impulses. He drew his evidence from literature, especially works written in English by Christian authors, and case histories.

According to James, *mysticism* is the term used to characterize ineffable and indescribable religious experiences. Mysticism is at the core of religion, he states, because "personal religious experience has its root and center in mystical states of consciousness."[3] Mysticism, in his view, refers to the essence of a particular human experience rather than to the specific technique by which such an experience is induced. No description of the substance of a mystical experience can adequately be expressed in words. Many people who have had mystical experiences describe them as fleeting, unanticipated occurrences which produce altered states of consciousness. James cites one such experience as an example of a mystical testimony:

> Suddenly, and always, I think, when my muscles were at rest, I felt the approach of the mood. Irresistibly, it took possession of my mind and will, lasted what seemed an eternity, and disappeared in a series of rapid sensations which resembled the awakening from anesthetic influence. One reason why I disliked this kind of trance was that I could not describe it to myself. I cannot even now find words to render it intelligible. It consisted in a gradual but swiftly progressive obliteration of space, time, sensation and the multitudinous factors of experience which seem to qualify what we are pleased to call our Self.[4]

This experience has no connection with initiation into a specific religion or cult. It is a highly individual experience with no reference to a particular content. There is no preparation, training, or initiation process prior to the advent of the experience. It occurs passively and involuntarily in a state of rest and repose rather than being actively induced through initiation, ceremony, or ritual. Members of the Eleusinian mystery cult experience contact with the gods and can describe the experience but choose not to. James' respondent, however, cannot put his experience into words. The account, moreover, relates a feeling of unpleasantness rather than the elation characteristic of some of the earlier mystery cults.

This account, however, includes several features that are common to many forms of mysticism. The experience produces an altered state of consciousness. Conscious awareness of mundane reality recedes, changing the physiological responses to external stimuli, and a hypnotic or other trance-like state is entered. The perception of time and space and orientation to the world changes in ways that cannot be described. The mystic experiences this as a change in consciousness and a new awareness of other levels of reality that are not accessible to normal consciousness. The experience leads to a change in his orientation to himself and to the world. Although the experience itself is transitory and cannot be sustained, the mystic remains changed by the experience. All subsequent experiences may be understood in light of this new awareness.

Many of James' subjects describe a mystical experience as more than just an emotional state. Their encounters have a noetic quality or an element of insight, knowledge, intuition, or revelation not normally acquired through rational means. Such knowledge, they testify, has an authority that endures and influences their lives long after the event itself has passed. R. M. Bucke, author of *Cosmic Consciousness,* a classic of futurist inspiration and mystical investigation, recounts one such experience after a quiet evening with friends discussing poetry and philosophy.

My mind, deeply under the influence of the ideas, images and emotions called up by the reading and talk, was calm and peaceful. I was in a state of quiet, almost passive enjoyment, not actually thinking, but letting ideas, images, and emotions flow of themselves, as it were, through my mind. All at once, without

warning of any kind, I found myself wrapped in a flame-colored
cloud. For an instant I thought of fire, an immense conflagration
somewhere close by in that great city; the next, I knew that the
fire was within myself. Directly afterward there came upon me a
sense of exultation, of immense joyousness accompanied or immediately followed by an intellectual illumination impossible to
describe. Among other things, I did not merely come to believe,
but I saw that the universe is not composed of dead matter, but is,
on the contrary, a living Presence. I became conscious in myself
of eternal life. It was not a conviction that I would have eternal
life, but a consciousness that I possessed eternal life then; I saw
that all men are immortal; that the cosmic order is such that . . . all
things work together for the good of each and all; that the
foundation principle of the world, of all the worlds, is what we
call love, and that the happiness of each and all is in the long run
absolutely certain. The vision lasted a few seconds and was gone
but the memory of it and the sense of the reality of what it taught
have remained during the quarter of a century which has since
elapsed.[5]

This testimony introduces several important additional factors
present in many accounts of mystical experiences. Some individuals may be predisposed to having mystical experiences by virtue
of their personality and training. The scene described in this
passage attests to the aesthetic and contemplative inclinations of
the respondent. He is a person deeply moved by sublime
thoughts and emotions and is, evidently, meditative and contemplative by nature. He also practices a form of attentional meditation which involves the restful visualization of and attention to
the sequence of ideas and images that enter his consciousness. He
turns his attention away from the external stimuli of the senses
inward towards his own consciousness. There is a logical transition from the technique of visualization to the visual experience
that soon overcomes him. In this case the nature of the experience is conditioned by the steps that he takes leading up to it. Like
many visualizing mystics, he sees himself bathed in a luminous
glow. Fire and light frequently form the visual frame for mystical
experiences.

The subject describes his experience in paradoxical terms.
Since philosophic thinking and visualization are the techniques
that lead to this particular encounter, it is not surprising that the

subject achieves a type of visual knowledge. He does not merely know things acutely – he sees what he knows. This paradoxical "seeing thought" carries with it a deep conviction of the truth of his discovery because of the specific sensual awareness of what is essentially abstract. The mystical mode of knowing is characteristically paradoxical.

The content of the noetic experience within mysticism is often described as an 'oceanic feeling' – a sense that the mystic is undifferentiated from the rest of reality. A mystical experience frequently culminates in the disintegration of the boundaries of individuality and the self and results in a sense of the "oneness" of the universe. Usually this awareness is transient, allowing the mystic to return to routine consciousness and to continue to function in the world. Some mystics, however, cannot shed this 'oceanic feeling' and continue to feel undifferentiated. Such individuals who cannot sustain routine consciousness frequently suffer from psychotic delusions. The difference, perhaps, between the mystic and the psychotic is that whereas both have oceanic experiences, the mystic is able to return to the world of mundane reality. Phenomenologically, mysticism may be indistinguishable from a form of temporary insanity. Although the mystic might not be psychotic, he is, nevertheless, transformed by his experience.

This fleeting experience, common to many people during the course of a lifetime, is often called a 'peak experience.' It is frequently accompanied by the sense that one is communicating with something other than the normal everyday world. The mystic often feels that he has transcended the world of the senses and has peered behind the veil separating this world from the reality beyond.

Transcendent experiences are, according to many, at the core of religious experiences. In religious contexts these experiences may assume a specific character. Sometimes they involve a visual sense of the entire self separating from and rising above the body. These are often called 'out-of-body experiences.' At other times the subject experiences an inner change in consciousness alone. The following example from The New Testament illustrates the ambiguity:

> I know a man in Christ (i.e., a Christian) who fourteen years ago was caught up to the third heaven – whether in the body or out of

the body I do not know. God knows. And I know that this man
was caught up into Paradise – whether in the body or out of the
body I do not know. God knows. And he heard things which
cannot be told, which man may not utter.[6]

These examples, which are only several among many recorded
mystical testimonies in world literature, exhibit some of the
primary characteristics of mystical experiences. Mystical experiences are frequently ineffable and indescribable states of altered
consciousness involving the deautomatization of normal percep-
tual modes. They may be brought about actively through
training and preparation or passively as the result of an individual's predisposition. The experiences themselves always have an
emotional content of either serenity or overwhelming awe.
They often have a noetic content involving the perception of
oneness and unity. This frequently manifests as either an 'oceanic feeling' of undifferentiatedness of the individual from the
rest of the world, a specific perception of contradictory or paradoxical phenomena, or an intense intellectual discovery of transcendence. All mystical experiences are transformative, and
many produce significant changes in one's orientation to the
world. Mysticism frequently involves some, but not all, of these
characteristics at the same time.

It is still difficult to define precisely what mysticism is.
Some argue that it is a fundamental category of human experience because it is known to occur to a wide range of individuals
in widely diverse cultures. One scholar, J. N. Findlay, author of
Ascent to the Absolute, describes it this way:

> The mystical way of looking at things enters into the experience
> of most men at many times. The so-called great mystics are
> merely people who carry to the point of genius an absolutely
> normal, ordinary, indispensable side of human experience.[7]

Others maintain that the mystical experience is an aberration of
human psychology and, therefore, should be seen as an illusion,
a neurosis, or, if it persists, a serious psychological disorder. As
one critic writes:

> Mysticism is that form of error which mistakes for a divine
> manifestation the operations of a merely human faculty.[8]

Sigmund Freud, for example, describes the 'oceanic feeling' as

> A sensation of eternity, a feeling as of something limitless,
> unbounded – as it were, oceanic, . . . [a] feeling of an indissoluble
> bond, of being one with the external world as a whole.[9]

He relates this not to objective reality but to a state of ego
regression. An infant cannot differentiate between himself and
objects, and so his ego includes everything. Later he separates the
external world from himself. The 'oceanic feeling,' in Freud's
view, is the result of regression to the infantile state or the
primitive persistence of this feeling in later life. In either case
Freud considers this mystical and 'oceanic feeling' to be a psychological state and not an objective experience.

Freud explains that there is only one state, other than
psychosis, in which the clean, sharp lines of demarcation between the ego and everything else melt away: love. It is not
surprising, then, that love should engender a feeling of mysticism
or that mystical experiences should involve the sensation of love.

The absolute conviction that one has achieved a type of
unification is the most common feature of all mystical experiences. As William James defined it:

> This overcoming of the usual barriers between the individual and
> the Absolute is the great mystic achievement. In mystic states we
> both become one with the Absolute and we become aware of our
> oneness. This is the everlasting and triumphant mystical tradi-
> tion, hardly altered by difference of clime or creed. . . . There is
> about mystical utterances an eternal unanimity which ought to
> make a critic stop and think.[10]

In the appendix to W. R. Inge's *Mysticism in Religion* appear a
variety of definitions of mysticism. These examples illustrate the
extent to which mysticism is a form of unification. At the same
time they are emblematic of the different interpretations of the
term *unity*:

> That we bear the image of God is the starting point, one might
> say the postulate, of all mysticism. The complete union of the
> soul with God is the goal of all mysticism.[11]

This definition would appear to be valid for practitioners of religions such as Judaism and Christianity in its assumption of the existence of a transcendent God and the human soul. It would apparently not apply to religions that are not based on the Hebrew Bible from which the idea of the "image of God" originated. Moreover, this definition would apply only in those circumstances where "complete union with God" is deemed possible and not in those cases where it is generally deemed impossible, as in Judaism.

The following is a broader definition of mysticism, but it leaves unanswered the question of how to differentiate between religion and mysticism:

> Mysticism is the immediate feeling of the unity of the self with God; it is nothing, therefore, but the fundamental feeling of religion, the religious life at its very heart and center.[12]

Another definition that emphasizes the union with God:

> Mysticism is the type of religion which puts the emphasis on the immediate awareness of the relation with God, direct and intimate consciousness of the divine presence. It is religion in its most acute, intense and living stage.[13]

Others emphasize mysticism as an intense form of consciousness that has little to do with traditional western conceptions of God:

> The thought that is most intensely present with the mystic is that of a supreme, all-pervading and indwelling Power, in whom all things are one.[14]

Other definitions emphasize the noetic rather than the religious elements within mysticism and may obfuscate more than they clarify:

> The essence of mysticism is the assertion of an intuition which transcends the temporal categories of the understanding, relying on speculative reason. Rationalism cannot conduct us to the essence of things; we therefore need intellectual vision.[15]

And still others, including that of the philosopher Bertrand Russell, see mysticism as little more than emotion:

> Mysticism is in essence little more than a certain intensity and depth of feeling in regard to what is believed about the universe.[16]

It is apparent, therefore, that mysticism is closely associated with some sense of unity and unification. It is equally apparent that the meaning of unity is not uniform and can mean different things to different people in different cultures.

James is mistaken in his belief that mysticism is a universal phenomenon of union because the notion of the 'absolute,' the object of the union, differs from culture to culture. The notion that all mystical experiences are essentially the same in character despite the different ways they are described is misleading. Recent studies have shown that the specific cultural and religious norms in which a mystic's consciousness is shaped make his experience culturally specific.[17] Although many mystics use similar language, thorough analysis of their experiences reveals that the meaning of oneness is not the same in each account.

Some modern scholars of mysticism, including William James, Aldous Huxley, and Fritjof Schuuon, have concluded that all mystical experiences are essentially identical in content regardless of differences in culture and religion.[18] In their view, Jewish, Islamic, Christian, and Buddhist mysticism are all similar expressions of a universal phenomenon.

One school of thought, represented by Rudolph Otto and Evelyn Underhill, maintains that all mystical experiences are similar in content. The differences between various forms of mysticism arise out of the different cultural contexts in which the experience occurs.[19] The only difference, then, between Jewish, Islamic, Christian, and Buddhist mysticism is that each mystic describes his experience in the language of his respective culture.

Another school of thought, associated with R. C. Zaehner, W. T. Stace, and Ninian Smart, maintains that there is no universal phenomenon of mysticism.[20] As is evident from the survey of popular definitions of mysticism, there is little unanimity in what constitutes mysticism. Moreover, as we shall see, there are a variety of distinct types of mysticism that differ experientially and phenomenologically from each other. Not only is there more than one type of mysticism, but the various types might appear in greatly different cultures. Therefore, mysticism is not necessarily culturally specific. It is often difficult, however, to identify the main types of mysticism that cut across cultural boundaries because the descriptions of mysticism are culturally specific and so their components must be analyzed. Recently Steven Katz has shown the complexities inherent in analyzing and defining mysticism. In his view the categorization of various types of mysticism is helpful, but it must take into account the fact that the culture in which a mystic lives shapes his consciousness and helps to determine the kind of experiences that he might have. Therefore, even the classification of various types of mysticism must take into account the complexities of culturally specific experiences.[21]

In actuality, therefore, it is impossible to define mysticism broadly except perhaps within a specific culture. It is possible however, to describe various types of mysticism that cut across cultural lines. One type of mysticism involves what many have called *the sense of unity*.

The meaning of unity can involve different and conflicting elements. As is evident in several of the definitions of mysticism, some mystics experience a oneness with God, whereas others experience a sense of the oneness of nature. There are mystics who experience an awareness of integration within themselves and others who have the 'oceanic feeling' of the unity of all beings. Each of these, as we shall see, is a fundamentally different type of mystical experience. For example, Wordsworth, the English poet, offers a wonderful testimony of mystical oneness with nature in his famous poem, "Tintern Abbey":

> And I have felt
> A presence that disturbs me with the joy
> Of elevated thoughts; a sense sublime
> Of something far more deeply interfused,
> Whose dwelling is the light of setting suns,
> And the round ocean, and the living air,
> And the blue sky, and the mind of man:
> A motion and a spirit, that impels
> All thinking things, all objects of all thought,
> And rolls through all things.[22]

For Wordsworth, mysticism is the feeling of the presence of "a motion and a spirit," a power that infuses all of nature with its presence. He never mentions "oneness with the Absolute" because his unity is the pervasive spirit of nature, the presence of something that others might call "God in nature." This idea that nature is united and contains something absolute beyond the entities that make up the physical universe is called 'pantheism.'

Meister Eckhart, a medieval Christian mystic, also expresses a pantheistic view of the oneness of nature:

> All that a man has here externally in multiplicity is intrinsically One. Here, all blades of grass, wood, and stone, all things are One. This is the deepest depth.[23]

This example illustrates the inadequacy of William James' definition of mysticism. For Eckhart, mysticism is not "union with the Absolute" but the awareness of the inherent unity of all being. Not all mysticism involves union with an absolute or transcendent being. Frequently nature mysticism is the awareness of the oneness of all things and the inherent unity of God within nature. In other religions, however, accounts of mystical experiences suggest that the world and nature are illusions. A deeper unity is achieved by annihilating one's awareness of and connection to the world. This is known as 'acosmic' or world-negating mysticism and is found in the *Upanishads,* the classic text of Hindu mysticism:

> It is pure, unitary consciousness wherein awareness of the world and of multiplicity is completely obliterated. It is ineffable peace. It is the Supreme Good. It is One without a second. It is the Self.[24]

This passage suggests that consciousness is the 'oceanic feeling' of undifferentiatedness. This strongly acosmist declaration suggests that the self is not the differentiated and individual ego. Paradoxically, the true self is achieved through the annihilation of self-consciousness and awareness.

Pantheistic mysticism and acosmist mysticism are generally foreign to the spirit of Judaism, with the exception of some Polish and Lithuanian Hasidic mystics of the eighteenth century. Judaism is a religion based on the idea of the existence of one transcendent God whose being transcends, and is separate from, that of the world. God creates and governs nature, but He also stands above it. The pantheistic idea that God is synonymous with nature, or the acosmic idea that the world is not real is not consistent with the biblical world view. Jewish mysticism starts from the premise that God and nature are fundamentally different. God cannot be identical with nature any more than the world can be said not to exist.

Jewish mysticism is generally 'theistic,' which means that God is a separate and distinct being whose nature is different from that of the world. It involves a supreme being who transcends and rules over nature. But this mysticism may assume a variety of forms. Sometimes Jewish mysticism may strive for the union of two beings who remain essentially distinct even in their unity. A good example of this 'nonabsorptive' mysticism can be found in this parable of the Baal Shem Tov, the founder of Hasidism, an eighteenth-century mystical movement:

> A king had built a glorious palace full of corridors and partitions, but he himself lived in the innermost room. When the palace was completed and his servants came to pay him homage, they found that they could not approach the king because of the devious maze. While they stood and wondered, the king's son came and showed them that those were not real partitions, but only magical illusions, and that the king, in truth, was easily accessible. Push forward bravely and you shall find no obstacle![25]

In this testimony, union with God is a feature of acquiring a special form of consciousness to realize that the obstacles to union exist only in consciousness and not in reality. Mystical consciousness is necessary in order to permit the subject to peer behind the veil or to bridge the abyss between himself and the supposedly unknowable and unreachable God. It assumes that God and man can never become one, but the obstacles that prevent the drawing together of God and man are only illusory. Only in rare instances, particularly in acosmist Hasidic mysticism, do Jewish mystics suggest that the actual union of man and God is possible:

> If we achieve this union, we will think about ourselves as well that we are nothing other than God who gives us life. He alone

exists and there is nothing other than Him. . . . And when we realize this, that we are like nothingness in truth and nothing exists in the world but God, just as before creation, He, as it were, takes genuine pleasure.[26]

Traditional Jewish theology gives little support to the idea that man and God can be identical. But a Muslim author, al-Ghazzali, describes a type of 'absorptive' mysticism not entirely foreign to Hasidism in which the ego of the mystic becomes submerged and indistinguishable from God, the object of his devotions. In such a case the individual not only achieves unity but becomes one with God:

> When the worshipper thinks no longer of his worship or himself, but is altogether absorbed in Him whom he worships, that state is called the passing away of mortality (*fana*), when a person so passed away from himself feels nothing of his bodily members, nor of what is passing without, nor what passes in his own mind . . . He is journeying first to his Lord, and then at the end, in his Lord. Perfect absorption means that he is unconscious not only of himself, but of his absorption.[27]

In Judaism the goal of the mystic quest is usually the attainment of nonabsorptive unity with the transcendent deity. Abraham Joshua Heschel, a leading Jewish theologian, describes Jewish mysticism as a theory of divine transcendence and a method for attaining transcendence.[28] This means that Jewish mysticism involves the experience of overcoming the barriers that apparently separate the world of God from the world of man.

Frequently the most incisive definitions of mysticism are offered by mystics themselves or those with first-hand experience with mystical traditions. In his own spiritual autobiography, Isaac Bashevis Singer, the Yiddish writer who won the Nobel Prize for Literature in 1978, offers the following observations on Jewish mysticism:

> Mysticism isn't a line of thought separated from religion. They both share a basis in the human soul – the feeling that the world is no accident or blind force and that the human spirit and body are closely linked with the universe and its Creator.

If there is a difference between religion and mysticism, it consists of the fact that religion is almost completely dependent upon revelation. All religions have preached that God revealed Himself to a prophet and communicated His demands through him. Religion never remained the property of a single individual. It appealed to a group. It often tended to proliferate and take in whole tribes and nations. Religious leaders often forced obeisance to their faith with the sword. Because of this, religion tended in time to become routine and closely linked with social systems. Mysticism, on the other hand, is individualistic. True mysticism has always belonged to one person or to a small group. It was and it has remained esoteric. The mystic never completely relied upon the revelations of others but sought God in his own fashion. The mystic often assumed the religion of his environment, but he tried to extend it by coupling it with the higher powers; actually to become a prophet himself.

My personal definition of religion is a mysticism that has been transformed into a discipline, a mass experience, and thus grown partially diluted and often worldly. The more successful a religion is, the stronger its influence, the further it recedes from its mystical origin.[29]

Singer points out that mysticism is the attempt to overcome routinized religion by reasserting the primacy of individual religious experience. Mysticism, representing a strong strain of individualism, may be linked to anti-institutional tendencies in formal religion. Individual religious experience is not necessarily the concern of established religion. Therefore, mysticism serves an important function by bringing religious movements back in contact with the powerful experiential impulses that were part of their origins.

The mystic quest is often a search to return to or to repeat the religious experience upon which a religion was founded. The content of the Jewish mystical experience often takes the form of a revelatory experience, an experience akin to what Moses experienced at Sinai.

The varieties of mystical experiences are as diverse as the range of human experiences in different cultures and periods. The term mysticism refers to a specific category of human experiences associated with certain characteristics. However, these characteristics often differ from one culture to another. It is impossible to define precisely what mysticism is except within a specific culture at a particular moment. A precise, universal definition of mysticism is not possible. Therefore, in order to understand mysticism, it is necessary to comprehend specific types of mystical experiences.

2

BRIDGING THE ABYSS:

The History of Jewish Mysticism

Nebuchadnezzar, the Chaldean king of Babylon, the most powerful nation in the region, defeated the Judean king, Yehoyachin of Jerusalem, in March of 597 B.C.E.[1] When Nebuchadnezzar conquered Jerusalem, he deported a large number of the city's aristocracy to his realm. Among them was Ezekiel, a widowed priest and aristocrat with a powerful devotion to Jerusalem. Ezekiel settled in the valley around Tel Aviv, along the Khabur River, a tributary of the Euphrates. Eleven years later the Babylonian commander Nebuzaradan laid siege and destroyed Solomon's Temple.

Ezekiel was consumed by remorse for the condition of the dispersed Jerusalemites. He was wracked by a powerful sense that his people's infidelity to God's covenant had brought on this disaster which he expected would persist. Ezekiel portrayed the terrible national consequences of the exile in starkly imaginative and baroque terms. He prophesied the doom and desolation of Jerusalem to be followed by the eventual physical restoration and moral renewal of Israel.

In the summer of 592 B.C.E., he was suddenly gripped by an unexpected and startling event in which a stunning apparition appeared to be moving toward him. Ezekiel saw a rumbling storm cloud of fire surrounded by a glow. Within the cloud there appeared to be a lustrous and metallic shell containing a vivid and dramatic scene. The shell seemed to contain four bizarre creatures who appeared to be made of metallic bronze. Each had the torso of a man, and each bore the face of man and a lion on the right side, and the face of an eagle and an ox on the left. Each creature had four wings, and under each wing was a hand and bovine hooves with circular soles. The creatures moved as one toward Ezekiel, each one's wings touching those of the adjacent figure, forming a square with their bodies. Their movement was accompanied by fire and lightning.

As the creatures approached him, Ezekiel saw another set of figures within the apparition. Next to each of the creatures were spinning wheels within wheels. On the rim of each wheel were countless eyes. The whole mechanism sparkled like topaz. The creatures and the wheels moved together, sometimes rising into the air, sometimes rolling on the ground, all the while moving toward Ezekiel with a roar.

Looking up, Ezekiel saw within the fiery storm cloud another apparition. Above the heads of the creatures, shrouded in fire and light, was a crystalline vault. Inside the vault was a luminous and radiant throne. Sitting upon the throne was a humanoid figure whose lower torso was fiery and whose upper torso looked like molten brass. The whole mechanism appeared to be rolling toward him rapidly, accompanied by thunder and lightning. Ezekiel took this figure on the throne to be God. He threw himself down on the ground to avoid being crushed by the storm cloud. When he recovered from this event, Ezekiel was fortified, and he proceeded to warn the community of exiles of the impending catastrophic destruction of Jerusalem.[2]

Ezekiel may have been the first of the Jewish people to have recorded and transmitted an account of a direct visual and mystical encounter with God. He is characteristic of those mystics who, like R. M. Bucke, have unanticipated mystical experiences while in a state of repose and attentiveness. Water, in this case the nearby river, often induces a meditative, contemplative state conducive to mysticism. Like other encounters, Ezekiel's experience is visual and contains a strong luminous quality. This event appears to be a wholly spontaneous encounter which is all the more powerful for its unpredictability. Ezekiel, of course, was transformed into a prophet by this gripping and obviously unpleasant experience.

The form of this encounter is especially shocking since it occurs in a state of wakefulness, not in a dream. The figures that he sees are phantasmagoric hybrids of humans and animals. The appearance of beings whose shapes are contradictory and counter to nature make the experience that much more terrifying. The apparition is antithetical to what his consciousness tells him is real. Yet, Ezekiel, like all mystics, has no doubt that what he experienced is real. He is so gripped by the experience that he has no reservations about its authenticity, and will not be persuaded to doubt what his own eyes saw.

This vision is all-encompassing and squeezes out all of the normal, familiar signposts to reality. As a result, Ezekiel is gripped by the power, mystery, and awe of this vision and submits to it. He cowers in fear until a voice from within the apparition calls to him, charging him to become a prophet and to deliver God's message to the other exiles. He is ready to do whatever the voice commands.

Ezekiel was seen by later Jewish mystics as the prototype of a Jewish mystic. The difference between Ezekiel and his successors is that the latter attempted to imitate his experience through rigorous and disciplined training. The earliest recorded attempts at consciously pursuing mystical, visionary, and ecstatic states appear in the second century C.E. Most of the evidence of this early phase of Jewish mysticism has not been preserved although traces of it appear occasionally in the writings from that period.[3]

Rabbi Akiva ben Yosef (50–135 C.E.), the leader of second century rabbinic society in the Land of Israel, was the master of a small group of practitioners of mysticism. They practiced an ecstatic and visionary form of mystical experience in which each rabbi prepared himself for his ascent to the celestial world through asceticism and rituals of purification. He visualized himself ascending through seven heavens and through the seven palaces in the highest heaven, the *aravot*. Along the way, he gained admission to each heaven and palace by presenting the correct password to the angelic gatekeeper. These passwords consisted of magical formulae and secret names of God or His angels. He traversed bridges across rivers of fire and had to pass a host of terrible creatures seeking to thwart his passage. He was mesmerized by the hymns of the angels in the highest heaven as they praised the figure on the throne. Often, the figure on the throne was concealed by a curtain. But on those occasions

when he was permitted to see behind the curtain, he saw himself
standing face to face with God's celestial throne, and he spontaneously composed and uttered hymns to God. Some of these
hymns have made their way into the standard synagogue liturgy
(e.g., the Sabbath hymn, *El Adon*; the morning *kedushah*; and
various *ofannim, sillukim,* and *kedushot*).[4] Some of these mystics
believed that the celestial throne that they visualized was identical with the luminous throne described by Ezekiel.

Rabbi Akiva, who frequently engaged in these practices
with three colleagues, probably began his study of Jewish law as
an adult. Although legend describes him as first having learned
the Hebrew alphabet together with his young son,[5] he was soon
almost universally recognized as a prodigious and exceptional
scholar. He was opposed by Elishah ben Avuyah who resented
the intrusion of this neophyte into the rabbinic elite. Eventually,
however, Elishah acceded to Rabbi Akiva's leadership and accepted him as a colleague.

Elisha and Rabbi Akiva were joined by Shimon Ben Azzai,
his son-in-law, and Shimon ben Zoma in a secret society devoted
to mystical meditation. According to legend the results of their
attempts to achieve the visionary ascent were fraught with
danger. This effort, described metaphorically as "entering a garden," is described in the Talmud as follows:

> Four entered a garden and these are: Ben Azzai, Ben Zoma, Aher
> (i.e., Elisha ben Avuyah), and Rabbi Akiva. Rabbi Akiva said to
> them: When you come to the stones of pure marble, do not say,
> "Water, water!" For it is said: "He who speaks untruth shall not
> stand before my eyes" (Ps. 101:7).
>
> Ben Azzai gazed and died. Of him the Torah says: "The death of
> his faithful ones is grievous in the Lord's sight" (Ps. 116:15).
>
> Ben Zoma gazed and was stricken. Of him the Torah says: "If
> you find honey, eat only what you need, lest, surfeiting yourself,
> you throw it up" (Prov. 25:16).
>
> Aher cut down the shoots.
>
> Rabbi Akiva departed in peace.[6]

Rabbi Akiva and his companions in this enterprise preferred to
keep this activity secret. They recognized the deep psychological

and religious dangers inherent in this system of meditation and trance inducement. Akiva warned his colleagues that when they achieve a vision of the entranceway to the sixth palace, they are likely to be deceived: "When you come to the stones of pure marble, do not say, 'Water, water!' " Rabbi Akiva meant by this to warn his colleagues that they should respect the limits to which the mystical imagination can reach. In their visionary state they might see great boulders obstructing the entrance to the chamber of the king. Rabbi Akiva admonishes them not to trust their imagination for it might deceive them into believing that these awesome obstacles to the last palace are really fluid and not solid barriers. He warns them not to proceed beyond these limits and not to enter where they are not permitted.

Rabbi Akiva's warning was intended to foster respect for the limits of mystical achievement. Visionary ascent was permitted, even encouraged, as high as to the highest palace. But he cautioned against going directly from the anteroom into the presence of the king. He warned them strictly against attempting to see God directly in such a vision.

Apparently the results justified the warning. The visionary experience was so powerful that Ben Azzai died in an ecstatic trance, and Ben Zoma was overwhelmed by his encounter and lost his mental equilibrium. Elishah ben Avuyah is known to have defected from Judaism to the Roman camp during the war with Rome (132–135 C.E.) and to have gone on to oppress his former co-religionists. Therefore, he was subsequently known as Aher, "the Alien." He persecuted Jewish youth and aided the Romans in closing Jewish schools.[7] This became known euphemistically as "cutting down the shoots." His apostasy is attributed here to the power of his mystical experience and, by implication, to the distortion and error of which Rabbi Akiva warned.

Ezekiel's experience served as a model and paradigm for Rabbi Akiva and other Jewish mystics. The practice of attempting to ascend through the heavens and palaces was seen as an effort to consciously replicate what had occurred spontaneously for Ezekiel. This was known alternately as 'palace' (*Heikhalot*) or 'chariot' (*Merkavah*) mysticism or "the visions of Ezekiel" (*Marot Yehezkel*). Their successors debated whether they actually ascended through the heavens on a celestial journey or

whether it merely seemed so to them.[8] There is little doubt that
the reality of the ascent was certain in their own eyes.

On the other hand, Ezekiel's experience was seen as an act
fraught with dangerous possibilities. Because mysticism itself
was seen as inherently dangerous, strict warnings against intentionally attempting to replicate Ezekiel's experience appear in
Jewish law.[9] Apparently even the public reading of the biblical
account of Ezekiel's vision was banned except on the holiday of
Shavuot.[10] Later commentators even criticize Ezekiel for not
being more reticent about relating what occurred to him.[11]

The techniques of visionary mysticism were practiced
during the next eight hundred years. As late as the time of Hai
Gaon (939–1038), the leader of Babylonian Jewry, these techniques were practiced among circles of devotees. Hai Gaon
recorded the techniques which were employed in order to induce
this visionary state:

> You may perhaps know that many of the Sages hold that when
> a man is worthy and blessed with certain qualities and he wishes
> to gaze at the heavenly chariot and the halls of the angels on high,
> he must follow certain exercizes. He must fast for a specified
> number of days, he must place his head between his knees
> whispering softly to himself the while certain praises of God with
> his face towards the ground. As a result he will gaze in the
> innermost recesses of his heart and it will seem as if he saw the
> seven halls with his own eyes, moving from hall to hall to
> observe that which is therein to be found.[12]

According to Hai Gaon this experience is an inner journey to "the
innermost recesses of the heart." It is not meant to be an actual
celestial journey of the soul through the heavens, nor does it have
any elements characteristic of 'out-of-body' experiences. The
techniques employed here lead to changes in the usual physiological responses to external stimuli and produce a reordering of
consciousness. This state, known as 'deautomatization,' is a
purposefully contrived effort to induce hypnotic and other
trancelike states. It is common to many 'Merkavah' experiences.

Two types of mystical experiences are common in rabbinic
Judaism. First, Rabbi Akiva's experience is representative of
'transportation' mysticism in which the subject experiences his

whole being traveling on a celestial journey. A variation on this is the 'out-of-body' experience in which the consciousness or soul of the mystic, but not the physical self, embarks on the celestial journey. Second, Hai Gaon's experience is representative of 'penetration' mysticism in which the subject experiences an inner voyage, a "journey into the heart," achieved through visualization techniques that are centered within the consciousness of the mystic. The difference between these two types of experiences in rabbinic Judaism is whether the encounter is understood by the mystic to occur externally or internally.

From the time of Islam's birth in the seventh century until the rise of the Mamluk Dynasty in the thirteenth century, Jewish mysticism flourished within the Islamic realm. In fact, the relationship between Judaism and Islam in this period was pivotal in the history of both religions. The prophet Muhammad was undoubtedly well acquainted with Jewish oral lore based on biblical and rabbinic legends as well as with some of the forms of Jewish practice common to Jewish tribes living in the Arabian peninsula during the seventh century. Muhammad may, in fact, have drawn inspiration for his understanding of personal piety and religious justice from tales he heard from Jews concerning the exemplary lives of the Hebrew prophets.[13]

Muhammad wished to bring about the conversion of the Arabian Jewish tribes on the grounds that Islam was the legitimate heir to the biblical calling and the fulfillment of the Hebrew monotheistic mission.[14] His favorable attitude toward Judaism changed when these powerful Jewish tribes rejected his efforts to consolidate them under his leadership. Consequently, Muhammad's disappointment with the Jews is reflected in the Koran's many pronouncements about the moral perversities, treacheries, evasions, and idolatries of the Jewish people. At the same time, the Koran expresses indebtedness to Hebrew prophecy as the original monotheistic tradition.[15]

The ambivalence of the early Koranic attitude served to complicate the later status of Jews living under Islam. The Jews' virtue derived from the fact that they were "the People of the Book," an appellation that was coined by the Koran itself and adopted later by the Jews. They were treated as a protected minority with property and religious rights under Islamic rule. However, they did not share in any of the political rights and other prerogatives of the members of "the community of the faithful," and they were the victims of occasional anti-Jewish outbursts.

The Jews willingly accepted their status under Islam because it, in fact, offered a greater degree of legal security than did Christianity. From the time of the destruction of the second Jerusalem Temple in 70 c.e. and the transfer of Judaism's spiritual hub to the rabbinic academies, Jews saw themselves as a minority people living under the authority of foreign, dominant political regimes. They eschewed pretensions for political sovereignty for themselves as long as they were guaranteed a measure of self-government and religious tolerance. This important strategy for diasporan living made it possible for Jews to adapt to their status as a protected minority within the Islamic world while preserving their own particular religious institutions and traditions.

The area around Baghdad, Kufa, and Basra provided an especially fertile ground for Jewish life between 635 and 1258 c.e. Baghdad, the seat of the Islamic Abbasid Califate, was the thriving center of Islamic culture during this period. Under Abbasid rule the institution of the exilarch (*resh galuta*), the lay leader of the Babylonian Jewish community, grew. Islamic authorities vested the exilarch with the power to assess and collect taxes, dispense justice, and supervise the charitable funds of the community. The famous rabbinic academies at Sura and Pumbedita were also located near Baghdad. They were presided over by the *Geonim* ("the Pride of Jacob"), the religious and intellectual leaders of Babylonian Jewry whose authority was recognized throughout the Jewish world. During this period the forty thousand Jews of Baghdad enjoyed a high degree of religious tolerance, integration within Islamic society, autonomous self-government, and religious interaction with Muslims.[16]

Jewish mysticism also flourished in the Islamic Empire especially in the area known throughout Jewish history as Babylonia, which is present-day Iraq.[17] Over the centuries this region, which included the city of Baghdad, produced such diverse personalities as Ezekiel and Hai Gaon. Muslim and Jewish mystics in and around Baghdad and Damascus had close contacts with each other. Some even shared an interconfessional outlook—a belief that Judaism and Islam were different but equally valid paths to achieving mystical union with God. There are known instances of Muslims who visibly wore the traditional Jewish headcovering under their turbans and professed belief in a universal religion. When one such Muslim sage was asked by a student for spiritual guidance, he responded, "Upon which road, the Jewish, Christian, or Muslim?"[18]

Jewish and Islamic mystics probably shared meditative techniques and other methods for achieving visionary and ecstatic mystical encounters. For example, in Hai Gaon's attempt to replicate the prophet Ezekiel's ascent to the heavenly chariot, he probably utilized amulets inscribed with magical names of God as passwords and immunization devices in the mystic ascent from heaven to heaven.[19] It is likely that Hai Gaon borrowed the technique of mystical amulets from Muslim magical and mystical calligraphy.[20]

Beyond the techniques of mystical ascent and 'throne mysticism,' little is actually known about the practice of Jewish mysticism in the Islamic world. In the latter half of the twelfth century, the center of Jewish mystical activity shifted from the area around Baghdad to Germany and Provence in southern France. The eleventh century Hebrew travelogue, *The Chronicle of Ahimaaz,* explains that Jewish mysticism was imported to Italy by way of a Jewish mystic from Baghdad, Abu Aharon. Other chronicles identify other figures who brought Jewish mysticism from "the east" (Baghdad) to "the west" (Europe).[21]

Jewish mysticism in western Europe sank its deepest roots in Germany and Provence and, subsequently, in Spain. Some of the mystical ideas concerning Ezekiel's "Account of the Chariot" were transmitted to European Jewry by the members of the Kalonymide family who learned them ostensibly from Abu Aharon of Baghdad. The Kalonymide family belonged to the religious aristocracy of German Jewry in the middle of the twelfth century, and they were the acknowledged masters of a spiritual movement known as *Hasidei Ashkenaz* (German *Hasidim* or Pietists).[22] Many of their ideas, in turn, were conveyed to Provence and Spain by their adherents in the last quarter of the twelfth century. The beginning of the thirteenth century marked the beginning of the most fertile period in the history of Jewish mysticism.

German Hasidism promoted a new religious ideal of spiritual equanimity. The *Hasid*, or truly pious individual, was one who could be indifferent to all the sufferings and temptations of the world. He would turn away both from physical pain and the joys of the physical world and absorb himself exclusively in the contemplation of God. The *Hasid* consciously attempted to inure himself to his passions and physical desires by avoiding their pleasures. He also wittingly faced and accepted scorn and suffering as a means of sharpening his ability to respond to all worldly stimuli with indifference. The *Hasid* was a solitary figure removed from the world and devoted exclusively to God.[23]

The mysticism of the rabbinic practitioners was replaced by a new understanding of meditative prayer among German *Hasidim*. No longer was the emphasis on the ascent to the highest palace of the God who remained inaccessible despite the abundant hymns of the mystics. The emphasis in German Hasidism shifted to the paradox of God's absolute uniqueness and remoteness on one hand, and his accessibility and immanence on the other hand. The earlier '*Merkavah*' mystical prayers were spontaneous and uncensored outpourings of praise for the hidden glory on the throne. German *Hasidim* understood prayer as the means of uniting the soul with the omnipresence of the divine.

The German *Hasidim* differentiated between the hidden God and his manifestation which was visible to Moses and to other prophets. The visible manifestation of God, called alternately *Shekhinah* (divine presence), *Keruv* (cherub), *Kavod* (glory), and *Gedulah* (greatness), is the "relational" aspect of God, which is revealed to the prophets and mystics. In fact, the *Shekhinah*, in their view, can assume a visible form in the guise of fire and clouds. The German *Hasidim* went farther than the '*Merkavah*' mystics by positing activity rather than passivity on the part of God. It is not the mystic who ascends through the palaces, but the relational aspect of God that descends to man.

German Hasidism integrated elements of 'throne' mysticism within a new theology according to which God can be made manifest in the world through prayer. By differentiating between the hidden and the revealed aspects of God, they introduced a new approach to the problem of divine oneness. God is one and unique, yet He can create occasional representations of Himself that can appear in a visible form in the world. Despite

the problems inherent in saying that God has a created representation on earth, they were able to preserve both the concepts of
God's absolute uniqueness and His accessibility to humanity.
At about the same time as Hasidism emerged in Germany,
the most important of the medieval Jewish mystical movements
was beginning to emerge in Provence. Provence, in the late
twelfth century, was the intellectual capital of European Jewry.[24]
Closely tied to Spanish Jewry, Provence was emerging as the
crossroads between two great cultures–Arab and Christian.
Under Arab rule, the Jews in Spain had produced an intellectual
and literary renaissance that lasted from the tenth to the twelfth
century.

Andalusia, or *Sefarad,* as Spain was called by Muslims and
Jews respectively, became the arena of greatest cultural interaction between these two peoples. From 711 C.E., when Muslim
forces under the command of Tarik ibn Ziyyad landed at Gi-
braltar (named after him in Arabic, *"jabl al-tarik"* [the mountain of
Tarik]), until 1145, when the fundamentalist Almohade movement sought to enforce religious conformity throughout the
Iberian peninsula, Muslim and Jewish scientists, philosophers,
statesmen, and physicians served side by side in the Andalusian
courts and contributed to a renaissance of learning which later
spread inland from Spain to the rest of Europe.

The cultivation and refinement of Arabic prose, poetry,
grammar, and philosophy and their influences upon the Jews
produced a lasting transformation in Jewish and Hebrew culture.
The activities of Muslims and Jews in Spain produced a rich
tapestry of cultural accomplishments which exhibit in bold relief
how advanced Muslim society became during this *"golden age"*
when compared to the concurrent *"dark ages"* of medieval Christian Europe.

Muslim Spain proved fertile soil for a Jewish intellectual and
literary renaissance. Shmuel ha-Nagid (993–1055), the preeminent leader of Andalusian Jewry, gained prominence, even
among the Moslems, as a poet, statesman, and military commander. Shlomo ibn Gabirol (1020–c. 1057) composed secular,
even erotic, poetry as well as deeply inspired religious poetry and
important philosophic works. Bahya ibn Pakuda (late eleventh
century) introduced the notion that the *"duties of the heart,"* the
spiritual and inner dimensions of human life, are as important

and obligatory for a Jew as the overt actions prescribed by Jewish law. Yehudah ha-Levi (c. 1075–1141) was the author of *Sefer ha-Kuzari,* an original and compelling conception of Judaism which, as much as the Bible and Talmud, articulates popular Jewish belief. The brightest luminary of the period, however, was Rabbi Moshe ben Maimon, Maimonides (1135–1204), the brilliant Jewish philosopher and legal scholar whose ideas and decisions have shaped all of subsequent Jewish thought and jurisprudence.

The accomplishments of the "golden age" of Muslim Spain are those of an elite class of courtiers, artists, and intellectuals who lived within a society that imposed strict religious conformity upon Muslims but that was relatively free of dogmatic attitudes regarding non-Muslims. The remoteness of Andalusia, an Umayyad Califate until the eleventh century, from Baghdad, the seat of the Abbasid dynasty, contributed to the Andalusian sense of cultural autonomy. The prosperity of the Andalusian courts made it possible to promote the growth of a materially rich culture and to patronize those individuals, irrespective of religious creed, who could best fulfill the ruler's political ambitions and adorn the reputation of his court.

Arabic literature in Spain reflected the ideal of *arabiyya,* the idea of the perfection of the Arabic language in the Koran and in classical poetry, and its centrality in the consciousness and identity of Islamic peoples. At times it appeared that many Andalusians saw themselves as living within a culture that was defined more by the importance of the Arabic language than by the Islamic religion. Andalusian Jewry adopted the Arabic language as the medium of their oral and literary expression because it defined for them a common cultural ground with the Muslims. They recognized that the very success of prominent Jews living in an Arabic civilization depended on their facility in the Arabic language. Arabic was adopted among the Jews to the extent that much of the Jewish religious literature and biblical commentaries of the period were written in Arabic rather than in Hebrew.

The ideal of *arabiyya* expressed the Muslims' sense of national identity through their language. Arabic poetry was revered by Muslims as the highest form of literary creativity, and the ability to master the art became the yardstick of cultural literacy. *Arabiyya* stimulated a parallel sense of linguistic nationalism among Jews who turned to the classical Hebrew of the Bible in order to develop a language of poetic expressiveness as refined as Arabic. Although Jews were fully acculturated in all areas of Andalusian society, the expression of the national consciousness of the Jewish people in Spain assumed the form of a renaissance of Hebrew literature, especially poetry. Poetry, secular and religious, was the one genre in which Jews wrote almost exclusively in Hebrew. The ideal of *arabiyya*, therefore, fostered a new growth in Hebrew literacy and cultural identity through the growth of Hebrew poetry.

The Almohade invasions of Spain in 1145, with their attendant anti-Jewish persecutions, and the disintegration of Muslim rule following the military successes of the Christian reconquest of Spain, brought this "golden age" to a tragic conclusion.

Since the eleventh century, Provence had been a center of rabbinic culture, including biblical scholarship, Talmudic study, pietistic thought, and liturgical composition. There is no evidence of any influence of the Andalusian secular culture in Provence prior to the second half of the twelfth century.

The beginning of secular Jewish culture in Provence dates from the arrival of Yehudah ibn Tibbon (1120–1190) as a refugee from the Almohade persecution. Tibbon, who brought with him an extensive library and knowledge of the intellectual tradition of Andalusian Jewry, found a receptive welcome among the Jewish intellectuals of Provence. He was commissioned soon after his arrival by a leading Talmudist to translate a number of major Jewish works from Arabic into Hebrew. Beginning with Bahya's work, *Duties of the Heart,* he devoted the next twenty-five years to a series of translations that introduced Hispano-Jewish culture into Provence and Christian Europe. This work was continued by his son, Shmuel (1160–1230), translator of Maimonides' *Guide of the Perplexed,* and other works. Provence emerged as a center of Jewish intellectual and literary life in Europe. Jews served as intermediaries and transmitters of Arabic civilization, and even of classical Greek and Hindu traditions, to Europe in the late twelfth and early thirteenth centuries.

Provence spawned the emergence of Jewish mysticism as well. The movement known as the *Kabbalah* began around 1175 among circles associated with one of the great families of Provencal rabbinic leadership.[25] Covert suggestions about mystical revelations from the prophet Elijah began to appear in statements attributed to leading rabbinic figures of the period.

Elijah, a zealous Israelite prophet of the ninth century B.C.E., is described in the Bible as the fierce opponent of all forms of paganism carried out within the boundaries of Israel.[26] The Bible also describes an encounter between Elijah and God that takes place at the same spot where God revealed the Torah to Moses. After a tumultuous array of thunder and fire, God's "still, small voice" addresses the prophet.[27] This account concludes with Elijah's disappearance as he is carried off to heaven in a chariot of fire.[28] According to tradition Elijah lives on in "concealment." He is also viewed as the messianic harbinger[29] who also appears to men as the revealer of heavenly secrets.[30]

Claims of such revelations by Elijah are attributed to Avraham ben Yitzhak of Narbonne (d.1179), the head of the Narbonne rabbinical court; his son-in-law, Rabbi Avraham ben David (RABaD) of Posquieres (d.1198), the leading Talmudist of his generation; and RABaD's son, Isaac the Blind (d. circa 1236), the first identifiable Kabbalist author.[31]

Toward the end of the twelfth century, copies of a manuscript called *Sefer ha-Bahir* (*The Book of Clear Light*), attributed to Nehunyah ben ha-Kanah, a rabbinic figure of the second century and colleague of Rabbi Akiva, began to circulate among the disciples of Isaac the Blind in Provence. Although the book was still considered part of the 'Merkavah' tradition, its authorship was certainly much later than the second century. *Sefer ha-Bahir,* a collection of fragmentary homilies and commentaries on biblical verses, was probably edited in the late twelfth century on the basis of earlier materials that were collected and reworked. The appearance of the book was accompanied by a sharp debate over the authenticity and antiquity of the book.[32]

The *Sefer ha-Bahir* introduced a decidedly new conception of God. No longer was God the transcendent king of 'Merkavah' mysticism. In *Sefer ha-Bahir* God is an amalgam of dynamic powers perpetually in a state of ebb and flow. This dynamic being is subject to continuous inner movement dependent upon the fluidity of his internal powers. At one moment certain aspects of God may be ascendant, and at other times those powers may be in decline. In *Sefer ha-Bahir* God is seen as an everchanging being whose inner dynamic is governed by human actions that have profound repercussions and reverberations for God.[33] The two most prominent powers within this pantheon of divine dynamism are the feminine and masculine potencies. These elements soon became central in the kabbalistic conception of God.

Isaac the Blind, the first identifiable Kabbalist in Jewish history, was called Yitzhak Sagi-Nahor (Isaac of the Great Light), euphemistically hinting at his actual handicap. Despite his blindness, he personifies the mystical experience of the human intellect that attempts to transcend its own limitations as it meditates upon the divine mind in colorful visual images. For Isaac, God is the "incomprehensible," the universal mind that is the source of all thought and being and whose scrutiny is the object of the penetrating mind of the mystic.

The early disciples of Isaac the Blind and followers of the *Sefer ha-Bahir* believed that it was impossible to reach God or understand God through rational means. God could only be understood through symbols and traces of His existence that He had planted throughout the universe. Everything is a symbol for God – the human soul, the Torah, nature – if one knows how to decipher its meaning. The early Kabbalists defined the meaning of the symbols by which God could be understood. They saw themselves as decoders who could reach God if only they could penetrate the code by which God lives.

The challenge of understanding the symbolism of God was picked up by disciples of Isaac the Blind in Spain. The center of Jewish mystical activity reverted to Spain around the turn of the thirteenth century. By 1225 the Christian reconquest of Spain from the Muslims was nearly complete. Jewish life then shifted from the provinces of southern Spain to the provinces of Aragon, Castille, and Catalonia in the north. The small Catalonian town of Gerona was home to the next generation of Kabbalists. The Gerona Kabbalists included many important mystics who contributed to early kabbalistic theory and practice.

The acknowledged leader of the Gerona school, Rabbi Moshe ben Nahman, Nahmanides (1194–1270), was also the most important figure in Hispano-Jewish history of the thirteenth century. His mystical views are contained in his many writings although he often attempted to conceal these views from non-Kabbalists. According to his students, his prodigious Torah commentary was originally intended as a kabbalistic work, but following a premonitory dream he rewrote it for a more popular readership. Many references to mystical secrets can still be found throughout this work. Many of his transcribed sermons and biblical exegeses contain kabbalistic "secrets" about God, angels, the soul, miracles, and the afterlife. Nahmanides is also distinguished as the first kabbalistic poet.[34]

Nahmanides successfully combined his pursuit of mysticism with traditional religious practice and the mantle of Jewish communal leadership. In 1232, when the rabbis of Northern France and Germany sought to condemn Moses Maimonides' writings as heretical, Nahmanides counseled moderation and compromise despite his own kabbalistic opposition to Maimonides' rationalism. He argued that Maimonides actually made religious ideas attractive for Andalusian and Provencal Jews who had been educated in an atmosphere of secular and philosophic rationalism that was inimical to the teachings of Judaism. In the context of Nahmanides' own culture, Maimonides was too much of a rationalist and his ideas too far removed from traditional teachings.

Not only was this a period of cultural struggle between traditionalists and intellectuals, but it was also a period in which Jewish fortunes in Christian Spain were in decline. One of Nahmanides' contemporaries, Shem Tov Falaquera, who introduced the Delphic maxim ("know thyself") into Hebrew, described it as, "A time of stress and danger [when] many troubles beset us and every man is poverty stricken by the wrathful rod of fate and must wander through the land in search of sustenance."[35] The restrictions upon Jewish economic activities imposed throughout Europe by the Catholic Church and the intolerance of the urban Christian populace resulted in the decline of Jewish prominence in government service, finance, science, and medicine.

Nahmanides was a physician by profession and the official representative of Catalonian Jewry in dealings with the ruling authorities. With the rise of the Dominican religious order in 1216, Catholic policy toward the Jews evolved from attacks upon the supposed anti-Christian heresies in the Talmud to mounting pressure to demonstrate that the Bible prophesies the coming of Jesus Christ. Dominican efforts in Spain to convert the Jews to Christianity mounted during this period and gained support through their alliance with the King, James I of Aragon. With the introduction of the Inquisition to Spain during his rule, the Jews were compelled to debate the Dominicans and listen to sermons that purported to show that Judaism proves the truth of Christianity.

The responsibility for advocacy on behalf of the Jewish people fell to Nahmanides. In 1263 he was commanded by King James I of Aragon to defend Judaism against the charges of the Dominicans who were led by a converted Jew, Fre Paolo Christiani. Despite Nahmanides' bold and outspoken defense of Jewish beliefs, the conversionist pressure upon the Jews mounted. In 1265 the Dominicans tried Nahmanides for his claim that the Jews actually "won" the disputation. The king interrupted the trial, but Nahmanides was forced to flee Spain for the Land of Israel.[36]

Nahmanides' devotion to the *Kabbalah* contributed to the dissemination of Jewish mystical teachings throughout Spain, Italy, and the Land of Israel. Although the *Kabbalah* remained an esoteric discipline confined to a select but significant few, it continued to grow among learned segments of Jewry throughout the next two centuries.

The most decisive event in the history of Spanish *Kabbalah* was the appearance of a new literary work, *Sefer ha-Zohar* (*The Book of Splendor*). The discovery of the *Zohar* around 1290 in Spain ushered in an entirely new era in the history of Jewish mysticism. Although the *Sefer ha-Bahir* continued to serve as the authoritative text of the *Kabbalah* for some time afterward, the *Zohar* soon replaced it as the primary kabbalistic text.

The *Zohar* was introduced by Moshe de Leon of Guadalajara in Spain around 1290.[37] De Leon copied and circulated manuscripts of the purportedly ancient *midrash* to kabbalistic acquaintances in Spain. His discovery was regarded with great excitement by some because the work attributed its authorship to Rabbi Shimon bar Yohai, a sage of the second century and student of Rabbi Akiva. This was indeed a precious discovery due to its antiquity and the prestige of its assumed author. Other of de Leon's contemporaries viewed his discovery with suspicion. After all, they wondered, how is it possible that such a seminal work should have been hidden and appear suddenly one thousand years later? One secondhand account even quotes the widow of Moses de Leon as saying:

> Let God punish me if my husband alone did not write this entire book. He wrote every word and letter of the *Zohar*. When I saw that he composed every word himself while telling people that Shimon bar Yohai was the real author, I asked him why he did not tell people the truth. He said to me, "If I were to tell people that I composed the words of the *Zohar* and its wonderful mysteries, it would not get the attention it deserves or the price which an ancient book commands. When people hear that Shimon bar Yohai revealed these words under the influence of the Holy Spirit, they will accept it."[38]

Controversy has always surrounded the *Zohar*. The small group of Kabbalists in Spain and the Land of Israel were divided between those who believed that this was an ancient *midrash* and those who believed it was Moses de Leon's prodigious literary forgery. What is most surprising is that the tenor of this debate in the thirteenth century was relatively mild. This indicated that while the *Zohar* was regarded as a matter of some contention, even the proponents of its antiquity regarded it as only one among other mystical classics.

It was not until several centuries later that the *Zohar* assumed preeminence as the most important classic literary work among Kabbalists. The *Zohar* is a comprehensive mystical commentary on many sections of the Torah. It presents a reading of the Torah as a novel of the inner life of God and the dynamics of the divine powers. It was the primary literary vehicle through which the mystical teachings and symbolism of the Spanish *Kabbalah* were conveyed along with major innovations in theory and interpretation. Because Spanish *Kabbalah* remained the province of a small coterie of devotees, the question of the authenticity of the *Zohar* excited very few.

In the two centuries following the appearance of the *Zohar*, Spanish *Kabbalah* thrived within these small circles. There were no academies devoted exclusively to the study of the *Kabbalah*, nor were there special associations or congregations. In Spain, the *Kabbalah* was the spiritual avocation of a small number of rabbinically literate and religiously conservative Jews. Teachings, theories, and devotions were transmitted from father to son, from teacher to disciple. The *Kabbalah* was an elite spiritual movement nurtured by the circulation of mystical manuscripts and private oral teachings.

The Kabbalists saw themselves as bastions of religious traditionalism guarding against the incursions of philosophic rationalism that they anathematized as modernism. The term *Kabbalah* itself means 'tradition' and was worn as an emblem of their conservatism. The Kabbalists maintained that this tradition originated at Sinai and had been adumbrated, albeit reluctantly, in a series of oral teachings and cryptic writings by ancient sages.

The Kabbalists opposed the modernist tendency to see the Torah as an allegory for moral and scientific teachings. They viewed this tendency as an attempt to make the Torah relevant by interpreting it to conform with contemporary mores. In the Kabbalists' view, the Torah was a mysterious tapestry woven of hints about the divine world, which was expressed in language comprehensible to humans. But they warned against understanding the Torah as a book that talks about real earthly and historical events. It may speak in human language, but its meaning is divine.

The Kabbalists saw themselves engaged in a battle with modernists over the meaning of the Torah. Still, due to the esoteric nature of their teachings and the paucity of their number, they had little general effect on Jewish life in Spain.

Despite the illustrious history of Jewish life in Spain, conditions worsened for the Jews during the fourteenth century. In 1391 anti-Jewish sentiment erupted into popular pogroms throughout Spain. Perhaps as many as one third of the seven hundred and fifty thousand Spanish Jews were slaughtered, and an equal number were forcibly baptized. The forced converts became known as *Marranos*. Over the next twenty-five years, the ranks of the *Marranos* were swelled by the voluntary conversion of many Jews, known as *Conversos,* who sought to escape the stigma and fate of their compatriots by abandoning Judaism.

The presence of a new social and religious phenomenon of converted Christians, some of whom maintained ties to Jews and Judaism, became a matter of great public concern. Debates raged in Spain regarding the fidelity of the new Christians to

Catholicism. Despite great differences in the circumstances of conversion and the degree of loyalty to the adopted religion, the new Christians were often regarded by Christians as a homogeneous group. The Church frequently saw the converts as crypto-Jews who continued to practice Judaism in secret. Rabbinic authorities distinguished between the legal status of the forced converts and the voluntary converts, and they sought to define criteria to establish who was and who was not considered to be a Jew in the eyes of Jewish law.

In 1449 the Franciscans moved to extirpate the real and imagined vestiges of Jewishness among the new Christians. The ascent of Ferdinand and Isabella to the throne in 1474 led to efforts to consolidate their political rule over all of Spain. The religious and political forces coalesced in 1481 with the establishment of the Royal Inquisition in Spain. Under the direction of Torquemada, the Inquisition pursued its goals with a legendary blindness to truth and devotion to brutality. Following a two-pronged policy toward the Jews, Ferdinand and Isabella sanctioned inquisitorial measures directed against the new Christians and expelled the remaining Jews from Spain in 1492. Having done so, they were able to establish national rule based on a foundation of ethnic and religious unity.

More than a thousand years of Spanish Jewish history came to an abrupt end in 1492, just as Columbus set sail for the New World. The remnant of Spanish Jewry fled to Portugal, the Ottoman Empire, and the major trading centers of Europe. They took with them a self-consciousness as the elite of world Jewry. After all, they believed that Spain was the home to which many of the exiles fled after the destruction of the first Temple in 586 B.C.E. at the time of the prophet Ezekiel. They believed that theirs was the oldest surviving continuous Jewish community in the world. They looked back with pride on the prominence of Jews as courtiers, financiers, scientists, philosophers, administrators, and scholars under Arab rule and to a lesser, but significant extent, under Christian rule. They were proud of luminaries such as Maimonides and Nahmanides, and they were proud of the traditions of Hebrew liturgical poetry. Many, too, were proud of the *Kabbalah* that had flourished in Spain.

The tradition of Jewish mysticism did not disappear with the destruction of Spanish Jewry. It had already spread to many other communities in Europe and the Mediterranean, but it was soon to undergo a decisive transformation under the weight of the experience of the Expulsion. As the great legacy of Spanish *Kabbalah* was transplanted to the town of Safed in the Galilee region of Palestine, one phase of the history of Jewish mysticism came to an end and a new one began.

At this point we shall turn to examine the major elements in the mystic quest in Judaism. Later we shall return to explore the history of Jewish mysticism from 1492 to the present.

3

LIVING WITH THE ABYSS:

The Character of Jewish Mysticism

Mystical and religious experiences are not necessarily identical. Before there is mysticism, there is religion. Mysticism is a type of religious experience, but not all religious experiences are mystical. Religion may be understood as the human response to the experience of the supreme reality of God whose being is beyond rational conception. Rudolf Otto (1869–1937), the theologian, explained that a religious experience is characterized by the experiencing of that which is beyond rational knowledge and which has been called variously "the wholly (or holy) other," or "the terrifying awesome majesty," not describable in common language.[1] Religion is associated with the feelings engendered by the experience and with the attempt to communicate that experience and elaborate it through ritual.

Mysticism is a specific theory and practice of how to intensify the religious experience. It involves the transformation of the religious experience into an intense relationship with the supreme reality. It is a more intense form of religion than is generally sanctioned within formal religions. Mysticism, in many religions, is also an esoteric phenomenon restricted to, or practiced by, select individuals rather than by the masses. Jewish mysticism is, therefore, a more intense form of religious experience than is generally found in normative, rabbinic Judaism.

Gershom Scholem (1897–1982), the leading modern scholar of Jewish mysticism, theorized that mysticism is a definite stage in the historical development of religion and makes its appearance under certain well-defined conditions.[2] He explains that Jewish mysticism is phenomenologically distinct from Jewish religious experiences known through biblical and talmudic records. He further argues that the development of Jewish mysticism was a relatively late development in the history of Judaism. In order to distinguish between religious experiences and mysticism, Scholem divides the history of Judaism into three stages:

- the mythical period,
- the institutional period,
- the romantic or mystical period.

In the "mythical" period, which coincides with the period from Abraham to Ezekiel (1500 B.C.E.–350 B.C.E.), man discovers that there is an order and harmony to his world that is not visible. He experiences the hidden hand of a god, gods, or other forces that direct the world and influence his existence. The explanation of the unseen forces in the world covers all contingencies from birth, harvests, and fortune to death, floods, and famines. Often he discovers hidden forces in nature and the presence of god in the wind, the sun, and the rain. The Hebrew genius, however, was the discovery of a god who was outside and beyond nature and who, in fact, ruled over and governed nature for good and for bad, depending upon the moral righteousness or failings of human beings. The God of Abraham and Moses was an awesome, unseen god, all the more powerful for His invisibility. Still, He was very familiar and near.

In the time of Adam, the Hebrew Bible recounts, "The voice of God walked in the Garden."[3] Man could communicate freely and easily with God. Abraham, too, had an intimate relationship with God throughout his lifetime. When God threatened to destroy Sodom and Gemmorah, Abraham bargains with Him as if He were a familiar merchant in the bazaar. After gaining God's assent to save the cities if fifty righteous men were found, Abraham tries to whittle down the number to ten.[4] This is certainly a god with whom one can reason.

When Moses speaks with God in the wilderness several centuries later, God is no longer the intimate stranger walking in the Garden or conversing freely with the patriarchs. Whereas man appears able to initiate dialogue with God in the narratives in Genesis, Exodus portrays God as initiating dialogue with man. God is somewhat less accessible, but certainly more awesome. When God tells Moses to take off his shoes, for the ground upon which he stands is holy ground,[5] God has changed the terms of the relationship. God is still present in the world, but His presence now seems to be localized on earth for just a brief moment in which He announces that, "I am what I am."[6] This is no longer the familiar partner of Abraham but the beginning of the hidden inscrutable God who soon appears on top of Mount Sinai shrouded in smoke and fog.[7]

The God of Israel, as He is known through the accounts of Genesis, is undifferentiated from the world and appears to be in constant dialogue with the patriarchs. The intimate relationship with God is like that between a child and its mother. The god of Exodus is still familiar and intimate but becomes increasingly remote, distant, awesome, and fearsome. The emotional tenor of the narrative shifts, and the affective mood is suggestive of what occurs when the child matures. The child may experience less of the all-encompassing nurturing of the mother and more of the power and authority of the father. The impression of God evolves from an almost prosaically familiar being to an increasingly remote, tremendous, and awesome power. The concealed God of Sinai is far more remote than the God of Eden whom Adam heard walking in the heat of the day.

The history of the religion of ancient Israel consists of the discovery of a personal, yet transcendent, God who, in the course of time, becomes increasingly remote and inaccessible to those who seek Him. The primary religious experiences of Abraham give way to the majestic and distant God of Moses. The Bible begins with an account of God's presence and follows His eventual withdrawal and distancing from His people. The earlier, intimate relationship is supplanted by a relationship mediated through a permanent and unchanging account of His wishes, the Torah. Having given His last word, so to speak, He bows out of the picture, leaving man to do the rest. God's voluntary self-withdrawal from the affairs of the people to whom He revealed Himself is not very different from the case of a parent who, having given his child a good upbringing and education, allows the child to mature and make decisions on his own. There is no question about the parent's desires, only about his whereabouts.

The Bible, according to this perspective, chronicles the history of the Jewish religious relationship with God and the subsequent creation of an abyss between man and God that cannot be bridged. By the time of the early rabbinic period (70 C.E.–200 C.E.), the Jewish people have no expectations of having a direct, unmediated relationship with God. All Jewish religious experiences become mediated through the Torah in the sense that, in the absence of direct contact, God and man meet when man follows God's will as prescribed in the law. Or, more emphatically, in the absence of God, all man has is His Torah.

Many of the rabbinic and talmudic teachings convey this sense of the unbridgeable abyss between man and God. Rabbinic literature contains many statements that reinforce the notion of God's increasing withdrawal from intimate contact with man over the course of time. Such passages seem to suggest that the history of God and the Jewish people is one of increasing remoteness and widening of an abyss as history progresses beyond the original moments of God's revelation to mankind. This rabbinic conception of history is explicit in the following popular legend in which God and Israel are compared to a king and his daughter:

> The case of a king who had a daughter who was a minor:
>
> Until she grew up and came of age, he used to speak to her when he saw her in the street; he spoke to her in the alleyways. But, when she grew up and came of age, he said, "It is not in keeping with my daughter's dignity that I should talk to her in public. Make her, therefore, a pavilion and I shall speak with her inside the pavilion." Thus, at first, it is written: "When Israel was a child, then I loved him."
>
> Said God: "They saw Me in Egypt; they saw Me at the Red Sea; they saw Me at Sinai." But, once they had accepted the Torah and became a complete nation unto Him, he said: "It is not in keeping with the dignity of My children that I should speak with

them publicly, but let them make Me a tabernacle and I shall speak with them from the midst of the tabernacle."[8]

This marvelous passage shows how the rabbis of the talmudic era understood the reasons for the end of God's spontaneous revelation to individuals and the subsequent localization of all contact with God in one stationary locale, the Temple of Solomon. The shift from mobile to stationary places of direct contact with God is portrayed here as a recognition of the increasing maturity of the Jewish people. When the Jewish people were a young nation, individuals were able to have free and easy access to their God. As the nation grew and came of age, they became less dependent upon regular contact with their God and had less need for direct intercourse. Now that they possess the Torah, a direct contact with God is less essential for guidance and direction. Therefore, the frequency of contact is diminished, and the place of meeting is restricted by God. It is even portrayed as a parental gesture of respect for the independence of the child. The passage implies that the Jewish people have less need for immediate revelations of God Himself once they have received His Torah.

The abyss between God and man is also portrayed as a feature of the historical condition of the Jewish people. After the destruction of the Second Temple in 70 C.E., Jewish sources reflect the view that the moral failings of the Jewish people were responsible for that catastrophe. The liturgy captures the sentiment that the destruction of the Temple and the forced exile from Jerusalem were due to Jewish sin: "Because of our sins, we were exiled from our homeland."[9] Some sources go so far as to imply that human sin caused God to withdraw his protection from the Temple and make it vulnerable to attack and destruction. These rabbinic passages forcefully convey the notion that this exile was the direct result of human acts that forced God to remove the immunity from destruction that He guaranteed by His presence from the Holy of Holies in the Temple. This permitted the Romans, who acted as agents of God's dissatisfaction with His people, to attack Jerusalem and send the Jewish people into exile:

When the Holy One, Blessed be He, wished to destroy the Temple, He said, "So long as I am in it, the gentile nations will

not harm it. I shall, therefore, cease to regard it and shall swear not
to give it heed until the time of the End." At that moment, the
enemy entered the Temple and burned it. When it was burnt, the
Holy One, Blessed be He, said: "I no longer have a seat upon the
earth; I shall remove my presence therefrom and ascend to my
first habitation." At that moment, the Holy One, Blessed be He,
wept and said, "Woe unto Me! What have I done? I caused My
presence to dwell for Israel's sake, and now that they have sinned,
I have returned to My original place."[10]

Thus, human sin also contributed to the abyss that grew between God and man. This passage describes the abyss in concrete
terms as the ascent and return of God to a higher habitation from
where He had earlier descended. In fact, other rabbinic passages
describe God as having ascended through seven habitations to
His permanent dwelling place in "the seventh heaven." Each of
these reinforces the notion of God's increasing distance from
man, a notion that runs directly counter to the biblical conception of God. There, God is at times described as a transcendent
being, hidden in the recesses of his inaccessible habitation, and at
other times, immanent within the world, accessible and near.

Some rabbinic authors such as the second century Aramaic
translator of the Torah, went so far as to suggest that the God of
the Bible did not really appear to the forefathers. The translator
subtituted a new term, *Shekhinah* (literally, presence), to characterize the appearances of God to man.[11] By differentiating between God and His *presence,* the translator sought to preserve
God's hiddenness and inaccessibility while maintaining that He
could also appear to man. The use of different terms, however,
does not suggest two different gods or aspects of God; it merely
serves to reinforce the dual nature of God – hidden and revealed –
through the use of different proper nouns. Still, the novelty of
suggesting that God has two natures was not lost on the readers
of the translation. They lived in the period after the destruction
of the Temple and consequently felt, in real historical terms, the
abyss that separated man from God. By their own account they
recognized that their religious experience differed from that of
their ancestors. They were acutely aware of the abyss.

While the abyss prevents man from approaching God, God
can still bridge the gap at His will. After all, it is an abyss of His

own creation. It does not prevent God from exercising His providential watch over the world:

> Rabbi Levi said: To what can the matter be compared? To an architect who built a city and made therein secret places, hideouts, and chambers and, eventually, he became the ruler. He then sought to seize the bandits in the city and they fled and hid themselves in those hiding places. He said to them: "Fools! Are you seeking to hide from me? I, after all, am the craftsman who built the city, and I, therefore, know all the secret places and the entrances and exits of the hideouts better than you." Likewise, the Holy One, Blessed be He, says to the wicked: "Fools! Wherefore do you conceal the wickedness in your hearts? It is I who have built man and I know all the secret chambers and recesses within him."[12]

The rabbis maintained a respect for the rare individual who possessed the combination of religious and spiritual powers that would allow him to overcome the abyss. They did not deny that it was possible to overcome the abyss. On the contrary, they recorded several instances of individuals who achieved states of mystical contact with God or attained direct communication with Him. The rabbis, however, in deciding points of law, did not give weight to such spontaneous contacts with God because these could lead the individual to claim that his experience gave him greater authority than the legal authority of the Torah or the rabbinic court. Since rabbinic Judaism is predicated upon the foundation of the Torah, the notion of majority rule, and the common consent of the Jewish people to accept rabbinic decisions as legally binding, the mystic posed a potential challenge to the rabbinic system of law.

The rabbis acknowledged the truth and validity of mysticism and other forms of intense personal religious experiences. As a practical matter, however, they deemed such personal experiences irrelevant as a basis for formulating legal decisions. Mysticism simply does not confer any special status upon the mystic. This is clear in the following talmudic legend:

> One day, Rabbi Eliezer was in dispute with the other sages on a matter of law. He brought all the proofs in the world in support of

his opinion but the other sages would not accept them. He said to them: "If the law is according to me, let this locust tree prove it." And the locust tree moved one hundred cubits. (Some say four hundred cubits.) The sages said to him: "The locust tree cannot prove anything."

Then he said to them: "If the law is according to me, let this stream of water prove it." And the stream of water turned and flowed backward. They said to him: "The stream cannot prove anything."

Then he said to them: "If the law is according to me, let the walls of the House of Study prove it." The walls of the House of Study began to topple. Rabbi Joshua reprimanded the walls: "If scholars are disputing with one another about the law, what business is it of yours?" The walls did not fall down out of respect for Rabbi Joshua and did not straighten up out of respect for Rabbi Eliezer. They are still so inclined!

Then Rabbi Eliezer said to them: "If the law is according to me, let the heavens prove it." A voice then came forth from heaven and said: "Why do you dispute with Rabbi Eliezer? The law is according to him in every case!"

Thereupon, Rabbi Joshua rose to his feet and said: " 'It is not in heaven' " (Deuteronomy 30:12). The Torah has been given once and for all at Mount Sinai. For you have already written in the Torah at Mount Sinai: 'After the majority must one incline' (Exodus 23:2)."

Later on, Rabbi Nathan came upon Elijah the Prophet. He said to him: "What was the Holy One, Blessed be He, doing at that moment?" Elijah said to him: "He was smiling and saying: 'My children have defeated me! My children have defeated me!' "[13]

The astounding conclusion reached in this passage is that the disagreements among rabbinic scholars about points of law are no business of God's! God freely transferred the right to interpret his Torah to competent rabbinic jurists. These jurists have established procedures for the resolution of differences in legal matters. No individual has the right to circumvent the process of jurisprudence by claiming special prerogatives or authority. Although the rabbis do not deny that prophets and mystics may converse with God, they do insist that such experiences are legally irrelevant. Among the rabbis of the talmudic period, mysticism is simply regarded as an extracurricular affair.

The rabbis point to another reason for discouraging individuals from attempting to bridge the abyss. In the legend of the four sages who entered the garden, three were afflicted with various unforeseen consequences: death, insanity, and apostasy. The rabbis warn against pursuing the mystical quest, not because it is unreachable but because it is dangerous. Jewish mysticism, they warn, promises great turmoil and unsettling awesomeness rather than calm and serenity. The mystic quest is a path of many dangers and threats even though the road is open to those who wish to tread on it. This is why the rabbis introduced the idea that God makes His presence, not His very being, known to those who study the Torah and follow a moral code of conduct.

God's presence, called the *Shekhinah,* is the term used to describe the perception of God in the world. Even though God's being is truly inaccessible, there are moments when individuals feel acutely aware of His nearness and involvement with human affairs. Such moments may occur when one witnesses God's activity in the world. In order to distinguish between the transcendent being and the occasional moments of religious intimacy, the rabbis coined the term *Shekhinah* to refer to the latter. This concept domesticates God's being and makes mysticism wholly unnecessary because God is near. Without the yawning abyss, there can be no mysticism.

One early rabbinic passage attempts to reject the literal interpretation of a biblical text that suggests that man can reach God. The rabbinic passage explains that one cannot expect to actually approach God or to have direct encounters with Him. It suggests that to approach God means to emulate His moral attributes.

> "After the Lord your God you shall walk" (Deut. 13:5). And is it possible for a man to walk after the *Shekhinah?* Rather, this means that one should emulate the virtues of the Holy One, Blessed be He.[14]

The rabbis were able to insure the continued belief in the nearness and immediacy of God in the world while preserving the unbridgeable abyss by introducing the concept of the *Shekhinah*.

There are few statements in Jewish religious literature that capture more fundamentally the notion that God is believed to be present in the act of study and observance than the following dictum:

> If two sit together and occupy themselves with words of Torah, the *Shekhinah* abides in their midst.[15]

Rabbinic Judaism is, ultimately, a religious system that substitutes rituals of study, priestlike purity, and moral goodness for direct religious experience between man and God. In this regard rabbinic Judaism is antimystical or at least attempts to neutralize the mystical impulse inherent in all religions. Judaism is a religion in which the abyss is filled with the rituals of prayer, study, purity, and morality.

Prayer, in rabbinic Judaism, is one of the most important means of achieving nearness to God and awareness of God's presence in the world. The God who guides history, who judges man from heaven, who hears and answers the petitions of His people, and knows the innermost reaches of the heart is the object of these prayers. Prayer is an act of great faith in the transcendent God's concern for the world. Without actually denying the abyss, prayer affirms that it can be traversed by the supplicating voice.

Mysticism is a form of religious experience that occurs when man is acutely aware of the abyss that separates him from God, knows that his predecessors had a relationship that he cannot have, and attempts to bridge the abyss. Therefore, from the vantage point of Jewish history, mysticism could only have occurred once the second, or *institutionalized*, stage of religion had developed. Jewish mysticism is the attempt to bridge the abyss that was formalized in the rabbinic period and to return to the religious experiences common in the first, or *creative* period. In religion as in history, however, time can never go backwards. Mysticism is a form of religion that comes to terms with the abyss between man and God.

Rabbinic Judaism established certain norms that shaped the

way Jews thought about religious issues. The rabbinic conception of God was, however, based on the paradoxical formulation
that God is both transcendent and immanent.[16] He is removed
and hidden by nature, yet the performance of his commandments allows us to become aware of His abiding presence;
indeed, through our actions we can permit His *Shekhinah* to dwell
in our midst. The problem that rabbinic Judaism solved was how
to make the experience of God accessible in a period in which we
do not hear voices from heaven. They rejected the legal admissi-
bility of the individual religious experience, direct contact with
God, or prophecy in favor of the indirect relationship with God
that is possible through the fulfillment of the Torah.

The solution of rabbinic Judaism, however, served only to
create another more serious dilemma: How can the individual
fulfill God's will without experiencing Him directly as did his
ancestors? If all of the force of religion is based on the compelling
revelation of God to his predecessors, as it is transmitted by the
Torah, why should not the experience of God be available to him
as well?

On an even more fundamental level, a religious Jew might
ask about the paradox of God's essential remoteness even as his
religion promotes nearness. Which shall it be? If God is transcendent, how is it possible for anyone to have a relationship with
Him? And if there is no relationship with the hidden God, what
is the meaning of the fundamental rituals of Judaism such as
prayer? Finally, it is impossible to repeat the accounts of the
ancestors' direct encounters with God without, at some point,
asking if these experiences are still possible. The desire to experience God as deeply as Abraham or Moses did lies at the heart of
the mystical impulse in Judaism as much as does the temptation
to bridge the abyss between the hidden God and the God who
listens to, cares about, and answers the prayers of man.

4

THE HIDDEN AND THE REVEALED:

The Principles of Jewish Mysticism

Rabbinic Judaism developed a comprehensive theology: a system of teaching about God and His relation to the world. That theology was based on several important principles. Although these principles were never codified, they are implicit in the teachings of all Jewish thinkers from the rabbinic period until the present. They are also important keys to understanding how Jewish mysticism developed out of rabbinic Judaism.

Shortly before the second Temple was destroyed by the Romans in 70 C.E., the Jewish community in the Land of Israel was torn apart by a bitter internal struggle. The issues that divided them involved the tactical question of how best to respond to the Roman presence and pressure in Palestine and the strategic question of how to define Judaism as a way of life. There were those who promulgated a policy of conciliation and appeasement and believed that it was possible to preserve the institutions of the Jewish people through concessions to the Roman Empire. Many of these were Sadducees, a group from among the priestly class, which was responsible for the Temple administration, tax collection, maintaining the treasury, and insuring the continuation of sacrifices. The Sadducees also believed that the Jewish people had only one central religious institution, the Jerusalem Temple, and that God was localized there in the Holy of Holies. In their view, there was no Judaism without the Temple and no Temple without Roman sanction. Therefore, they pursued a dual policy of submission to Roman rule, accompanied by a degree of assimilation to Roman urban culture, and a staunch defense of the centrality of the Temple and the priesthood within Judaism.[1]

A second segment of the community, the Pharisees, criticized the Sadducees for having assimilated too much of Roman culture and for overemphasizing the centrality of the Temple. They believed that the essence of the Jewish religion was more than sacrifices offered by the priests in the Temple on behalf of the Jewish people who supported the Temple through donations, tithes, and contributions. Moreover, they did not adhere to the Sadducean notion that only priests were able to expiate sin and petition God. They also challenged their claim that only priests were qualified to interpret the Torah, for this led to the impression that only priests could serve God.

The Pharisaic challenge was directed against the Sadducee's fundamental conception of the Torah. The Pharisees believed that the written Torah supported the Sadducean claim to priestly privilege, but the ancient judges and prophets also possessed authority equal to that of the priests. They based this view on the fact that upon Moses' death, leadership passed both to the priests and the elders. The latter were succeeded by the judges and, eventually, the prophets. The Pharisees believed that in addition to the written Torah which served as the basis of priestly authority there is another source of authority that goes back to the time of Moses, which they called "the Torah that was [transmitted] orally" (*Torah she-be-al peh*). This source of authority is enunciated in the opening of one of the earliest Pharisaic manifestos, the Mishnaic tractate *Avot* (Fathers):

> Moses received the Torah at Sinai and transmitted it to Joshua. Joshua [passed it on] to the elders, the elders to the prophets, and the prophets to the men of the Great Assembly.

Since they were the successors of the men of the Great Assembly, this tractate supported the Pharisees' opposition to the Sadducean view that only priests have the right to interpret the Torah. The Pharisees asserted the legitimacy of another interpretive tradition, that of orally transmitted guidelines governing the religious rights and responsibilities of nonpriests and religious rituals outside the Temple.

The Pharisaic beliefs were based on an understanding of Judaism that challenged the Sadducean notion of an exclusively Temple-centered religion. The Pharisees taught that every man is a priest, every Jewish home a temple, every table an altar, and every meal a ritual sacrifice.[2] Moreover, any meal that was conducted without words of Torah being spoken was like a sacrifice conducted improperly. The Pharasaic rituals were an attempt to extend the holiness and sanctity of the Temple to the home by expanding upon the notion that the written Torah was accompanied by an orally transmitted interpretation of the Torah that mandated new responsibilities for Jewish householders.

The war between the Jews of Israel and the Romans raged between 66 and 70 C.E. The Roman victory and their destruction of the Temple put an end to the Sadducean or priestly aspirations for a Temple-centered Judaism. The Pharisaic religious outlook made it possible to conceive of the continuation of Judaism without the Temple.[3] The issues of authority and legitimacy that divided the Sadducees and Pharisees became moot, and the groundwork for the continuation of Judaism was guaranteed. What the Pharisees did not realize was that their Oral Torah was soon to become as important in determining the future course of the Jewish people as the Written Torah.

The Pharisees made a virtue out of necessity. They soon developed new institutions and rituals to preserve the religion of Israel. They expanded the "houses of assembly" (synagogues) where the people assembled on market days and Sabbaths to hear the Torah read publicly as they had done in the Jerusalem Temple. The sacrifices, now extinct, were replaced by prayers of thanksgiving and petition that were offered in the houses of assembly before and after the Torah reading. Soon a regular liturgy developed, and the houses of assembly became central places of prayer and teaching.

The rituals of priestly preparations for sacrifices were now transferred to the home where the head of the house was to assume the holiness of the priests. He was to conduct himself in a ritually and morally pure manner through rituals of washing and reciting blessings. The very act of eating an ordinary meal was transformed into a dramatic reenactment of the priestly sacrifices of wine, grain, fruit, and meat to God and was thereby invested with priestly holiness. Individuals who were trained in the specific requirements of the priestlike rituals were called *rabbis* (masters) because of their mastery of the Oral Torah.

The Judaism of the last two thousand years is the legacy of Pharisaism and the innovations that were based on their understanding of the Oral Torah. All subsequent movements to introduce change in Judaism have attempted to claim that their reforms were part and parcel of the oral tradition in Judaism. In particular, efforts are usually made to justify innovations through citing corroborating biblical verses or statements by talmudic sages who make up the continued oral tradition.

In the twelfth century Moses Maimonides (RaMBaM) (1135–1204) introduced a sweeping new codification of Jewish law called *Mishneh Torah* (*Repetition of the Law*). The title boldly suggests both a repetition, or recapitulation, of the Oral Torah law code and a book second in importance only to the Torah. This fourteen-volume work was strongly attacked by some because it did not quote earlier rabbinic authorities. The suspicion that Maimonides went too far beyond some of his predecessors and thereby set himself up as a greater authority than the oral tradition was raised about this and his other writings as well.[4] His *Mishneh Torah,* however, soon gained acceptance and assumed great importance as the basic codification of Jewish law.

Maimonides' *Guide of the Perplexed* presents an interpretation of two of the most important theories contained within the Oral Torah. These teachings, "The Account of Creation" and "The Account of the Chariot," are interpretations about the nature of the origins of the world and the nature of the prophet Ezekiel's ecstatic vision of God, respectively.[5] Since the biblical accounts of these two events are rather brief and enigmatic, various speculations and theories had been advanced orally, transmitted as unwritten interpretations as part of the Oral Torah, and eventually some of these ideas were recorded in the Talmud and other writings.

Maimonides, who was interested in the question of the origin of the world and the problem of whether one can know God, found these biblical accounts perplexing. He did not find the rabbinic explanations of creation and theology wholly satisfactory because they were contradicted by current scientific knowledge and philosophic beliefs. He was drawn to the teachings of ancient Greek and medieval Islamic philosophers. There he found compelling explanations for these problems but, as a rabbi, he was troubled by the fact that he found these interpretations closer to the truth than the ones he knew through the Talmud. In order to avoid claiming that Aristotle had more to say on these issues than Judaism, he ingeniously tried to prove that the real meanings of "The Account of Creation" and "The Account of the Chariot" are identical with the teachings of Aristotle. His claim that Aristotle's philosophy was compatible with the Oral Torah was strongly attacked as an abuse of the integrity of authentic Jewish oral traditions.

The *Kabbalah,* which originated in Provence and Spain shortly after Maimonides' death, faced a similar challenge. The *Kabbalah* sought to introduce a new notion of spirituality without appearing to be new. The very term *Kabbalah* means *that which is received.* In fact, the name *Kabbalah* derives from the very same word (*kibbel*) used in the tractate *Avot* to explain the chain of transmission of the Oral Torah. *Kabbalah,* therefore, means *tradition* in the sense that it claims to be another stage in the unbroken transmission of the Oral Torah going back to Sinai.

The early Kabbalists used another technique, pseudepigraphy, to identify their new teachings as part of the oral tradition. Pseudepigraphy is the publishing of literature under an assumed name. The Kabbalists published many of their most important works under the name of some of the most distinguished figures of the oral tradition. In some cases forgeries were knowingly introduced as genuine. In other cases false authorship was ascribed to certain texts over the course of time and circulation. *Sefer ha-Bahir (The Book of Pure Light),* whose real author is unknown, was attributed to Rabbi Nehunya ben ha-Kanah, a sage who lived in the second half of the first century. *Sefer ha-Zohar (The Book of Splendor),* the most important literary work of the *Kabbalah,* was probably written in the late thirteenth century by Moses de Leon of Guadalajuara who attributed it to Rabbi Shimon bar Yohai, a pupil of Rabbi Akiva. Still, the Kabbalists believed that their theories were indeed the true teachings of the Oral Torah, which they had rediscovered.

The belief of the Pharisees and their rabbinic successors, the talmudic sages, in the principle of the authenticity and continuity of the oral tradition made it necessary for every subsequent movement of reform or innovation in Judaism to prove that it was based upon, or part of, the Oral Torah. Jewish mystics could not claim that their experiences entitled them to special knowledge or status within Judaism, nor could they claim to be above the Torah law. There is little encouragement in Judaism for those reformers who openly claim originality; continuity and tradition are held as greater virtues. Jewish mystics were usually rabbis who followed the Torah and tried to assimilate their mystical experiences into traditional Judaism by using prayer as the vehicle for the mystic quest. The Torah, written and oral, became the idiom through which Jewish mystics explained their illumination.

The rabbinic conception of God, discussed in the last chapter, is based on the paradoxical formulation of God's essential closeness to man even as He remains remote and hidden across the unbridgeable abyss. Rabbinic Judaism is based on rituals such as prayer whose purpose is to bridge the abyss with the human voice. The Written Torah contains many accounts of the ancestors who maintained a close relationship with God, whereas the traditions of the Oral Torah emphasize the abyss between man and God and the means of crossing it. Attempts to bridge the abyss found their justification within the oral tradition itself. A Jewish mystic would naturally be guided by the biblical and rabbinic conceptions of God in embarking upon his quest.

Maimonides may not have been thoroughly persuasive in his claim that his interpretation of creation and Ezekiel's vision was based on the Oral Torah. His discussion of God, however, clearly is based upon its rabbinic traditions. In fact, Maimonides accepts the rabbinic notion of the abyss and refines the concept in many novel ways.

Maimonides, like the rabbinic sages, teaches that God is unique, transcendent, uncaused, incorporeal, and without limit.[6] He goes further than they did, however, in claiming that God is, therefore, unknowable. All we can know, he asserts, is that God exists. If that is the case, however, how are we to explain all the biblical and rabbinic descriptions that portray God as having physical characteristics such as a face, hand, and arm and emotional attributes such as compassion and anger?

Maimonides explains that these descriptions are the result of events in the world whose cause we attribute to God. In fact, God does not have an "outstretched arm" or a "face," nor does He show anger or compassion. God, however, acts, and the consequences of His actions are described in human terms as being similar to what we know is the result of an action of a hand or an action done with anger or compassion. But, Maimonides warns, we should not confuse human and divine actions by attributing to God what are merely human physical or emotional characteristics. God is by nature above that.[7]

Maimonides was troubled by many of the biblical and talmudic expressions that portray God in very human terms. The Bible speaks of God's hand, face, front, back, and eyes as well as his hearing, seeing, and anger. The rabbinic literature even portrays God as crying and wearing a prayer shawl. Were these to be taken literally as suggesting that God has the same characteristics, emotions, and habits as humans? There were, in fact, several books popular in the Middle Ages that asserted that God literally has physical dimensions of awesome proportion. Or were these to be taken as metaphors, symbols, or mere figures of speech? If that were the case, how are they to be interpreted and understood?

Maimonides explained the biblical anthropomorphisms, expressions that attribute human physical characteristics to God, as being necessary to convey to the ancient Israelites a sense of God's existence, actions, and providence. The anthropopathic expressions, which attribute emotions to God, really mean to convey God's moral attributes and the myriad ways in which He governs the universe. Maimonides was also disturbed by passages in the Oral Torah that describe God as crying and praying. In response to this Maimonides states: "Anyone who is led to believe that God has a body is a heretic!"[8] Still, in the thirteenth century, his view was criticized by Rabbi Avraham ben David (RABaD), Isaac the Blind's father and one of the leading rabbis of France, who defended the belief that God has anthropomorphic and anthropopathic qualities.[9]

Gradually, Maimonides' conception of God gained accep-

tance and replaced many of the more popular views of God as
having physical and emotional characteristics. Maimonides' God
was the hidden God of the rabbinic tradition. Maimonides explained that the biblical and talmudic passages that speak of God
in human terms are not meant to be taken literally. They are
mere figures of speech since "The Torah speaks *as if* in the
language of the sons of man."[10]

Maimonides professes that there can be no real relationship
between God and man since God is unique, incorporeal, and
transcendent. There is nothing that God and man share since
man is corporeal and rooted in the physical world. There can be
no relationship between two beings who share nothing in common. Maimonides, in an attempt to refine and purify the rabbinic conception of God, makes God so removed from humanity
that there is almost no human contact with Him. Maimonides
attempted to destroy the paradox inherent in the rabbinic view
that God is both remote and near by concluding that since God
cannot be both, He must be one or the other. His philosophic
consistency led him to the conclusion that God must be remote
and inaccessible.

Maimonides widened the abyss separating God and man.
He taught that God is unique and unknowable. From the time of
Maimonides, few challenged his notion of God's essential
uniqueness and remoteness. The challenge that remained was
how to reestablish a relationship between man and the unknowable God. That challenge was met by the Kabbalists who sought
to recover the lost unity. The *Kabbalah* originated, simultaneously to the rise of German Hasidism, among mystics in
Provence and Spain who also sought to bridge the abyss.

The common term for God among Maimonides' philosophic contemporaries was not the biblical and traditional
written name of God *YHVH* (known as the Tetragrammaton)
pronounced *Adonai.* God was designated as *bilti baal takhlit* (translated from the Arabic term *la nihaya,* one who has no limit), *sibbat
kol ha-sibbot* (the cause of all causes) and *shoresh ha-shorashim* (the
root of all roots). The philosophers stressed the impersonal aspect
of God in order to emphasize the differentness of God. For them
there was no personal God; the personal God of the Bible was
only a myth, a means by which primitive people imagined their
God. For those who could live in the rarefied atmosphere of

philosophy and had no need for a personal God, it was hard to imagine how one could attribute personality to God without diminishing His greatness. In most respects the Kabbalists and German *Hasidim* accepted Maimonides' concept of a unique and unknowable God. The mystics found it difficult to understand how one could dispense with the concept of a personal God. The God of philosophy was hardly one to whom a Jew could pray. Nevertheless, there was little disagreement on the notion of the absolute impersonality of God's essence.

Late in the twelfth century, Elazar of Worms, the leader of the German *Hasidim* and a contemporary of Isaac the Blind, composed a poem to God in which the difference between the personal yet hidden God of rabbinic Judaism and the impersonal, hidden God of Maimonides is apparent. The passage is from his *Chapters on Mystery, Unity, and Faith*:

> God is one, there is no boundary to His wisdom, no measure to His understanding, no limit to His power, and no end to His unity. He has no beginning and no end. The Shaper of all and the Knower of all has neither front nor back, height nor depth, for He has neither boundary nor end in all that He has. The Creator of the world has neither limits nor limbs.[11]

If this impersonal God has none of the attributes given to Him in biblical and rabbinic literature, how are the traditional attributes to be understood? The answer of the Kabbalists and the *Hasidim* is bold: All references to anthropomorphisms and anthropopathisms in Scripture and rabbinic literature do not refer to the hidden God! One of the later kabbalistic writers explained that the true, unknowable, transcendent God is never even mentioned once in the Torah, Prophets, or Writings.[12] To whom, then, are these references made?

The Kabbalists introduced a distinction between the hidden and revealed aspects of God. The hidden, infinite aspect of God is called *Eyn Sof* (without end). This name came to be understood as the proper name for the hidden aspect of God: *The Infinite.* It only suggests that God exists without implying anything about His character. In fact, according to the Kabbalists, God should be referred to as *It* rather than *He,* although there is no neuter gender in the Hebrew language. Because of the great sublimity and transcendence of God, no name at all can be applied to It. The term *Eyn Sof* only conveys that God is unlike anything we know. According to these mystics, *Eyn Sof* is not the object of prayers, since *Eyn Sof* has no relationship with His creatures. The personal aspect of the hidden God is called the *Eser Sefirot,* which literally means *the ten numerals.* Simply put, the Kabbalists believed that *Eyn Sof* possessed ten aspects of His being. There are, therefore, two natures to God's being—the infinite, unknowable essence and the ten identifiable noninfinite aspects of His being. The major literary work of the *Kabbalah, Sefer ha-Zohar,* contains few passages about *Eyn Sof* but many about the *Eser Sefirot.* It is possible to examine several of the important passages in the *Zohar* that convey novel conceptions of God.

The first passage in the *Zohar* begins with a discussion about the nature of prayer and sacrifices. It is based on a biblical verse that explains that a sacrifice is a "burnt offering to the Lord, a pleasing odor."[13] The *Zohar* asks whether the pleasing odor ascends to God. The underlying problem in this passage is whether sacrifices can actually please God who is exalted above all finite matters:

> Rabbi Elazar asked Rabbi Shimon: "The connection between the burnt offering [and God] is made in the Holy of Holies in order to bring illumination [to the world]. How high does the union of the priests', Levites', and the Israelites' purposefulness ascend?"
>
> Rabbi Shimon said: "Our masters [of Oral Torah] taught: The union ascends to 'the Infinite.' Every connection, unification and perfection is hidden in the hiddenness of the One who is not reached or known and in whom the highest purposefulness is found. 'The Infinite' is not knowable and has neither beginning nor end.
>
> But there is 'the Infinite' which has neither purposefulness nor lights nor illuminations within its own infinity. All the lights and illuminations depend on it for their existence and are, themselves, imperceptible."[14]

How high does the pleasing odor rise? Does it reach God? Can an individual bridge the abyss and reach God with his sacrifice? The answer is unambiguously positive: "The union ascends to *Eyn Sof!*" Thus, it is indeed possible to bridge the abyss through certain ritual actions and under certain specific circumstances. *Eyn Sof*, however, is absolutely impersonal and beyond all characterization. All that can be said about this God is that He is above everything and is called *Eyn Sof*.

The Kabbalists understand God as Maimonides describes him, with one crucial difference. Their impersonal God is influenced by man and can therefore be said to have a relationship with man. In another passage of this same work, *Eyn Sof* is described as being impersonal; at the same time, he is characterized as the God of the Bible:

> Rabbi Shimon continued [with an explanation of the verse]: 'See now that I, even I, am He and there is no God but Me' (Deut. 32:39) [Shimon] said: Friends, hear these ancient words, for it is my intention to reveal [a secret] after receiving permission from on high. What is the meaning of 'See now that I, even I, am He?' This is the Supreme Cause, the one called 'the Cause of Causes' because He is the cause of all those known causes (i.e., the *Sefirot*). None of those known causes can act at all unless they receive permission from a higher cause, as I explained above with reference to 'Let us make man.' I mean, 'let *us* make,' literally! It refers to two, one of which says to the one above it, 'Let us, etc.' It did nothing until it had permission and assent from the cause above it which could not act unless it, in turn, had the agreement from the cause above it. But about the one who is called 'the Cause of all Causes,' above which there is none and below which it has no equal, it is said, 'To whom shall you liken Me and compare Me says the Holy One?' (Isaiah 40:25). This is the one who says, 'See now that I, even I, am He and there is no God but Me.'[15]

The hidden God is active and causative of other stages of being. He causes the *Sefirot* to come into existence. They, in turn, are causes that produce other stages of being. Each cause has a cause except for *Eyn Sof*, which is the uncaused cause. It causes but is not caused. The highest cause is identical with God who is unlike, and cannot be compared with, any of the lesser causes. This is also one of the rare instances in which the Kabbalists state that *Eyn Sof* is mentioned in the Bible. The lesser causes, the *Sefirot*, constitute the personal aspect of God that is manifest in the narratives of the Bible. For example, it is not *Eyn Sof* but the *Sefirot* who create man. Together, the infinite and the finite, the impersonal and the personal, the higher and the lower aspects of God constitute the being known as God.

In the century before the appearance of the *Zohar*, a Spanish Kabbalist, Azriel of Gerona, composed a catechism of Jewish mystical beliefs. Written in the form of questions and answers, it attempts to convey in direct language the mystical conception of the infinite God:

> If one should ask, 'Why should I believe in *Eyn Sof*?' You should tell him: You ought to know that everything which is visible or perceptible to the heart is finite. Every limited thing has an end and every finite thing is not perfect. Therefore, there must be that which is without limit and which is called *Eyn Sof*. It is absolute perfection in complete unity which does not change. If it is without limit, there is nothing beside it. Since it is sublime, it is the root of all things visible and unseen. Since it is hidden, it is the basis of faith and of disbelief. The masters of speculation admit that we are unable to grasp it except by saying what it is not.[16]

Azriel employed a simple deductive method of proving that since there is a universe of finite, knowable beings, they must have their cause in a being that is infinite and unknowable. Azriel represented the school of kabbalistic thought that sought to retrace the stages of being back to the first cause. He concluded that the first cause is unique, infinite, impersonal, and unknowable. Little else can be said about this being.

This understanding of God's nature goes far beyond the notions of divine transcendence found in the Bible. It directly contradicts the more intimate and personal characterizations of God found in biblical and rabbinic literature. This kabbalistic conception was philosophically consistent with the premise of God's uniqueness, but it carried the notion to its extreme. The Infinite is certainly not the God with whom one can have a relationship or to whom one might pray for help. It is even hard to imagine that this might be the God who spoke on top of the mountain in the wilderness.

The introduction of the concept of *Eyn Sof* was the common

legacy of Maimonides and the early *Kabbalah*. The Jewish mystics followed the basic conception of God introduced by Maimonides, who distilled the concept of God of all anthropomorphic and anthropopathic properties. They did not follow the philosophic conception which went so far as to assert that God was above all relations with man. The Kabbalists preserved the impersonality and infinity of God while preserving the essential religious relationship between man and God. The Kabbalists, paradoxically, prayed to the unique, unknowable God of Maimonides, thus preserving the notions of God's transcendence and nearness in a new way. They accepted the widening of the abyss yet, at the same time, made the challenge of reaching this infinite God the central element of their religion. Their mysticism is based on their pursuit of the unique and unreachable God.

5

THE CALCULUS OF THE DIVINE WORLD:

The Teaching of the Sefirot

In an anonymous thirteenth-century text, *Sefer Maarekhet ha-Elohut* (*The Structure of Divinity*), the following definition of Jewish belief appears:

> [The basis of belief is] the negations which ought to be made in reference to God for the sake of the perfection of His unity and the proper sequence in which one makes these negations. Everyone following our religion ought to believe that God is one and unique in absolute unity.

> The ancients' statement about unity is an affirmation of perfect oneness. Their statement obligates every one who is perfect in his belief in [God's] unity and every person who is enlightened concerning unity to make three explicit negations, and they are: [the negation of] corporeality, composition and change [in God].

> The denial of corporeality means that God is not limited and is neither a body nor a force in a body. The principle of this negation is that God is not limited by either place or time. For He is, was and always will be.

> The denial of composition means that God is a pure Mind. One ought to believe that pure Mind is not simply a mind separate

from a body. . . . He is pure Mind, unique in absolute oneness
with no end or limit to the perfection of His unity.

The denial of change excludes two types of change: change of
thought and change of action.[1]

The chief characteristics of God are His incorporeality, His
absolute immateriality, and His unchangeability. The impersonal description of God is the result of God's absolute dissimi-
larity to anything known to humans and their consequent inability to say anything positive about God. All that can be
known about God is that He is not like anything human.
Therefore, the only possible description of God comes through
excluding all those human qualities by which we describe our-
selves such as our corporeality, our composition of body and
mind, and our changeable actions and thoughts. The Kabbalists
believed that all that could be said about Him is what He is not.
This did not mean, however, that man is ignorant of God's
existence. On the contrary, it is only God's nature that is unfa-
thomable.

These mystics thought the most likely description of God
was as pure Mind. He is a mind without body, a universal
intelligence that is unlike any other mind, the infinite and incon-
ceivable mind of the universe. This infinite mind is always
thinking, never changing, and thinks only infinite thoughts
about itself. Thus "the Infinite," is the perfect mind thinking
perfect, infinite thoughts completely unrelated to anything but
itself. God is the one who is thinking, the very act of thinking,
and the object of His own thought.

This would be an apt and appropriate characterization of a
universal intelligence if there were no world. God, the pure mind,
does not think about anything but His own essence and so has no
concern with the world. But Judaism teaches that there is a world
created by a God who cares for and has a relationship with the
world. The Kabbalists teach that this infinite mind neither created a world nor has any relation to it. This is not the God of the
Bible nor the object of traditional prayer. How do they solve the
problem of preserving God's unity while at the same time
preserving the traditional relationship between God and man?
Moreover, how is it possible to describe God as unchangeable if
at times He has spoken to man and at other times He is silent? Do

these Kabbalists mean to say that all of the traditional teachings of Judaism about God are wrong? Or do they suggest that the object of our prayers is not the true God but some lower, less infinite manifestation of God?

The Kabbalists introduced the idea that *Eyn Sof* possesses ten aspects of His revealed Being, or instruments of activity, called *Sefirot*. The term *Sefirot* originally meant *numerals* and was taken from the earliest Hebrew text on the nature of numbers and letters, *Sefer Yetzirah* (*Book of Formation*). It is a generic term that, in itself, just means that the aspects of God's being, or the instruments of God's activity, can be counted; there are ten *Sefirot* just as there are ten cardinal numbers. Some mystics explain that the term *Sefirot* comes from the Hebrew root *sapper*, which means *to tell*, suggesting that these aspects *tell* us about God. Others have suggested that it derives from the Hebrew word for *sapphire* since the *Sefirot* illuminate our knowledge of God like a precious and radiant gem. The term itself tells us little about the meaning and nature of the *Sefirot*.

There have been a variety of attempts to translate the term *Sefirot* into English. They have often been called 'spheres,' 'radiances,' and other terms suggesting occult meanings. The *Sefirot*, however, are symbols of the various aspects of God's being or activities and are identifiable as being ten in number. A more faithful English rendition would be *Calculi*, a term that signifies both a means of reckoning and the use of symbols, for the *Sefirot* are numerically identifiable symbols of God's being and activities. Although a good English translation of *Sefirot* would be desirable, the use of the original Hebrew term is still preferable.

The *Sefirot* are the bridge across the abyss, the connective tissue between the infinite God and the finite world. They are the link that makes it possible to preserve God's absolute unity while preserving the relationship between God and man. They, and not *Eyn Sof*, are the object of human prayers and the subject to which all biblical anthropomorphisms and anthropopathisms refer. The *Sefirot*, not *Eyn Sof*, are the God of the Bible.

By differentiating between *Eyn Sof* and the *Sefirot*, it is possible to say that God is incorporeal, immaterial, and unchangeable while still preserving the traditional notion of the God who spoke at Sinai. All the references to the traditional notion of an active, personal God refer to the *Sefirot*, which are the subject of anthropomorphic and anthropopathic references. All the references to God that imply corporeality, composition, and change refer to the *Sefirot,* not to *Eyn Sof.* Therefore, *Sefer Maarekhet ha-Elohut* can justifiably claim that *"Eyn Sof* is nowhere mentioned in the Bible." The Bible refers only to the *Sefirot,* not to the hidden God.

The theory of the *Sefirot* is an attempt to explain how the infinite God can have a relationship with any finite thing and how an unknowable God can be known by man. The relationship of *Eyn Sof* to the *Sefirot* can generally be explained only by drawing an analogy. One of the most common kabbalistic analogies is that of the relation of the soul to the body. The soul, invisible and unknowable, dwells within the body. Although there is only one soul in each body, the soul acts through a variety of physical organs. The soul is, therefore, the essence that uses the "instruments" of the body for its activity. The manner in which the soul is connected to the body is still a mystery. Nonetheless, we claim to know that there is a soul even if it remains inscrutable because of its incorporeal nature.

The *Sefirot* are understood by one school of Kabbalists as the vessels or instruments through which God acts.[2] *Eyn Sof* is like the soul in relation to the *Sefirot* which are its vessels or organs. In order to avoid suggesting that *Eyn Sof,* itself, acts, these Kabbalists, who may be called *instrumentalists,* explain that the *Sefirot* are God's vessels. In their view, *Eyn Sof,* whose infinite nature has nothing in common with the *Sefirot,* remains totally passive and unchangeable. What appear to be changes are only the various modes by which the *Sefirot* channel, reflect, and employ the essence of *Eyn Sof.* Change, to paraphrase *Molly Bawn,* is in the eye of the beholder.

Other Kabbalists, who might be called *essentialists,* believe that the *Sefirot* are God's essence, and that there is a common nature to *Eyn Sof* and the *Sefirot.* They adopted this position in order to avoid suggesting that we pray to *Sefirot* that are different from God. If prayer is directed to the *Sefirot,* the worshipper would be praying to a false god or, worse yet, to different gods, unless the *Sefirot* were indistinguishable from *Eyn Sof.*

These two views, the theory of 'vessels' and the theory of 'essence,' were one of the few major points of difference among the Kabbalists. Although there was only one *Kabbalah,* these two schools of thought represented two fundamentally different approaches to the problem of how God could be both hidden and revealed.

The 'instrumentalist' doctrine of the *Sefirot* as vessels seeks to avoid attributing change or composition to God's essence by relating them to His vessels, not His essence. The only essence of God is His infinite, unchangeable essence. The *Sefirot* are mere instruments of its activity. None of the changes attributed to God through the anthropomorphic or anthropopathic descriptions in the Bible refer to the hidden God; they refer to the *Sefirot,* which are distinct from the hidden God. Each *Sefirah* is separate and distinct from the hidden God because each one is an instrument through which *Eyn Sof* acts. Each instrument is another dimension of divine activity. When the Bible speaks of God's compassion or judgment, it does not refer to *Eyn Sof,* which is above all definition, but to the *Sefirot,* instruments called *compassion* or *judgment.* When the Bible speaks of God's hand, eye, front, or back and the like, it refers symbolically to the *Sefirot.* Therefore, all attributes of God refer to the *Sefirot,* the vessels through which God acts and that are distinguished from God's essence.

The *Sefirot* can be seen as containing the divine essence like the body contains the soul. They share, in some way, the infinite nature of the essence that acts through them. The *Sefirot* are not the hidden God, but neither are they not the hidden God. They are both infinite and finite because they are the bridge that links God's infinity to everything else. They are infinite because they are the vessels of *Eyn Sof;* they are finite because they are not *Eyn Sof.* God acts through the *Sefirot* in bringing all other things into existence and in governing the world. Prayers, praises, and descriptions of God are directed at the *Sefirot,* not to the infinite God who remains recondite and inscrutable, infinite and impersonal, unrelated and indifferent to the world. The doctrine of the *Sefirot* as vessels succeeds in avoiding attributing change or activity to the hidden God at the expense of the concept of a personal God.

The portion of the *Zohar* known as *Raaya Mehemna* (The Faithful Shepherd) contains many selections that reflect the 'instrumentalist' theory. In one such section, God is described as acting without being known because He acts through the instrumentality of the *Sefirot:*

Woe to one who compares God [i.e., *Eyn Sof*]
to any of the [human] characteristics
or even to one of His own attributes,
all the more so to one who compares Him to humans . . .
who are born and die.
God may be characterized according to His governance
upon a particular attribute (i.e., one of the *Sefirot*)
or even upon all the created beings.
When He disappears
above and beyond that attribute,
He cannot [be said] to have that attribute,
characteristic or form.

God is like the ocean
for the waters of the ocean
cannot be grasped and have no shape
except when they are channeled into a vessel,
such as the land,
and take on a shape;
then we are able to measure them:
the source, the waters of the ocean are one;
then, a tributary comes forth
and is channeled into a round basin . . .
the source is one
and the channel which comes from it is two.
Next, a large vessel [is formed],
as if one dug a large basin
which becomes filled by the waters of the channel;
this becomes three . . .

Now, if the artificer
would break these vessels which he created,
the waters would return to the source
and only broken vessels would remain,
dry and without water.
Likewise, the Cause of Causes
made ten *Sefirot,*
calling the Crown 'the Source.'
There is no end
to the fullness of [the source's] light

and, therefore, He called himself *Eyn Sof* . . .
Everything is within His power,
to withhold from the vessels
or to replenish them with fullness
and withhold according to His will.
There is no other God
above Him who can add to Him
or diminish Him.[3]

The first three *Sefirot* are described as follows: *Eyn Sof* is described as being indistinguishable from the first vessel. This first *Sefirah*, the infinite and undifferentiated expanse, is the source of everything else. Then the essence of *Eyn Sof* is channeled into a tributary that gives the first definition to the boundless expanse. This tributary is the second *Sefirah*. Next the channel empties into a basin that is defined by the contours of the land around it. The basin is the third *Sefirah*, and the land around it constitutes the other *Sefirot*. This analogy suggests that the *Sefirot* are vessels or channels that limit the infinite *Eyn Sof* and give finite definition to everything else. The description is also reminiscent of the creation narrative in Genesis and suggests a parallel between the creation of the *Sefirot* and the creation of the world.

The 'instrumentalist' conception of *Eyn Sof* is profoundly impersonal. *Eyn Sof* is thoroughly removed from everything and never reveals itself. All that is traditionally associated with the personal concept of God as the being who reveals Himself, cares about man, and answers his prayers is relegated to the *Sefirot*. In order to consider *Eyn Sof* as God, the mystic must be willing to engage in an unusual degree of remoteness and abstraction.

The doctrine of the *Sefirot* as the essence of God is an attempt to preserve the concept of a personal God. It does, however, imply that God's essence changes according to the differences among each of the *Sefirot*. Kabbalists of this persuasion believed that it was more important to preserve the notion of a personal God than it was to preserve the unity of God. These Kabbalists describe the relation of *Eyn Sof* to the *Sefirot* by an analogy to a candle. Many candles can be lit from one candle without ever changing the nature of the first candle. Therefore, one unique essence can be the source of many other essences without undergoing any essential change.

The essentialists also believed that the descriptions and attributes that appear in the Bible refer to the *Sefirot* and not to *Eyn Sof*. Unlike the instrumentalists, however, they claim that God is portrayed in the Bible since the *Sefirot* are God's essence. Thus they are able to preserve the personal concept of God while referring all of the anthropomorphisms and anthropopathisms to the *Sefirot*, not *Eyn Sof*.

The difference between *Eyn Sof* and the *Sefirot* is one of degree. *Eyn Sof* emanates or radiates the *Sefirot* like a powerful transmitter that broadcasts signals through space. This process is called *Atzilut* (emanation). The *Sefirot* are the signals, which do not differ essentially from the original broadcast no matter how far it is sent. The *Sefirot* are the same as *Eyn Sof*, but the distance from the source produces a slightly different reception. Therefore, the only difference between *Eyn Sof* and the *Sefirot* is according to the receivers. God is *Eyn Sof*, but sometimes He is *perceived* as one *Sefirah*, whereas, at other times He is perceived as another. God never changes; only our perception changes. The changes in our perception, or reception, correspond to the different *Sefirot*.

In the 'essentialist' scheme, each *Sefirah* differs from the other according to its distance from *Eyn Sof*. There are altogether ten *Sefirot*, and each one emanates from *Eyn Sof*. The first is more sublime and more pure than the tenth, but each one contains the essense of *Eyn Sof*. Each one reflects another aspect of God's nature, or essence. When it appears that God acts in different ways, it is really a different *Sefirah* acting.

If, as the essentialists maintain, the *Sefirot* are just different aspects of one infinite essence, the personal aspect of God is preserved although the unity of God is somewhat compromised. On the other hand, the instrumentalists preserve the integrity of the divine unity while sacrificing the personal aspect of God. While neither theory is able to preserve both personality and unity, the two schools of thought flourished side by side according to the predilections and theological inclinations of the Kabbalists.

The term *Sefirot* first appears in *Sefer Yetzirah* and later in *Sefer ha-Bahir*. These texts, however, do not employ the term in the same sense that it came to mean in the *Kabbalah*. The earliest kabbalistic treatises in Gerona, particularly the writings of Azriel, describe the *Sefirot* in ways that came to be accepted among all subsequent kabbalistic writers. The Gerona Kabbalists also codified the names of the individual *Sefirot* although some variations in the names persisted.

The Kabbalists, following the definition found in *Sefer Yetzirah,* taught that there are ten *Sefirot.* It was left to the Gerona Kabbalists, the disciples of Isaac the Blind, to identify the *Sefirot* by name. Six of the names were derived from the biblical verse:

> Yours, Lord, are greatness (*Gedulah*), might (*Gevurah*), splendor (*Tiferet*), triumph (*Netzah*), and majesty (*Hod*) . . . to you, Lord, belong kingship (*Mamlakhah*) . . .[4]

Each adjective was understood as an attribute of God that the Kabbalists included in their list of ten *Sefirot.* To these six they added three others to represent the idea that God is pure mind. These three, *Keter* (crown), *Hokhmah* (wisdom), and *Binah* (understanding), were placed at the top of the list. A ninth, *Yesod* (foundation), was inserted, and the decad was complete.

Keter (crown), is the first *Sefirah* emanated from *Eyn Sof.* It is the highest and most glorious of the *Sefirot* and *crowns* them all. It stands as the barrier between *Eyn Sof* and the other *Sefirot* and, so,

KETER (*crown*)

HOKHMAH (*wisdom*)

BINAH (*understanding*)

GEDULAH (*greatness*) usually called **HESED** (*mercy*)

GEVURAH (*might*) usually called **DIN** (*judgment*)

TIFERET (*splendor*)

NETZAH (*triumph*)

HOD (*majesty*)

YESOD (*foundation*)

MALKHUT (*kingship*)

Figure 5-1   The canonical list of *Sefirot*

encircles and *crowns Eyn Sof.* Because each *Sefirah* is emanated
from another, the highest one, *Keter,* stands hierarchically above
them all.

Sometimes *Keter* is identified with *Eyn Sof.* Most often,
however, *Keter* is the first *Sefirah* radiated, or emanated, by *Eyn Sof*
which stands above it. Those who identify *Keter* with *Eyn Sof*
lean toward the 'essentialist' point of view and believe that the
Sefirot are only different stages in the unfolding of God's infinite
essence. Those who believe that *Keter* is the first *Sefirah* and is not
identical with *Eyn Sof,* generally follow the view that *Eyn Sof* acts
through vessels, the *Sefirot,* and that God and His vessels are not
similar. Therefore, the essentialists favor the 'personalist' notion
of God and theorize that *Keter* is the same as *Eyn Sof.* The
instrumentalists believe that God is impersonal, and *Eyn Sof* is
above *Keter.*

There are many other names for *Keter* in the *Kabbalah.* It is
often called *Ayin* (nothingness) because it is beyond all existence
and is nonetheless the cause of all existing things. In the *Prayer of
Nehunyah ben ha-Kanah,* written in the thirteenth century, a hymn
to *Keter* appears:

> Everything is in it,
> for the internal powers of the *Sefirot* are in it.
> The vitality and existence of everything stem from it.
> It is analogous to the soul
> which gives life to the body
> and constitutes it.
> The constitution of everything is in *Keter.*
> There is no front or back,
> right or left, in this *Sefirah.*
> It is called 'Indifferent Unity.'[5]

It is also called *Hokhmah Penimit* (internal wisdom) because it is the
hidden potentiality of divine wisdom before it is revealed or the
Mahshavah Elohit (divine thought) because it is produced by *Eyn
Sof,* the pure Mind. *Keter* is similar to *Eyn Sof* in many of these
respects but different in others. It differs in that it is the highest
aspect of God which moves into activity out of the repose of *Eyn
Sof.* Both *Eyn Sof* and *Keter* are unknowable and imperceptible.
Keter is the more active representation of God's will which

cannot be known except during the rare moment when God chose to reveal Himself as *Ehyeh Asher Ehyeh* (I Am What I Am). The Kabbalists display a certain ambivalence about whether *Keter* can be known.

In the following passage *Eyn Sof* and *Keter* are described paradoxically as the hidden and revealed will of God, respectively. *Keter*, however, cannot be known except through the unique intuition that comes about through mystical revelation.

> Rabbi Shimon said:
> I raise my hands upward in prayer.
> When the divine will up above (i.e., *Eyn Sof*)
> shines upon the will
> which is eternally unknown and imperceptible,
> the first hidden upper will (i.e., *Keter*)
> produces its unknowable creation
> and radiates what it does secretly.
> Then, the will of divine thought
> pursues the first will
> in order to be illuminated by it.
> A curtain is then opened
> and, from inside, with the divine will
> pursuing [the upper will],
> it reaches and yet does not reach [up]
> and the curtain begins to radiate.
> Then, the divine thought
> is illuminated secretly
> and remains unknown, hidden.
> The illumination coming from
> the hidden upper unknown will strikes the
> light of the curtain
> which is lit up by the will
> which is unknown, unknowable and concealed.
> The light of the concealed thought
> strikes the light of the curtain
> and they both radiate,
> creating nine palaces.[6]

This passage illustrates how in moments of deep revelation Rabbi Shimon bar Yohai, the voice of the *Zohar*, reveals his mystical knowledge. *Eyn Sof* emanates its essence upon *Keter* and activates it. *Keter,* in turn, turns back to *Eyn Sof* to draw down further essence linking them together. As *Keter* turns back to reflect its light toward *Eyn Sof,* its source, it strikes a barrier that stands between it and *Eyn Sof.* The barrier reflects the light of *Keter* back to it and creates the third *Sefirah.* This process of emanation and reflection creates the ten *Sefirot.*

The Kabbalists placed great importance on the inner workings of God especially on the relationship of *Eyn Sof* to *Keter.* They attempted to explain how the infinite God can bridge the abyss between Himself and the world. In the passage above there is very little difference between *Eyn Sof* and *Keter* except the slight gradations of difference between the divine will and the upper will. Still, there is a curtain that separates them. When they sweep aside that separation, they radiate against each other and create the other *Sefirot.*

Some Kabbalists were disturbed by the idea that there is little difference between *Eyn Sof* and *Keter.* They believed that there were a series of three imperceptible luminous beings that interposed between *Eyn Sof* and *Keter.* They radiate out from *Eyn Sof* and become embedded in *Keter. Keter* then becomes God's pure Thought. This is described in the following passage quoted from the *Responsum of Hai Gaon:*

> The three supernal lights have no beginning for they are the name and essence and root of all roots. Thought cannot apprehend them because apprehension is impossible and the knowledge of all creatures is too weak to comprehend the Holy Name. We have learned their names: 'primordial internal light' which radiates in the hidden root and shines from its radiant power the likeness of the two great luminaries. The 'polished light' and the 'clear light,' all of which are one light, one essence, and one root hidden infinitely.[7]

Keter cannot be known because it is either identical with, or only slightly different from, *Eyn Sof.* Like a king who is hidden from most of his subjects, he can be known by his venerable crown which is filled with precious gems and diamonds. *Keter* is, however, identified as divine thought and the source of all the other *Sefirot.* The thirteenth-century *Tradition of Wisdom from the Sages of Mata Mehasya* describes *Keter:*

Supernal *Keter* is a world hidden unto itself. All the *Sefirot* receive from its emanation even though it is separate, recondite and bound up with the root of all roots which cannot be apprehended by thought. *Keter* receives from the root without any interruption in a subtle whisper. It emanates and pours forth from its reservoir upon the other crowns which are always close to its emanation.[8]

The unknowability of *Keter* is due to its identity with, or proximity to, *Eyn Sof*. Yet it is also the root of all the other phenomena of the world especially the other *Sefirot*. It is the cause of the *Sefirot* and produces them through *Atzilut* (emanation). Emanation, according to most Kabbalists, is a process of hypertrophy, or overflow, from *Eyn Sof*. *Eyn Sof* is, by nature, effulgent and tends to spread its essence outward. The *Sefirot* are there to receive this essence.

Emanation, according to other Kabbalists, most notably Nahmanides, is a process in which *Eyn Sof* limits its own infinity through contracting or constricting itself. God cannot create anything directly from His own boundless and infinite essence unless He voluntarily limits Himself.[9] The Kabbalists use the analogy of the sun to explain this process. The radiant light of the sun shines endlessly due to its great power and brilliance. Nothing could be seen, however, unless the unbridled light of the sun is restricted, allowing for the emergence of shapes, contours, and details. In the same manner the radiance of *Eyn Sof* must be contracted and limited through the emanation of *Keter*, a channeling of the infinite mind and will into the more defined thought and will. *Keter* is the means by which the infinite God makes all other creations possible. It is the transition between God's infinity and the finite world.

It is ironic that the Kabbalists should have so much to say about an unknowable God. They speculated endlessly on the nature of God and on His *Sefirot*. Although much consideration was given to *Eyn Sof* and *Keter*, the Kabbalists recognized that human knowledge could never adequately penetrate the secrets of the infinite God. Much more analysis was devoted to the *Sefirot* below *Keter*, beginning with *Hokhmah*.

In the Book of Proverbs several passages speak of God's wisdom, which existed alongside Him before He created the world:

The Lord created me at the beginning of His course as the first of His works of old.[10]

Later, the rabbinic sages developed this notion with the suggestion that God employed His wisdom (*Hokhmah*) in the creation of the world.[11] The Kabbalists elevated His wisdom, gave it individual existence, and made it the second *Sefirah*. They called it *Hokhmah* (wisdom), *Reshit* (beginning), *Yesh* (being), and *Abba* (father), because it is the first being to have existence outside of *Eyn Sof*.

Hokhmah contains within itself the archetypes, the ideal prefiguration of all things. It is the divine realm of the perfect model and blueprint of everything that might come into existence at some later stage of God's unfolding of His being. Since *Eyn Sof* and *Keter* are the divine will, *Hokhmah* is the sum total of all the possibilities of existence. Everything that might conceivably come into being anywhere and at any time exists within *Hokhmah* as sheer possibility. In *Hokhmah* things exist in a general way as concepts, ideas, or principles, not as individual phenomena. The archetypes are static and undifferentiated and the blueprint upon which the universe is ultimately modelled. *Hokhmah* contains God's idea of what the world should be.

Hokhmah is considered to be the ideal pattern for the world which exists deep within the recesses of the divine mind. Because *Hokhmah* is associated both with the essence of God and the blueprint of the universe, the Kabbalists imply that the universe must first exist within *Hokhmah* before it can stand on its own. The universe is ultimately indistinguishable from God's essence. Everything that is later to be found in the universe is found first in *Hokhmah*.

The very tendency to emanate the archetypes of existence is also associated with *Hokhmah*. *Hokhmah* is the generative and active power within God that emanates the archetypes into reality. Because *Hokhmah* is understood to be active and even procreative, it is often described in masculine terms as the "father" (*Abba*) of the other *Sefirot*. *Hokhmah* is, therefore, the archetype of masculinity and activity.

The sexual overtones and the association of masculinity with activity lead to a differentiation between so-called masculine and feminine *Sefirot*. If *Hokhmah* is masculine, *Binah* (understanding), which is emanated from it, is feminine. Kabbalistic treatises describe how *Hokhmah* emanates the third *Sefirah, Binah,* also called *Imma* (mother). *Binah* is impregnated with the archetypes found within *Hokhmah.* Within *Binah,* the embryonic archetypes become more distinct and differentiated into specific phenomena.

Hokhmah becomes associated with masculinity and the trait of activity. *Binah* becomes associated with femininity and receptivity. While these notions reflect the way the Kabbalists understood the process of emanation, they also reflect medieval ideas about sex-role differentiation. With these two *Sefirot,* the Kabbalists set the stage for the establishment of opposing, or contrary, powers that would carry out the process of emanation. From this point on the *Sefirot* are divided into masculine and feminine vessels or essences.

The fourth and fifth *Sefirot,* called *Hesed* (mercy) (other sources call it *Gedulah*) and *Din* (judgment) (other sources call it *Gevurah*), are emanated from *Hokhmah* and *Binah.* They, too, represent archetypes of contrary powers that act in the world. *Hokhmah* emanates *Hesed,* which symbolizes the power of unmitigated love and mercy. Surprisingly, *Hesed* is associated with the masculine domain. *Binah* emanates *Din,* which signifies the power of severity and absolute justice. *Hesed* and *Din,* like the two before them, are seen as opposites because they represent extremes.

Hesed illustrates the divine inclination to emanate and fill the universe. It is associated with the tendency to radiate the infinite essence of *Eyn Sof* without end. Were this to occur, the divine essence would permeate all corners of the universe leaving no room for anything but God. Therefore, God had to constrain Himself from acting this way by limiting Himself. This necessitated that His *Hesed* be tempered by His *Din. Din* represents the ability of God to limit His goodness by halting its emanation. This attribute is associated with the archetype of femininity, which the Kabbalists understood in terms of severity and limitation. *Hesed* is the tendency to emanation; *Din* is the tendency to withhold the emanation. Since too much emanation would not allow room for the universe to exist, both are necessary.

Primitive notions that associated femininity and sinister forces also entered the *Kabbalah.* Although the literal meaning of *sinister* is *left side,* the Kabbalists linked together the *Sefirah Din* with femininity, left-sidedness, and the demonic. As the feminine, *Din* curtails the activity of *Hesed.* *Din* itself is said to be capable of issuing its own emanation which takes shape outside of the world of the *Sefirot* as the realm of demonic forces. The "left emanation" from *Din* creates a universe of evil that stands locked in permanent and mortal combat with the power of the *Sefirot.* The mythology of *Din* is meant to convey that there is not a great difference between good and evil, and that one God has created them both.

The archetypes of *Hokhmah, Binah, Hesed,* and *Din,* respectively, represent the ideal types of intellectual and moral qualities that are found in man. The archetypes are the blueprint upon which God lays out the plan of the world. But ideal archetypes rarely exist in nature because they are rarely found except in combination with other qualities. Also, these ideal types are extremes that tend to stand in conflict with their opposites. Therefore, the Kabbalists introduced the sixth *Sefirah, Tiferet* (splendor), in order to harmonize the intellectual and moral opposites within the *Sefirot.*

The Kabbalists taught that the world is a place of conflict between opposing forces: good and evil, life and death, holiness and impurity, obedience and sin, reward and punishment, masculinity and femininity, knowledge and ignorance. They further believed that these polarities were rooted in the *Sefirot,* particularly in the polar *Sefirot* of *Hesed* and *Din.* On the other hand, they believed that no one power is able to act by itself. The masculine *Sefirot* need the feminine in order to act. Without its opposite each of the *Sefirot* could only act in a distorted fashion. *Hokhmah* could not be truly creative unless *Binah* gave definition to the archetypes within it. *Hesed* could not bring about a universe unless *Din* gave definition and limit. Alone, the polarities of the *Sefirot* – right and left, active and passive, male and female, good and evil – remain ineffectual. A universe of extremes cannot endure. All opposites need to be moderated by another element in order to be brought into a state of harmony and balance.

The moderation of opposites among the *Sefirot* of *Hesed* and *Din* occurs with the emanation of *Tiferet.* This *Sefirah* harmonizes the boundless love of *Hesed* and the strict judgment of *Din.* It is often portrayed as the masculine offspring of the *Sefirot Hesed* and

Din. It is the point of harmony between the upper *Sefirot* and the ones that come after it. Because of its pivotal role as harmonizer of the various opposing tendencies, *Tiferet* is regarded as the axis and stable center of the *Sefirot.*

Because *Tiferet* symbolizes the state of harmony among the *Sefirot,* it came to be associated with the traditional name for God in rabbinic literature–*Ha-Kadosh Barukh Hu* (*The Holy One, Blessed be He*). *Tiferet* was understood to be the subject of many traditional prayers. Prayers that emphasized God as father and king were usually prayers referring to *Tiferet* in particular or, through it, to the *Sefirot* in general. In this way *Tiferet* was often portrayed as the representative of the other *Sefirot. Tiferet* came to symbolize the aspect of God that was known as the traditional God of Judaism, the God of the Hebrew Bible. *Tiferet* was the *Sefirah* that most closely symbolized the transcendent deity. It was the *Sefirah* that spoke at Sinai as the representative of the other *Sefirot.*

The *Sefirot Netzah* (triumph) and *Hod* (majesty) are often described as the means by which God governs the world. They correspond respectively to *Hesed* and *Din* and represent a lower manifestation of these upper *Sefirot.* Divine providence, or governance, was understood as the phenomenon of God's emanation of His essence upon the world. The further away this emanation flows from God to the world, the more diluted it becomes. In fact, if God would withhold his favor from the world, the emanation would temporarily cease and leave the world vulnerable to demonic forces or chaos. The *Sefirot* serve as the conduits for the transmission of this divine grace upon the world. The *Sefirot Netzah* and *Hod* were understood as filters that pass along the emanation from *Hesed* and *Din* to the *Sefirot* below. These two *Sefirot* are the conduits by which the divine essence is transmitted from the upper *Sefirot*–to *Tiferet*–to the lower *Sefirot,* especially *Malkhut.* They are the means by which divine preservation of the world is assured.

The tenth and last *Sefirah, Malkhut* (kingship), is also called the *Shekhinah* (divine presence), *Atarah* (diadem), and *Kavod* (glory). It is the last vessel of God's activity and the vessel through which the rest of the *Sefirot* act. It is the boundary of the divine realm and the outermost vessel through which God acts. When the Kabbalists describe the *Sefirot* in a hierarchical scheme, this is the last of the *Sefirot.* Below this is the beginning of the nondivine realm, the end of God. *Malkhut* is also the least infinite of all God's aspects and the most accessible dimension of his personality. Thus, this *Sefirah* is the one that is most frequently known to man and the one most aimed at in prayer. *Malkhut* is the funnel through which the divine essence, carried along through the vessels of the *Sefirot,* overflows upon man and the world.

This overflow *creates* the worlds below God and gives substance and sustenance to humanity. By means of this emanation, which is channeled across the abyss from God to man through this *Sefirah,* individuals are able to retrace the path to God and bridge the abyss. Knowledge of how God conveys His essence to the world through this *Sefirah* provides the key to unraveling the mystery of how one can bridge the abyss. To paraphrase the neo-Platonist Plotinus: "Everything comes from the One, and everything returns to the One." The secret of the *Sefirot* is the secret of reaching oneness with God.

The *Zohar* contains many passages that describe the emanation of the *Sefirot* in rich symbolic detail. Rarely does it present the *Sefirot* in a vocabulary that a modern reader can comprehend. It uses symbols for these divine processes that are taken from the language of the Bible. The Kabbalists had an unusual approach to the Bible and read it differently than a modern reader would. They believed that the *Sefirot,* and not *Eyn Sof* itself, are described in the Bible and that biblical descriptions of God refer to the *Sefirot.* This approach can be illustrated by their interpretation of the different Hebrew names used to describe God in the Bible. For example, *Elohim* (Lord) refers to the *Sefirah Binah* and *YHVH* (God) refers to *Tiferet.* In addition biblical narratives were not taken at face value. They refer to the *Sefirot* that are portrayed symbolically in all of the biblical stories. Stories about the patriarchs in Genesis are read as symbolic accounts of the various *Sefirot.* Abraham represents *Hesed,* Isaac symbolizes *Din,* Jacob refers to *Tiferet,* and Joseph points to *Yesod.* This meant that the biblical narratives were not only about real people but about cosmic dramas involving the *Sefirot.* Even the story of creation in Genesis depicts the creation, or emanation, of the *Sefirot,* not just the physical creation of the world.

The *Zohar's* commentary on the creation narrative from Genesis vividly exemplifies the mystical interpretations of the *Kabbalah:*

"In the Beginning . . ."

When the King conceived ordaining
He engraved engravings in the luster on high.
A blinding spark flashed
within the Concealed of the Concealed
from the mystery of the Infinite,
a cluster of vapor in formlessness,
set in a ring,
not white, not black, not red, not green,
no color at all.
When a band spanned, it yielded radiant colors.
Deep within the spark gushed a flow
imbuing colors below,
concealed within the concealed of the mystery of the
   Infinite.
The flow broke through and did not break through its aura.
It was not known at all
until, under the impact of breaking through,
one high and hidden point shone.
Beyond that point, nothing is known.
So it is called Beginning,
the first command of all.

"The enlightened will shine like the splendor of the sky,
and those who make the masses righteous will shine like
the stars forever and ever" (Dan. 12:3).

Zohar, Concealed of the Concealed, struck its aura.
The aura touched and did not touch this point.
Then this Beginning emanated
and made itself a palace for its glory and its praise.
There it sowed the seed of holiness
to give birth
for the benefit of the universe.
The secret is:
"Her stock is a holy seed" (Isa. 6:13).

Zohar, sowing a seed for its glory
like the seed of fine purple silk.

The silkworm wraps itself within and makes itself a palace.
The palace is its praise and a benefit to all.

With the Beginning
the Concealed One who is not known created the palace.
The palace is called Elohim.
The secret is:
"With Beginning, [the Concealed One] created Elohim"
(Gen. 1:1).[12]

This passage poetically describes how the impulse to emanate its
fullness upon the universe welled up within *Eyn Sof* and finally
burst through in a dazzling display of radiance. The flow of
divine essence congealed into the *Sefirah Hokhmah,* the first point
in the new universe. This mystical world remained paradoxically concealed within itself and yet revealed in the point called
Hokhmah. This point was then enveloped in *Binah,* also called by
the divine name *Elohim* (Lord), a garment for *Hokhmah.* The *Zohar*
concludes the passage with an intentionally playful misreading
of the first verse in Genesis. Instead of reading the verse as "In the
beginning, God created . . .," it offers the verse as follows: "By
means of the [*Sefirah* called] 'Beginning' (i.e., *Hokhmah*), [*Eyn
Sof/Keter*] created *Binah* [which is called *Elohim*]." Thus the creation
story is really about the origins of the *Sefirot* not the earth.

The *Sefirot* may be either God's essence or His instruments
of activity, but they are, nevertheless, divine. The incorporeal
world of divinity, the realm of the *Sefirot,* is the first stage in the
unfolding of God's relationship to the world. This realm was
explained by the Kabbalists as the aspect of God that was
unknown to those who believed only in the hidden God. This is
the revealed dimension of God, the personal aspect, the God to
whom we pray, the object of the mystic quest. It is the essence
that fills the vacuum of the abyss and allows man to establish a
relationship with God.

It is not surprising, therefore, to find that the Kabbalists
composed their own prayers to God that were directed at *Eyn Sof*
and the *Sefirot.* The introduction to *Tikkunei Zohar,* a book written
in the style of the *Zohar,* begins with the following prayer to be
recited before embarking upon the mystic quest for God:

Master of the worlds,
You are one but not according to number.
You are elevated above all heights,
more hidden than all hidden things.
No thought apprehends You at all.
You are He who brought forth ten perfections
which we call the ten *Sefirot*
through which You govern the worlds,
hidden, concealed and revealed.
Because there are ten *Sefirot*,
You are also hidden from man.
You join the *Sefirot* together
and cause them to be one.
Since You are present in them,
one who considers one in isolation from the rest
is considered himself
as one who thinks of You
as having separate parts.

Master of the worlds,
You are the cause of causes,
the first cause
who waters the Tree from your spring.
This spring is like the soul to the body,
the life of the body.
Nothing can be compared to You,
within or without.
You created the heavens and the earth,
the sun and the moon,
the stars and the constellations.

There is no one who knows You at all,
and there is nothing as unique or unified as You,
above or below.
You are called the Lord of all.
You have no proper name since
You are the very essence of the divine names,
the perfection of the names.
When You withdraw from your names,
they are left
like a body without a soul.[13]

The *Sefirot* through which *Eyn Sof* reveals itself and establishes a relationship with the world span the abyss between man and God. The emanation of the ten *Sefirot* from God unfolds in a sequential process in which the hidden God reveals Himself through His attributes, thereby weaving the strands of His own personality. The *Sefirot* are not as infinite as the hidden God but, together with Him, constitute God. God is primarily *Eyn Sof,* but He is also the *Sefirot.* Together they are divinity and the God that, according to the religious tradition, is the object of prayer. The Kabbalist acknowledges thereby that God is both transcendent and immanent.

The *Sefirot* form triads or groupings that represent aspects of God's creativity and goodness. *Keter, Hokhmah,* and *Binah* respectively symbolize the triad of God's pure Mind, His act of thinking, and the object of His thought, which is His own infinity. A perfect being must only contemplate itself, but, consequently, His thought takes on a life of its own. Thus God's thought, the idea or archetype of perfection, becomes a *Sefirah* and takes on an independent life of its own. This archetype is the perfect representation of God's wisdom, the highest of His qualities, and the symbol of divine perfection.

The second configuration of *Hesed, Din,* and *Tiferet* is the triad of archetypes of God's ethical perfection. These *Sefirot* are, respectively, the symbols of God's moral attributes of unqualified love, strict and unforgiving justice, and tempered judgment. The first two characteristics are extremes that are mitigated by the third attribute. The third triad, *Netzah, Hod,* and *Yesod,* represents the agents of God's governance and providential guidance of the world.

The first nine *Sefirot* form three triads of archetypes – intellectual, moral, and providential – that God employs in creating a blueprint for all of existence. God then employs these archetypes as would an architect who refers to the symbols or blueprint that he has drawn up before actually creating his edifice.

The Kabbalists frequently chart the *Sefirot* in a drawing that depicts them in the form of a human body. The chart, rendered below, suggests that the *Sefirot* correspond to the human constitution: the first three intellectual archetypes within God are the blueprint for the human intellect and are depicted by the head;

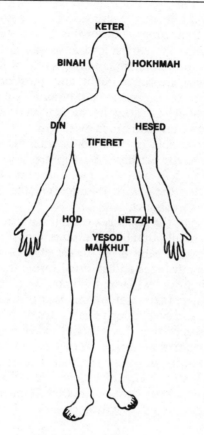

Figure 5-2 The *Sefirot* of Being

the second triad of moral virtues corresponds to human moral actions associated with the hands and regulated by the heart; the triad of providential or governing archetypes is symbolized by the human thighs and sexual organs, the seat of power.

The Kabbalists explain the relation of the world of the *Sefirot* to the other realms in terms of this triadic principle. The world of the *Sefirot* gives birth to the world of spiritual forms, the realm of "pure forms" in which all of the archetypes of God's attributes assume independent existence outside of God. This realm of forms contains the ideal model and prefiguration of all of the forms of the world. In this realm, however, they are only the forms or ideas of all things and not the things themselves. For example, this is the storehouse of the souls, the abode of the heavenly Torah and Jerusalem, and the world of forms of such human attributes as greatness, might, and splendor.

These forms take on matter and become real things in the "natural world" which is below the spiritual world. In this realm, the spiritual forms are combined with "matter" and become sensible and perceptible objects. Souls enter into bodies, the earthly Torah and the earthly Jerusalem are built according to their heavenly models, and the divine attributes become the moral qualities that the Jewish tradition enjoins man to adopt and exhibit in daily conduct.

The doctrine of the *Sefirot* is a complex and comprehensive attempt to explain all of reality. It teaches that what we see of this world is only the visible tip of the iceberg, outward manifestations of divine attributes and spiritual forms that come from God. All of existence pulsates and vibrates with an inner life of form and attributes. Like matter composed of atomic particles, nothing is static, and everything reverberates with inner spiritual forms and an essence that flows from God. Everything in the world is an essence that comes from God and is clothed in vessels. Some vessels are more spiritual, like the Torah, and others are more material, like the human body. But every object contains divinity in one form or another, and, therefore, it is possible to retrace the steps of existence back to God, the source.

6

THE *SHEKHINAH*:

The Feminine Aspect of God

Malkhut, the tenth *Sefirah,* elicits a special fascination for Kabbalists. It is the vessel that gathers the essence that has been transmitted through the other *Sefirot* and channels it outward. It is, for the Kabbalists, the symbol of God's presence in the world and the aspect that is most readily accessible to mankind. This function of the tenth *Sefirah* is called the *Shekhinah* (divine presence).

In the Talmud the term *Shekhinah* refers to the personification of God's presence in a particular location, and it is the noun used to describe the human perception of God's presence on earth. It is the synonym for God that is used by the sages to describe God's nearness and presence, to be distinguished from the term *Ha-Kadosh Barukh Hu* (*The Holy One, Blessed be He*), which they used to describe God's hidden persona. They are both the same God except that the former term describes His immanence and the latter, His transcendence.

The term itself was coined by the rabbis from the verb root "to dwell" (*shakhan*) since it was associated primarily with God's localized presence in the portable tabernacle in the desert and later in the Temple. God commands Moses on Sinai to build a tabernacle that will house the divine covenant:

> And let them make Me a sanctuary that I may dwell (*shakhanti*) among them.[1]

The term is used interchangeably with other names for God especially when He is said to be present in the world. For example, the rabbis offer the following explanation of the biblical verse, "After the Lord, your God, you shall walk" (Deut. 13:5):

> And is it possible for a man to walk after the *Shekhinah*? Rather, it means that one should emulate the virtues of the Holy One, Blessed be He.[2]

Thus, in order to avoid suggesting that God walks or that man can walk after God the rabbis suggest that *walking* means *emulation*. It was more acceptable to suggest that one can emulate the moral actions of the immanent presence of God rather than His transcendence. Thus, it is the *Shekhinah,* not *The Holy One, Blessed be He,* that is mentioned.

The sages of the rabbinic period introduced new concepts to explain the reality that they experienced. In doing so they institutionalized the concept of the abyss and required that it be taken into account as a religious fact. Thus all religious experiences must be based on the premise that God is both transcendent and immanent. The remedy for this abyss, in the rabbinic period, was the concept of the *Shekhinah,* which helped explain how God could be remote and near at the same time. After Maimonides widened the abyss, undermined the concept of immanence, and made God wholly transcendent, the concept of the *Sefirot* served to restore God's immanence.

The *Shekhinah* became a synonym for God's nearness and the personification of God's presence among practitioners of Jewish rituals of study, worship, and eating in a state of purity. With the destruction of the Temple and the transference of priestly purity to Jewish homes, the presence of God that had been in the Temple was now extended to those same homes and to the academies in which the Torah was studied. The replacement of the Temple by the home and Torah academy is indicated in the following rabbinic aphorism:

> If two sit together and occupy themselves with words of Torah, the *Shekhinah* abides in their midst.[3]

God's immanence was not destroyed with the destruction of the Temple. Generally, rabbinic sources propagate the belief that

God's immanence is permanently attached to the Jewish people, guarding over them wherever they may be. Rather than arguing that the destruction of the Temple suggests God's abandonment, most sources reassure the people of God's abiding interest in and concern for their fate:

> Wherever Israel went into exile, the *Shekhinah*, as it were, was exiled with them. They were exiled to Egypt, the *Shekhinah* was with them. They were exiled to Babylon, the *Shekhinah* was with them.[4]

The moral charge that the destruction of the Temple was due to human sinfulness was not vitiated by this reassuring position. Jewish immorality, responsible for the loss of the Sanctuary, could still cause the banishment of God's nearness from the world:

> Whoever is humble will ultimately cause the *Shekhinah* to dwell with men on earth. But whoever is haughty will bring about the defilement of the earth and the departure of the *Shekhinah*.[5]

The rabbis attempted to conceptualize the notion of God's nearness in such a way that allowed it to be localized in a particular place without being restricted to one address. The *Shekhinah* could be in any place:

> Why did the Holy One, Blessed be He, reveal Himself to Moses in a [lowly] thorn bush? This teaches us that there is no place on earth void of the *Shekhinah*.[6]

The nearness of God does not imply that there are different *Shekhinot* (plural of *Shekhinah*) for each localized presence of God:

> The [Roman] Emperor said to Rabban Gamliel: "You say that wherever there is a company of ten [Jews], the *Shekhinah* abides in their midst. How many *Shekhinot* are there then?" Rabban Gamliel replied: "The sun shines upon each individual and, at the same time, upon the world as a whole. Now, the sun is just one of the thousand myriad attendants of the Holy One, Blessed be He.

How much more so the *Shekhinah* of the Holy One, Blessed be He."[7]

The rabbinic conception of the *Shekhinah* did not entail a being separate or distinct from God. Any time the name *Shekhinah* appears, the term *God* could just as easily be substituted. The rabbinic *Shekhinah* has no character of its own and serves only to refer to God in His nearness to man.

The concept of *Shekhinah* undergoes a major transformation in the *Kabbalah*. It is no longer synonymous with God but appears as a separate and distinct being with a character all its own. The character is feminine, and the kabbalistic descriptions of the *Shekhinah* accentuate her separateness from the hidden God and her own femininity.

The earliest kabbalistic portrayal of the *Shekhinah* describes her as God's daughter whom he gives to the world as its wife. He longs to hold on to her but recognizes that she now belongs to a different realm. Therefore, God creates the *Sefirot* as a window between himself and the *Shekhinah* who dwells in the world. The *Sefirot* are now the link between God and his daughter. God can relate to the world by means of the *Sefirot,* and his *Shekhinah* can approach him by the same avenue:

A certain king had a good, beautiful and perfect daughter. He married her to a prince and dressed her, crowned her and adorned her. The king also provided a large dowry for her.

Now, can the king dwell apart from his daughter? Of course not.

But can the king dwell with her all day long? Of course not.

So what does he do? He places a window between himself and her, and whenever the daughter needs her father or the father needs his daughter, they meet together at the window.[8]

This resembles the earlier passage that describes God as making a meeting place for his daughter. There the meeting place is the Temple, not the *Sefirot*. More significantly, however, the daughter in that passage is the Jewish people, and here it is God's daughter, the *Shekhinah*.

In Jewish mysticism, *Eyn Sof* is inaccessible, and so are most of the other *Sefirot*. The last *Sefirah*, the *Shekhinah*, is accessible through the mystic quest and gives some insight into the other *Sefirot*. Because the *Shekhinah* is the vessel in which all of the other *Sefirot* are gathered, it reveals the higher aspects of God to those who know it. The sources caution against attempting to penetrate directly through the divine realm to *Eyn Sof* and instead direct the mystic toward the *Shekhinah*, the gateway to the other *Sefirot*. God is not accessible except through the *Shekhinah*:

A certain king dwelt within the inner chamber of his palace. There were thirty-two chambers in all and each chamber had its own path.

Now, is it proper for everyone to come to the king's chamber by simply following all the paths? Of course not.

And is it proper for the king to openly reveal his pearls, brocades and hidden, precious treasures? Of course not.

So what did the king do? He appointed his daughter and set in her and in her garments all the different pathways. Anyone who wishes to enter the palace should look to her.[9]

The term "thirty-two chambers" has symbolic significance in Jewish mysticism. It is an ideal number that signifies the totality of all possible phenomena that might exist in the world. The mystics believed that the ten *Sefirot* and the twenty-two Hebrew letters were the building blocks of the universe. Thirty-two thus represents the infinite possibilities that can emerge from the combination of divine essences and human language.

The *Shekhinah* is referred to as *her* in kabbalistic literature. This represents both a linguistic and substantive innovation. The word itself is classified among the Hebrew nouns that are governed by noun endings of the feminine gender. The term also has substantive connotations as the feminine aspect of God, the divine mother and protector of the world.

The abyss between God and the world cannot easily be bridged. The *Shekhinah*, however, is that aspect of God that can serve to link the two realms. The *Shekhinah* is the lowest of the *Sefirot* and the boundary between the divine and nondivine world. Thus, the *Shekhinah* has a certain ability to link the two realms.

The *Shekhinah* is God's delegate from the realm of the *Sefirot* to the world. Although the *Shekhinah* is never described as an emissary that literally descends into the world in an earthly form, it is still more imaginable than any other aspect of God. The *Shekhinah* is the caring part of God which can be felt as God's immanence in the world. The *Shekhinah* dwells in the midst of her people without ever leaving the abode of the *Sefirot*.

In some sense the *Shekhinah* can stand apart from the other *Sefirot*. It acts at times as the delegate of the *Sefirot* to the world and at other times as the intercessor on behalf of the world to the *Sefirot*. The *Shekhinah* thus serves as the link between the realms of God and the world.

Only this *Sefirah* can enter into contact with humanity. God's presence is felt in the world when one observes the ritual requirements of Judaism. Through observance, the world is reminded of the origin of the *Shekhinah* in the realm of the *Sefirot*. She is called God's *Kavod* (glory) and comes from a far more remote origin than did the rabbinic *Shekhinah*:

> Why is it written: "Blessed be God's Glory from its place?" (Ezek. 3:12). Because no one knows its exact place.
>
> A parable: The daughter of a king came from far away and people did not know from where she had come. After a while, they saw that she was strong, beautiful and perfect in all that she did. They said: "She must surely have been taken from the Realm of Light because through her deeds, the world shines."
>
> They asked: "Where are you from?"
>
> She answered: "From my place."
>
> They said: "Then, the inhabitants of your place must be noble. May you and your place be blessed."[10]

Sometimes the *Shekhinah* is inaccessible and remote to all but the other *Sefirot*. But her eventual presence in the world is always insured. In the following passage the *Shekhinah* is now the queen, not the daughter, and is hidden in the king's chambers. The *Sefirot*, and not the king, mate with her and produce children, angels, for the king. The *Shekhinah* is a mother of all life even when she is not present in the world fulfilling her role as God's emissary and presence:

> What is meant by "God's Glory?"
>
> A parable: To what can this be compared? To a king who had a queen in his chamber. All the king's soldiers took delight in the queen. She had children and they would come every day to see the king and bless him. The children asked: "Our mother, where is she now?"
>
> The king answered: "You cannot see her now."
>
> They responded: "May she be blessed wherever she is."[11]

If the *Shekhinah* is portrayed as God's daughter, other *Sefirot* are understood as having given birth to the daughter. The second and third *Sefirot, Hokhmah,* and *Binah* are often described as having male and female properties, respectively. Every *Sefirah* is seen as standing in a tense or even contrary relationship with another, and the opposites are resolved through the production of a third and mediating power. Thus the opposites *Hokhmah* and *Binah* are resolved by the emergence of *Tiferet.* The Kabbalists often resort to explicitly sexual metaphors to portray the emanation of the *Sefirot.* The emanation of *Tiferet* is seen as a son to *Hokhmah* and *Binah* and a balance to their opposing natures. Then the *Shekhinah,* the daughter, completes this ideal "family":

> *Hokhmah* spread out and brought forth *Binah.*
> They were found to be male and female.
> *Hokhmah,* the father, and
> *Binah,* the mother.
> Then, these two united and
> Lighted up each other.
> The mother conceived and gave birth to a son.
> Through the birth of a son,
> The mother and father found perfection.
> This led to the completion of everything,
> the inclusion of everything—
> father, mother, son and daughter.[12]

The perfection and unification of the divine world depends on the harmonious balance between individual *Sefirot* as well as harmonious interrelationships between all the *Sefirot*. When there is an absence of harmony above, it is a reflection of disharmony in the world, and the tension above in turn exacerbates the situation in the world. The mystic is one who attempts to perform the necessary steps that will preserve the unity of the divine realm. His work begins with the *Shekhinah* but affects the rest of the *Sefirot*.

> As long as Israel is found with the Holy One, Blessed be He, He, so to speak, is in a state of completion.[13]

The process of preserving God in a state of completion places a heavy burden of moral and mystical responsibility upon the individual. Fortunately, the *Sefirot Hokhmah* and *Binah* are always united:

> The father and the mother,
> Since they are found in union all the time
> And are never hidden from each other or separated,
> Are called companions.
> They find satisfaction in perfect union.[14]

The Kabbalists make a daring equation of *Tiferet* with *the Holy One, Blessed be He,* thereby suggesting that God, as He is known in the religious tradition, is the *Sefirah Tiferet*. Moreover, the *Shekhinah,* God's presence, is His mate, *Malkhut*. The union of *Tiferet* and *Malkhut* signifies the state of unity among the upper and lower, or masculine and feminine, *Sefirot*. It also represents the state of divine harmony necessary in order for peace to prevail in the world. These two *Sefirot* can be, but are not always necessarily in, the state of harmony.

The Kabbalists conclude that the union of *the Holy One, Blessed be He* and His *Shekhinah* is the desirable state of affairs in the divine realm and in the world. This union is brought about by human efforts and is disrupted by sin. Whatever occurs below determines what occurs above; whatever occurs above is a reflection of what occurs below.

The notion of the feminine aspect of the deity may be the

boldest conceptual innovation in Jewish mysticism. The fascination with the feminine aspect of God has its origin in human sexual consciousness. The Jewish mystics believed that everything in the terrestrial world has its roots in the divine realm. Since femininity must have its roots in God, there must indeed be a feminine aspect of God. This doctrine elevates human sexuality to a divine principle and thereby legitimates human sexuality. At the same time it humanizes God by attributing the vicissitudes of human sexuality to divinity. Most important, the concept of the feminine aspect of God paves the way for understanding human sexuality as a metaphor for the mystic quest in Judaism.

The mystics were fascinated by the relationship between *Tiferet* and *Malkhut,* the son and the daughter. They portray the union of these two *Sefirot* as being in constant jeopardy whereas the union of the father and mother (*Hokhmah* and *Binah*) was intractable. This notion does not have any incestuous implication because the mystics alternate freely between the son and daughter and the husband and wife metaphors. Whereas the parents are in perpetual union, human sinfulness prevents the permanent union of the *Shekhinah* with *Tiferet.*

The holy marriage of *Tiferet* and *Shekhinah* is the most important task that the mystic assumes in his quest. The Jewish mystic does not seek his own union with God but rather attempts to influence the last *Sefirah* to cause her union with her mate, *Tiferet.* Marriage between male and female on earth is considered one of the mystic techniques for influencing the holy marriage above. The proper and dedicated fulfillment of the marriage is a means for uniting the masculine and feminine *Sefirot*:

When is "union" said of man?
When he is male together with female
And is highly sanctified and
Zealous for sanctification.
Then, and only then,
Is he designated "one,"
Without any flaw of any kind.

Hence, a man and his wife
Should have a single inclination

At the hour of their union.
The man should rejoice with his wife,
Attaching himself to her with affection.
So joined they make
One soul and one body.
A single soul through their affection.
A single body –
For only when male and female are joined
Do they form a single body.

When male and female are joined,
God abides upon "one"
And endows it with a holy spirit.[15]

The *Kabbalah* teaches the incredible notion that humans are able to manipulate God through the performance of Jewish rituals. The most important effect that one's actions can have is the unification of *Tiferet* and *Shekhinah*. The *Zohar* contains many extensive passages that detail this thesis. For example, the simple declaration of monotheistic faith, "*Shema Yisrael Adonai Eloheinu Adonai Ehad*" (Hear, O Israel, The Lord Our God, The Lord Is One"),[16] becomes the occasion for elaborating a dramatic myth of the divine marriage between *Tiferet* and *Shekhinah*.

In order for a modern reader to follow the intricate symbolism of the mythology, it is necessary to provide a list of kabbalistic terms that appear in the passage:

Illumination: the overflow from *Eyn Sof*, which is often portrayed as a radiant light.

The Flame of Darkness: this symbol is an oxymoron, an inherently contradictory expression. It refers to the *Keter*, the only *Sefirah* to contain within itself contradictory powers.

The Tree of Life: a symbol for *Tiferet*.

The Garden [of Eden]: a symbol for *Shekhinah*, the garden in which *Tiferet* is planted.

The Bride: a symbol for *Shekhinah*.

Husband: a symbol for *Tiferet*.

Israel: another name for *Tiferet.*

The Heavenly Limbs: six of the other *Sefirot: Hesed, Din, Tiferet, Netzah, Hod* and *Yesod.*

The Lord: a symbol for *Tiferet.* This *Sefirah* is the referent also of the divine name, *The Holy One, Blessed be He.*

Limbs or Directions: another term for *Sefirot.*

The Hebrew letter *Vav:* this letter corresponds to the letter *V* in the word *YHVH.* In Hebrew, it has the numerical value of six and is related to the *Sefirah Tiferet.*

Attendants: the ministering angels.

Name: a symbol for *Shekhinah.*

This glossary should be used in deciphering the following passage from the *Zohar*:

> At the hour
> When Israel effects the unity
> Of the mystery of "Hear, Israel,"
> With complete devotion,
> An illumination deep within
> The sublime supernal world
> Issues forth
> Immediately.
>
> This illumination
> Collides with the flame of darkness
> And divides into
> Seventy lights.
>
> These seventy
> Become the seventy branches
> Of the Tree of Life.
> At that moment,
> This Tree emits odors and fragrances
> As all the trees of the Garden [of Eden]
> Do toward their master.

At that moment,
The bride is adorned
In order to enter
Beneath the canopy
With her husband.

All the heavenly limbs bind together
In one desire,
In one devotion,
In order to be one,
With no division
At all.

Then, her husband
Turns his attention to her
In order to bring her
Under the canopy
In one union,
To unite with his bride.

Therefore, awaken to her and say:
"Hear, [O, Bride], Israel [is coming]!
Prepare yourself!
Your husband is approaching
In his adornments.
He is ready for you."

"The Lord our God,
The Lord is One—"
In one union,
In one devotion,
With no division.
All the limbs are united
And enter into one devotion.

When Israel says, "The Lord is One,"
Through the arousal of the six directions,
They unite
And enter into one devotion.

This is the mystery of the Hebrew letter "Vav."
One extension alone
With nothing else adhering to it,
Only it alone,
Apart from the rest,
Complete.

At the same moment,
The bride
Is being prepared and adorned.
Her attendants present her
To her husband
In a thin whisper,
Saying:
"Blessed be the Name of the Glory of His Kingship forever."

This is said in a whisper
For this is how
She must be presented to her husband.

Happy are the people who know this
And prepare an exalted service
Of faith.[17]

The Kabbalist presents a new reading of the prayer "Hear, O Israel." It is no longer only the fundamental credo of Jewish monotheistic belief but a dramatic enactment of a holy marriage between two *Sefirot.* "Hear, O Israel," is not an invocation to the Jewish people to enunciate their belief in one God. It becomes a call:

" 'Hear,' *Tiferet,* [Israel]–you who are in unity with the other *Sefirot!*" In the process, *Tiferet* and *Shekhinah,* which is also called *Malkhut,* become one in holy marriage ("The Lord is One"). Thereupon the wedding party announces, "Blessed be the *Shekhinah* ("the name of Glory"), his *Malkhut,* forever, which now is united with *Tiferet.*"

The Kabbalists were acutely aware, however, that this holy marriage was far from accomplished. If it were, the world would be governed by harmony, and God's everlasting abundance would illuminate the world. On the contrary, the Kabbalists saw the world in which they lived as hostile and threatening. The *Kabbalah* flourished in medieval Spain at the time of increasing Christian persecution of Jews. The Seven Part Codes, which prohibited Jews from conducting their affairs like their Christian neighbors, and the restrictions of the Lateran Council in Rome curtailed Jewish civil, economic, and religious rights. The anti-Jewish attacks of 1391, the forced conversions of the Marranos, and the inquisitions finally led to the expulsion from Spain in 1492. This was hardly a period in which *Tiferet* and *Shekhinah* were in union.

The mystics were more conscious of their failure to "unite" God than of their success. The mystic quest centered upon a mission to rise above the vicissitudes of this world and address the problem at its source—the world of the *Sefirot*. Only if the *Shekhinah* were banished from her mate, only if she indeed were in exile, could the world be in such a condition as it appeared to be. The Kabbalists knew, believed, experienced, and felt that "the *Shekhinah* is in the dust," separated and exiled from her realm. The elevation of the *Shekhinah* becomes a precondition for bringing her under the nuptial canopy. On page after page the *Zohar* portrays this sense of anguish and exile in vivid imagery:

> Think of a king
> Who in anger against his queen
> Banished her
> From his palace
> For a stated time.
> That time elapsed
> And she returned to the king,
> Thus, it came to pass
> Several times.
>
> Then came a time
> When she was banished
> From the palace of the king
> For a long time.
>
> The King said:
> "Now is not like before

When she returned to me.
This time,
I shall go,
Taking all my followers to seek her out."

When he found her,
She was in the dust.
Seeing her thus trampled,
And yearning anew for her,
He took her by the hand,
Raised her up,
Led her back to the palace,
And promised
On his oath
He would never send her away.[18]

This kabbalistic reading of history proposed that the period of slavery in Egypt and the destruction of the first Temple were temporary exiles of the *Shekhinah* that ended with her voluntary return. The Kabbalists viewed the era in which they lived as qualitatively worse than previous epochs. Since the time of the destruction of the Second Temple in 70 C.E., the Temple had not been rebuilt, and the sense of exile persisted. The redemption from this exile which had already lasted more than a millennium required stronger measures. God, according to the *Zohar*, was not content to wait for the *Shekhinah* to return. It was now the task of God and the Jewish people to actively pursue the return of the exiled *Shekhinah*. The *Zohar* sanctioned utopian activism and perhaps even active messianism.

The sense of exile that each Jew felt palpably was explained as being the result of the exile of the *Shekhinah*. With God's presence "in the dust," the mystic assumed the burden of lifting her up out of the ashes of despair, cleansing and purifying her once again, and dressing her in preparation for her long post-poned wedding with her groom. If this could only be accomplished, the world would be a better place.

This feeling of anguish was familiar to the Kabbalists throughout Jewish history. The destruction of the first Temple was portrayed by Isaiah through the image of the fallen Jerusalem. The prophet anticipated the rebuilding of Jerusalem through a descendant of King David, the Bethlehemite, the descendant of Peretz: the Messiah. The imagery and hope of Isaiah consoled generations and nourished Jewish hopes even in the period after the Expulsion of 1492. There was, however, one significant difference. The Kabbalists knew that it was only through human efforts that the bride would enter the bridal chamber and the Messiah would wait until man did his share. The Kabbalist saw his duty as preparing the bride and ushering her into the ceremony. In real terms this meant that once a week, at the sundown that marks the beginning of Sabbath, the mystic could actually reunite the bride and the groom. The Sabbath, for the Kabbalist, is an auspicious moment, an anticipation of a better age.

The Jewish mystic knew Isaiah's prophecies about the rebuilding of Jerusalem, which is portrayed as an aggrieved mother, the symbol of Jewish hope. The prophetic characterization of Zion's desolation captured the feeling of the personal experience of the Spanish exiles. In the mind of Kabbalists living in the generation after the Expulsion, Isaiah's prophecies appeared to speak directly to the condition of the *Shekhinah* "in the dust." It is not surprising, therefore, that Isaiah should have provided these mystics with the vocabulary of redemption.

The Kabbalists of this period created new rituals whose purpose was to bring about the resurrection of the *Shekhinah* and her reunion with *Tiferet*. The most significant and enduring contribution of this period was the introduction of special hymns to the *Shekhinah* that were incorporated into the liturgy with which Jews usher in the Sabbath. The most outstanding hymn of this genre is the famous *Lekhah Dodi* (Come, My Beloved) composed by the Kabbalist Rabbi Shlomo ha-Levi Alkabetz in the Galilean town of Safed around 1560.

This hymn transformed the Friday sundown liturgy into a drama of the highest order in which the congregation, dressed in white as if at a wedding, literally went out into the fields around Safed to greet the *Shekhinah*. This notion is based on the talmudic invocation for the Sabbath: "Let us come and go out to welcome the Sabbath bride."[19] The rabbinic metaphor of the Sabbath as a bride is linked with the kabbalistic notion of the Sabbath bride as the *Shekhinah*. The *Shekhinah* arrives from the west with the setting sun, greeted by *Tiferet* who arrives from the east. The congregation is the wedding party that symbolically ushers the groom toward the bride by saying to *Tiferet:* "Come, my beloved, to meet the bride. Let us greet the Sabbath."

The Sabbath is transformed into a cosmic wedding between the masculine *Tiferet* and feminine *Shehkinah* of God. The role of the congregation is to bring the lovers together, for this cannot be accomplished without their assistance. In most congregations today, this hymn is repeated without any real awareness of the implicit kabbalistic significance. A vestige of the medieval custom is preserved when the congregation rises for the final stanza and faces the rear of the sanctuary, the west, to greet the Sabbath bride. The symbol of the Sabbath bride, however, has entered popular Jewish culture stripped of its peculiar kabbalistic nuances.

In order to understand *Lekhah Dodi,* a word of introduction is necessary. The language is drawn from Isaiah, Psalms, and from the Song of Songs. The latter is a love poem between the male "beloved" (*dodi*) and the female "lover" (*raaya*). Here the two lovers are equated with *Tiferet* and *Shekhinah,* respectively. The Sabbath itself is associated with the *Sefirah Malkhut,* which rains down blessings upon the world if the union between the two lovers is consummated. The *Shekhinah* is also identified with the heavenly Jerusalem, the voice of God at Sinai, God's name, and the divine crown.

The opening line, "Keep (*shamor*) and remember (*zakhor*) in one divine word," requires special explanation. The original Sabbath injunction appears in the list of the Ten Commandments. The list of commandments, however, appears twice in the Bible, in Deuteronomy 5:12 and Exodus 20:8. In the former the commandment regarding the Sabbath reads "Keep (*shamor*) the Sabbath day," and in the latter, "Remember (*zakhor*) the Sabbath day." The sages explain the variation by saying that God issued one commandment, and it was heard by the people in these two different ways. The Kabbalists associate *shamor* with *Malkhut* because *Malkhut* "keeps" and protects the world. *Zakhor,* which can mean *remember* or *to be masculine* (*zakhar*), is associated with *Yesod,* the phallic symbol within the *Sefirot.*

Many of the other phrases in this hymn are cryptic references to other names of the *Sefirot.* For example, "beauty" (*Tiferet*), "king," "glory" (*Kavod*) and "God" (*YHVH*) are synonyms for the

Sefirah Tiferet. "Praise" (*Tehillah*) refers to *Binah.* With this glossary in mind, the hymn takes on a new level of meaning. The *Lekhah Dodi* can easily be decoded and its kabbalistic significance uncovered with these keys. The following is a literal rendition of the hymn with references to the primary biblical allusions. It is followed by another rendering that presents its kabbalistic meaning:

LEKHAH DODI

Come, my Beloved (Song of Songs 7:12)
To meet the Bride.
Let us welcome the Sabbath.

"Keep" and "Remember" (Deut. 5:12; Ex. 20:8) in one divine
        word
Thus, the unified God to us made heard.
God is one, His name is one (Zekh. 14:9);
As is His name, His splendor, and His praise.

Toward the Sabbath, let us now go.
For she is the source of blessing,
Appointed since the earliest time, the beginning
Last in creation but first in thought (*Ber. Rabba*).

Shrine of the king, the royal city.
Rise up from your ruins,
Too long have you dwelled in the valley of tears (Ps. 84:7).
To you He will act mercifully with compassion.

Arise and shake off the dust (Isa. 52:2).
Dress yourself with your clothes of splendor, My people,
With the help of the son of Jesse [i.e., David], the
        Bethlehemite king.
Come near to my soul, redeem it!

Awake, Awake! (Isa. 51:17).
For your light has come, Arise, my light (Isa. 60:1).
Wake, wake (Isa. 52:1)–sing out with song.
The glory of God upon you is displayed.

Be not ashamed, be not distressed (Isa. 45:15; Jer. 22:22).
Why are you bowed, and why do you yearn? (Ps. 42:12).
In you shall the poor children of my people be comforted.
    (Isa. 14:32).
The city upon its ashes will be rebuilt (Jer. 30:18).

They who destroyed you will themselves be destroyed. (Jer.
    30:16).
Your foes will be routed (Isa. 49:19).
Your God will then rejoice in you
As a bridegroom rejoices in his bride (Isa. 62:5).

Spread out to the right and the left (Isa. 54:3),
Revering God
With the help of a descendant of Peretz [i.e., David] (Ruth
    4:18),
We will rejoice and celebrate (Ps. 118:24).

Come, in peace the crown of her spouse (Prov. 12:4).
Come in joy and radiance,
To the faithful of the chosen people.
Come, O bride! Come, O bride!

Come, my Beloved
To meet the Bride.
Let us welcome the Sabbath.

The following is the translation of *Lekhah Dodi* from mystical
symbolism to the underlying kabbalistic meaning:

Come, my beloved *Tiferet*
To unite with the bride *Shekhinah-Malkhut.*
Let us welcome the *Shekhinah* into our midst.

Malkhut and *Yesod* were emanated
By *Tiferet*, God's voice, at Sinai.
On the Sabbath, *Tiferet* and *Malkhut* are united.
In unity are *Malkhut*, God's name,
Tiferet and *Binah.*

To greet *Malkhut,* let us now go.
For *Malkhut* is the spring which draws from *Binah.*
Malkhut, anointed by *Hokhmah,*
Was the last *Sefirah* to be emanated
But the first to be conceived in God's *Hokhmah.*

Malkhut is heavenly Jerusalem, the sanctuary,
The vessel for *Tiferet,* the king.
Rise up from disunity!
Too long have you been separate from *Tiferet.*
Tiferet will invoke *Hesed* upon you
And reunite with you.

Awake! End your exile from *Tiferet!*
Adorn yourself with the garments of *Tiferet*
With the aid of the messiah, from the house of David,
Who is nourished by *Malkhut.*
Shekhinah, come close to my soul,
Redeem it!

Awake, Awake!
For the light of *Tiferet,* your mate, has come.
Wake, wake – sing out with song.
Tiferet, God's glory, will be joined to you.

Be not ashamed, be not distressed.
Why are you bowed, and why do you yearn?
By you, *Shekhinah,* the Jewish people will be restored
And the earthly Jerusalem will be rebuilt.

They who destroyed you will themselves be destroyed.
Your foes will be routed.
Tiferet will then rejoice in you
As a bridegroom rejoices in his bride.

You will spread out to *Hesed* and *Din,*
The right and the left.
And *Tiferet* you will revere.
The Sabbath will foreshadow the messianic age
Brought by a descendant of Peretz

[i.e., the messiah from the house of David]
In this we shall rejoice and celebrate.

Come, now, *Malkhut,*
The lower crown of *Tiferet,*
Come in joy and radiance
Come to the Kabbalists among the chosen people
Come, O bride! Come, O bride!

Come, my beloved *Tiferet*
To unite with the bride *Shekhinah-Malkhut.*
Let us welcome the *Shekhinah* into our midst.

The bold conceptualization of the *Kabbalah* is the notion that God's masculine and feminine aspects can be reunited by religious actions. The traditional notion of God as father and king has been dramatically transformed to God as the sum total of all the possibilities and polarities in the world. God is a dynamic whose strongest polarities are the masculine and feminine *Sefirot.* Jewish mysticism is predicated, therefore, on a series of abysses. The abyss between God and the world mirrors an abyss deep within God between two aspects of his being. The mystic quest in Judaism is the effort to bridge the abyss between God and the world by healing the rift within God.

7

LANGUAGE AND BEING:

The Torah as God's Emanation

Emanation from *Eyn Sof* is a substantive process in which God's being is distributed and conveyed through the *Sefirot*. *Keter*, coeternal with *Eyn Sof*, contains within itself the roots of all subsequent being in an undifferentiated state. Through the process of emanation these roots of existence change from a state of no-thing-ness to the potentiality of everything. *Keter*, however, is identical with *Eyn Sof* in respect to its infinity and, on the other hand, it is related to the other *Sefirot* in respect to its being the source of emanation.

The first moment of emanation is an act of self-contraction, or constriction (*Tzimtzum*), of the infinity of *Eyn Sof*. *Eyn Sof*, because it is infinite, remains inaccessible to anything else. It must become limited and diluted in order for the divine essence to become accessible. God cannot be made known to the world unless He presents Himself in a worldly form. The role of the *Sefirot* is to serve as the intermediate link that translates infinity into more limited essences. God's being is then communicated to humanity in a worldly form through the revelation of the Torah. The beginning of this process of translating God's being into comprehensible forms is an act whereby God brings Himself down to a less infinite level.

Some mystics describe the phenomenon of God limiting

Himself in order to make Himself more available to the world by an analogy. The father of an infant often needs to act in childish ways in order to communicate with his young child. Talking to the infant in "baby talk" can be a necessary strategy of self-limitation that must be employed in order to establish communication. The father remains an adult even though he must temporarily speak the language of the infant. So it is, they explain, with God who limits Himself for the sake of humanity.

This self-limitation of God creates *Keter,* the unbounded, infinite potentiality for existence. *Keter,* also called *Ayin* (nothing), is not a nonbeing; it is the undifferentiated unity of all being. It is the indeterminate *nothing* from which all *being* unfolds, and it exists only through an act of self-limitation by *Eyn Sof.*

The conception of emanation as 'self-contraction' is based on the idea that God can only bring things into existence from that which already exists. God, therefore, cannot create anything directly from His own infinite essence. Thus he constricts his own infinity into *Keter,* the fullness of all, the undifferentiated source of all being. The infinity of God is described as the radiant light of the sun which shines endlessly due to its overwhelming magnitude. But this unbridled light must be directed and channeled in order for details, shadows, contours, and shapes to emerge. In the same manner the radiance of *Eyn Sof* must be restricted in order to allow for the emergence of the *Sefirot.* It is not, however, a change in *Eyn Sof,* only within the vessels that receive the light. Contraction is not an essential change within *Eyn Sof* as much as it is the creation of possibility and differentiation through *Keter.* The subsequent process of emanation is a dynamic process in which *Keter* radiates the light of *Eyn Sof* through the other *Sefirot.*

The first act of divine expression consists of *Keter's* emanation of *Hokhmah,* God's sublime wisdom, which is hidden deep within *Keter.* This manifestation of the hidden essence of *Keter* produces the *Sefirah Hokhmah.* Whereas *Keter* is hidden and indistinct from *Eyn Sof, Hokhmah* is distinct from *Keter. Hokhmah* is the first essence, or vessel, to exist separately from *Eyn Sof* even though it contains the infinity of *Eyn Sof.* The emanation of *Hokhmah* is the first self-expression of *Eyn Sof* in which the infinite deity represents itself in a more limited form. This phenomenon of God expressing Himself, called *autorepresentation,* occurs through an act of self-limitation. The mystics call this *Tzimtzum* (contraction), the act of divine autorepresentation in which God limits His own infinite intelligence and causes it to be contained in a vessel.[1]

The *Sefirot* are also the linguistic expression of God. All beings reveal their essence through thought that eventually assumes the form of speech, and the *Sefirot* are the divine language. Even the term *Sefirah* conveys the notion of the *Sefirot* as God's language in the verse, "The heavens tell (*mesapprim*, from the same root as *Sefirah*) the glory (*Kavod*) of God."[2] The common Hebrew root of the terms *sefirah* and *sapper*, the Hebrew letters *spr*, which mean *to tell*, suggests that God's means of expression, the *Sefirot*, are also His language.

Each *Sefirah*, beginning with *Hokhmah*, constitutes a distinct stage in the process of the unfolding of the divine language. The sequence of divine self-expression begins with the manifestation of God's essential *Hokhmah*. The Kabbalists characterize this as the creation of a primordial "text," a vessel in which the author's wisdom is inscribed. Like any text, the implicit wisdom needs to be revealed by one who also interprets it and draws it out for all to see. Therefore, *Hokhmah* is followed by the emanation of *Binah*, the interpreter, or commentator, that draws out the hidden thoughts and gives them meaning. This *Sefirah* is the intellect that understands the infinite wisdom of God concealed in the text of *Hokhmah* and reveals it. *Understanding* is the third stage in the process of divine autorepresentation. It differentiates the undifferentiated wisdom of God hidden in *Hokhmah*.

The emanation of the first three *Sefirot* is a process of intellectual autorepresentation in which God's thought achieves existence distinct from His hidden essence. As this process continues beyond *Binah*, God's wisdom becomes increasingly particularized and differentiated and culminates in the linguistic expression of this wisdom through divine language. Divine language is both the particularization of God's own thought and the extension of His own intellectual essence. Divine language eventually becomes concretized as the language of the Torah. The Torah is the ultimate repository, or vessel, of God's essence and wisdom and is the final stage in the process of divine autorepresentation.

Hokhmah is the repository of divine wisdom and a treasury

in which the potentiality of divine linguistic expression is inscribed. In this *Sefirah* wisdom is inscribed as the ideal prefiguration of the letters of the Hebrew alphabet. The Jewish mystics understood letters as the outward means of expressing inner thoughts. *Hokhmah* is a repository, a matrix upon which are inscribed God's thought as Hebrew letters. These letters remain hidden deep within *Hokhmah* throughout the process of the emanation of the *Sefirot*. The process of differentiation in which these ideal letters become real letters occurs only after the process of divine autorepresentation concludes with the emanation of *Malkhut*.

The *Sefirot* are the principles of all existent things, the ideal prefiguration of all being, vessels, or instruments of divine activity and expressions of divine wisdom. With the conclusion of the emanation of the last *Sefirah,* the divine world comes to an end. The next lower world, the spiritual world, begins below *Malkhut* and consists of the distinct and differentiated forms that were hidden in an undifferentiated form within the *Sefirot*. This spiritual realm of forms separate from matter exists in an intermediate state between the world of divinity above it and the natural world below it that contains corporeal objects of form and matter together. The letters that were hidden in *Hokhmah* and that were brought out by *Binah* come into their own in this spiritual world of pure forms.

The radical innovation introduced by the *Kabbalah* is the idea that all of creation, the corporeal world below the spiritual realm, is made up of the letters of the Hebrew alphabet which contain God's own essence. In other words God's essence is His thought, and the expression of His essence is the emanation of the Hebrew letters. The letters assume concrete form in a series of stages that culminate in the Hebrew language.

The linguistic process of emanation is the process of creation. The Kabbalists explain that the etymology of the Hebrew word for *letter* (*ot*) is the root *come from* (*ata*). They suggest that the letters of the Hebrew alphabet *come from* the spiritual forms of the Hebrew letters which, in turn, come from the hidden letters or thoughts of God within the *Sefirot*. Although the letters have a mysterious and unknowable character in the upper worlds, they are still the building blocks of creation because they are the instruments of God's self-expression.

Creation is portrayed as the unfolding of divine language from the *Sefirot* into ideal letters of the spiritual realm which were then impressed upon the physical world. Seven of the Hebrew letters correspond to and create the seven known celestial planets; twelve other letters correspond to and create the twelve constellations of the Zodiac; three Hebrew letters create the material elements – air, water, and fire – out of which the world itself was thought to be created.[3]

Hokhmah is the repository of divine wisdom and contains within it the undifferentiated potentiality of the letters. In the midrashic literature of the rabbinic period, the Torah is identified as the outward manifestation of divine wisdom. The *midrash* explains that the Torah is one of six things that existed prior to the creation of the world.[4] The Kabbalists point out that the word for *things* (*devarim*) and the term for *words* (*dibburim*) share a common root. Therefore, the *midrash* supports the kabbalistic idea that the world was created by the preexistent divine language. In support of this the rabbis cite the verse that describes God's wisdom: "The Lord created me at the beginning of his course."[5] Wisdom was created before anything else. The Kabbalists also based their belief on another *midrash*, which described the preexistent Torah as "the vessel of God's craftsmanship" (*keli omanuto*).[6] They concluded that the *Sefirah Hokhmah* is the ultimate source and cause of existence.

The appearance of the written Torah is the final expression of this linguistic process and is the very instrument by which God created the world. The process that began with the emanation of *Hokhmah,* the unfolding of the letters, their differentiation in the spiritual realm, and their inscription in the preexistent Torah culminated in their final appearance as the letters of the written Torah. The Torah is, therefore, the final stage in the process of divine autorepresentation.

The gradual and sequential process of divine autorepresentation through linguistic expression brings the world into existence. The spiritual forms of the letters create the constellations, the planets, and the earthly elements. The preexistent Torah is the blueprint that God employed to create the world out of the elements that came from God's essence. The world is ultimately the final expression of divine language.

The act of revelation is the transformation of thought into

word. The word itself is, reciprocally, the means toward understanding the original thought. The text of the Torah is not
remote from God's original wisdom since it is nothing more than
another stage in the manifestation of God's thought. The Torah
is called *Hokhmah* because it is the last stage in the elaboration of
God's wisdom. The Kabbalists explain this notion through the
metaphor of human speech. God's wisdom is His internal
speech, the product of His eternal activity, His thought. The
Torah is the direct manifestation of this internal speech just as
language is itself the extension of thought. The process of emanation infuses the individual letters of the earthly Torah with
meaning; the vessel of the Torah contains the essence of the
Sefirot. The difference between the internal and the external
speech, the Torah, is one of degree.

Another way of understanding the unfolding of divine
language is to see emanation as the process of creating names.
Names are vessels that contain essences or refer to subjects that
exist. The Kabbalists describe the emanation of the vessel
Hokhmah as God giving Himself His first and most important
name, *YHVH,* traditionally pronounced as *Adonai* and called *the
four-letter name* (Tetragrammaton). The combination forming this
name is the first emanation of the divine letters through *Hokhmah.* All other divine names are elaborations of the Tetragrammaton.[7]

The *Sefirot* are now seen as a series of elaborations of the first
divine name, as linguistic vessels that contain the divine essence.
Since the first name is *Hokhmah–YHVH,* God's name is identical
with the preexistent Torah. Since the written Torah is the
elaboration of the preexistent Torah, the written Torah is also
the elaboration, or manifestation, of God's name through other
words and names. Nahmanides has this in mind when he
declares that "the entire Torah is composed of the names of
God."[8] This means that the Torah is the earthly manifestation of
the *Sefirot,* which are God's own names and the means by which
He created the world.

The Torah has two natures. It is the medium of divine
expression and the vehicle through which the mystic can retrace
the steps of the process leading back to God. The words of the
Torah are not merely combinations of letters that constitute
narratives; they are vessels that point to hidden essences, the

Sefirot. The relation of the *Sefirot* to the words of the Torah is analogous to the relation of the soul to the body. The words of the Torah are "bodies" that contain the "soul" of God's *Hokhmah.* The names, or words, of the Torah are ultimately expressions of divine power not just words referring to earthly things. One who knows how the divine power is infused in the words of the Torah is able to harness and utilize the power contained in them. In other words the mystic who understands the proper connection between the language of the Torah and the *Sefirot* is able to manipulate the power in the names and establish a connection between himself and God.

Jewish mysticism, therefore, is a system of creating relationships with God across the abyss through the medium of the Torah. One who can perceive the divine names in the Torah is able to cleave directly to God's *Sefirot* and transcend the world in which he lives. The study of the Torah is, therefore, the highest form of knowledge.

The kabbalistic theory of language is based on the notion that there is a real connection between a name and the object that it represents. The name is the concept of the thing to which the name applies. As an example, they point to the Torah where God gives names to the forefathers that fit their destiny, such as Jacob who is renamed *Israel* because he "struggled" (*sarita* from the same root as *Yisrael* [*Israel*]) with God. Many biblical figures are so named such that their names convey something significant about who they are. This indicates that names are not arbitrary but are correct or incorrect according to the degree to which they express the nature of their bearers.

The Kabbalists opposed the theory of names that was common among many rationalist biblical commentators in the Middle Ages including Maimonides.[9] Maimonides believed that there is no essential connection between a name and the object to which it refers, thus all names are conventional or arbitrary.[10] Most names are merely sounds that people mutually agree to assign to objects. The same objects could just as well be called by different names. Some names, however, are definitions such as when man is called a "rational animal." Generally, however, there is no real connection between a name and an object, there are no specifically "correct" names, and names do not express the nature of a thing. Moreover, there is no knowledge of the essence of something in knowing its name. According to Maimonides even divine names found in the Torah are conventional designations, not essential names.

According to the Kabbalists names express the nature of things. Language is fundamentally divine because all names have a connection with the *Sefirot* and unfold from *Hokhmah* in the process of emanation. Actually, all names are elaborations of the name of God – *YHVH* – the origin of existence and the genesis of language. The kabbalistic theory of language maintains that all names are symbols that refer to the *Sefirot*. Names do not really have meanings as much as they *point to* their correct referent, a *Sefirah*.[11] The Torah is a "code book" of divine names that refer to *Sefirot*. A Kabbalist is one who decodes the Torah and traces the meaning of terms back to their source. *Kabbalah* is also a theory that sees the world as a series of names, or vessels, that contain and even conceal God. The Torah, therefore, is full of symbols that hint at the divine essence, not a collection of words that can be read like any other story. The Kabbalist does not read the Torah for its narrative meaning; he reads it in search of the essence that is symbolized in the words of the Torah.

The words of the Torah might tell stories, but that is only incidental. The Torah is more a texture than a text. Even the names of the forefathers, Abraham, Isaac, and Jacob do not refer only to earthly humans. The Kabbalist is not concerned only with the historical figure of Abraham; he is interested in understanding the proper, divine referent that is symbolized by the name *Abraham*. *Abraham* is an essential name, according to the *Kabbalah,* whose referent is the *Sefirah Hesed.* This association is suggested by the verse: "Deal graciously (*Hesed*) with my master Abraham.[12] The Kabbalists identify countless names in the Torah and specify the *Sefirot* to which the names refer. Each of the various names of God, for example, refers to a different *Sefirah.*

The following is a brief glossary of some of the important names of God:

Y (first letter of *YHVH*)	**Hokhmah** (wisdom)
H (second letter of *YHVH*)	**Binah** (understanding)
V (third letter of *YHVH*)	**Tiferet** (splendor)
H (fourth letter of YHVH)	**Malkhut** (majesty)

YHVH	Tiferet (splendor)
Elohim	Binah (understanding)
The Holy One, Blessed be He	Tiferet (splendor)
Adonai	Malkhut (majesty)

The letters of the Hebrew alphabet are hidden in *Hokhmah,* which is the beginning of the name of God. The linguistic process of the unfolding of divine language through the particularization of these letters corresponds to the unfolding of the divine name. The stages in the process of the emergence of these letters corresponds to the stages in the process of emanation.

The first letter of the divine name, *Y* (ך *yod*), is symbolic of this process. The Hebrew letter begins with a "point," indicating that *Hokhmah* is the beginning of the process of linguistic expression and the start of emanation. The flourish on the tip of the Hebrew letter signifies and points to *Keter* and *Eyn Sof* that are above it. The second letter, *H* (*hei*), is associated with the *Sefirah Binah.* This *Sefirah* gives form to the letters which are hidden and undifferentiated in *Hokhmah.* The third letter, *V* (*vav*), is written as a straight line and has a numerical value of six, symbolizing the emanation of the six *Sefirot* from *Hokhmah* to *Yesod.* The final *H* brings all the potencies and forms of the *Sefirot* into actuality below this realm just as *Binah* did in relation to *Hokhmah.*

This theory of language and names is fundamental to understanding the kabbalistic view of the Torah. The Torah is the vehicle by which the mystic knows God. The notion of the Torah is different from the contemporary idea that the Torah is a book to be read like other books. One does not, according to the *Kabbalah,* read the Torah; one searches out the hidden or secret meanings. These meanings are the *Sefirot,* their dynamics, and how the realm of God is related to our world. It is against the background of a mystical understanding of the Torah that Kabbalists present their ideas in the form of biblical commentaries and homilies. After all, this is no ordinary book.

The following passage from the *Zohar* illustrates this idea:

> Rabbi Shimon said:
> Woe to the human being who says
> that Torah presents mere stories and ordinary words!

If so, we could compose a Torah right now with ordinary
    words
And better than all of them!
To present matters of the world?
Even rulers of the world possess words more sublime.
If so, let us follow them and make a Torah out of them!
Ah, but all the words of Torah are sublime words, sublime
    secrets!

Come and see:
The world above and the world below are perfectly
    balanced:
Israel below, the angels above.
Of the angels, it is written:
'He makes His angels spirits' (Psalms 104:4).
But when they descend, they put on the garment of this
    world.
If they did not put on a garment befitting this world
They could not endure in this world
And the world could not endure them.

If this is so with the angels, how much more so with Torah
who created them and all the worlds
and for whose sake they all exist!
In descending to this world,
If she did not put on the garments of this world
The world could not endure.

So this story of Torah is the garment of Torah.
Whoever thinks that the garment is the real Torah
And not something else –
May his spirit deflate!
He will have no portion in the world that is coming.

That is why David said
'Open my eyes
So I can see the wonders out of Your Torah!' (Psalms
    119:18).
What is under the garment of Torah.

Come and see:
There is a garment visible to all.
When those fools see someone in a good looking garment
They look no further.
But the essence of the garment is the body;
The essence of the body is the soul!

So it is with Torah.
She has a body:
The commandments of Torah.
Called 'the embodiment of Torah.'

This body is clothed in garments:
The stories of this world.
Fools of the world look only at that garment,
The story of Torah;
They know nothing more.
They do not look at what is under the garment.
Those who know more do not look at the garment
but rather at the body under that garment.
The wise ones, servants of the King on high,
Those who stood at Mt. Sinai,
look only at the soul, root of all,
Real Torah!
In the time to come
They are destined to look at the soul of the soul of Torah![13]

The study of the Torah is the loftiest purpose of human life because it is the self-revelation of God and the means by which God created the world. To the Kabbalist the entire world is Torah because all of existence is a garment for the Torah, which is itself a garment for the *Sefirot*. The *Sefirot* are garments, or vessels, for God's essence. Everything is essence within garment and garment within garment. The mystic quest is described as the act of unpeeling the layers of the garment in order to reach the essence at the very core. This is the basis of Jewish mysticism and the path to God. The Torah is the roadmap to God.

8

THE ONENESS OF BEING:

The   Destiny   of   the   Soul

The mystical dimension of Judaism is as evident in its doctrine of human nature as in its theory of God. The Jewish mystical conception of human psychology is based on a spiritual theory of the origin and destiny of the human soul. Unlike modern psychology, Jewish mysticism posits the existence of a spiritual realm beyond the individual that animates and energizes the life of the soul. The mystic believes that the boundaries between his inner world, the outer world in which he lives, and the spiritual realm of divinity can be traversed easily. The Jewish mystic believes that the soul is the vehicle that links heaven and earth. He is especially conscious of the power of actions that can elevate the soul from its bodily residence to its heavenly origins. For the Jewish mystic, this is the very meaning of Judaism.

In the Bible there is no dualistic concept of body and soul.[1] A living man or woman is seen as a unified organic being described, in Hebrew, as *nefesh*. *Nefesh* refers to human life in general and to human character in particular.

> The Lord God formed man from the dust of the earth. He blew into his nostrils the breath of life (*nishmat hayyim*), and man became a living being (*nefesh hayyah*).[2]
>
> And they seek my life (*nafshi*), to take it away.[3]

You shall not oppress a stranger, for you know the feelings (*nefesh*) of the stranger.[4]

Ruah refers to the *breath,* the power that brings about life and that is its visible manifestation.[5]

"In whose hand is the soul (*nefesh*) of every living thing, and the breath (*ruah*) of all mankind."[6]

There is no differentiation between the body, *nefesh,* and *ruah* in the Bible; man is of one nature.

By the second century the rabbinic sages had accepted the view that the human being was composed of two distinct entities – soul and body. This represented not only the view that man had two natures, but also that these derived from two dissimilar types of existence – heaven and earth.

All created beings [i.e., angels] that were created from heaven, their soul and body are from heaven; all creatures that were created from the earth [i.e., animals], their soul and body are from the earth, except man, whose soul is from heaven and his body is from the earth.[7]

In this view, man is a being with two distinct natures and is intermediate between angels and animals.

Consequently, man is capable of achieving great transcendence through the exercise of his soul or degradation through the actions of his physical body. Dualism replaced biblical monism as an expression of the strong spiritual bias of the rabbinic sages. In rabbinic theology the purification of the human soul through study, worship, and good deeds is the path to the kingdom of heaven. This does not lead, however, to a negative estimation of the physical aspects of human life. It merely serves to promote the view that the soul must regulate the activities of man.

Greek philosophy exerted a powerful influence upon rabbinic thinking about the soul as the result of two decisive encounters between Judaism and Hellenistic civilization. First, Hellenism spread Greek philosophic ideas throughout the Near East between the fourth century B.C.E. and the second century C.E. Rabbinic Judaism, which emerged in the period when Palestine was under Roman domination, was acquainted with Hellenism although it opposed it. Second, the revival of ancient Greek philosophy by the Muslim world during the Islamic Abbasid period led to the dissemination of Greco-Arabic philosophy from Baghdad to Cordova between the ninth and twelfth centuries. It was during this latter encounter that Jews, integrated culturally and intellectually into the Islamic world, were particularly receptive to philosophy and to the harmonization of rabbinic and philosophic teachings.

The Greek conception of the soul penetrated Jewish thinking during both of these encounters and was incorporated into rabbinic theology and medieval Jewish thought. Plato defined the soul as an essence that penetrates the body from without and gives it power. The soul comes from the realm of pure forms that exist as universal, ideal prototypes of worldly phenomena independent of matter and individuality.

Subsequently, Aristotle defined the soul as the "capacity" (*entelechy*) or "principle" (*logos*) of the body that gives it actuality. The soul cannot exist independently from the body although it is not, itself, identical with the body.[8] The human soul, according to Aristotle, has three faculties. The first, the appetitive faculty, is found among vegetable, animal, and human life. It is responsible for the self-preservation of the individual through nutrition and growth. The second, the cupiditive faculty, common to animal life, seeks the achievement of pleasure and the avoidance of harm and operates through the five physical senses. The third faculty, reason, found only in man, is the power of judgment, memory, and thinking.

In the first encounter between Hellenism and Judaism, the rabbinic sages generally accepted the Platonic premise that the soul and the body are opposites and that the soul penetrates the body "from without," which the sages understood to mean "from God." In the second encounter medieval Jewish intellectuals accepted a version of Aristotle's philosophy refracted through many interpretations. The human soul was understood as a hierarchically ordered capacity of the human body of which only the intellect comes from God. Still, they adopted the nomenclature from Aristotle of the vegetative, animal, and rational soul. Most important, however, both the concepts and the nomenclature were integrated with the rabbinic theories of *nefesh, ruah,* and *neshamah.* The Jewish mystical conception of the soul was influenced by these traditions.

The human soul, according to the Jewish mystics, consists

of *nefesh, ruah,* and *neshamah. Nefesh* is the physical force in all living beings, the soul that gives life. This faculty is common to all living beings: "This is the power given to animals, beasts and fish which are created from the earth."[9] *Ruah* is a higher faculty that enables man to rise above his limited physical existence to achieve religious transcendence. Once man has achieved the *ruah* through contemplative Torah study and religious living, the *neshamah* is conferred upon him.

The *Zohar* explains the functions of the different souls in a sense different from the Aristotelian scheme. The purpose of the *nefesh* is

> sustenance of the body by means of religious observance which it arouses. The [purpose] of *ruah* is to arouse [the body] to Torah and to guide it in this world. And if one is deserving, the *nefesh* through religious observance and the *ruah* through involvement in Torah, an exceptional benefit [*neshamah*] immediately descends upon it from above according to his actions.[10]

Nefesh serves the nutritive and preservative function for the body as in Aristotelian psychology. The *Zohar,* however, defines the performance of Jewish ritual observances as the real cause of human survival. The religious actions of man are motivated by the *nefesh,* and they in turn preserve his physical existence. *Ruah* is the faculty that motivates man to understand the deeper, spiritual meaning of the Torah beyond the merely physical observance of the commandments. If one perfects his under-standing of the Torah on this deeper level, he achieves a greater spiritual station, the *neshamah.* The *neshamah* is attainable only by followers of the Torah who lead exemplary lives. This is the soul that enables man to achieve mystical insight into the Torah and that leads to religious communion with the *Sefirot* and, ulti-mately, immortality. It is the mystic faculty in humans.

The souls are hierarchically arranged in man, beginning with *nefesh,* and the higher soul is attainable only after the lower soul has been acquired.

> *Nefesh* is the lowest awakening. It is attendant to the body which it nourishes. The body clings to it as it clings to the body. If it reaches its fulfillment, it becomes a throne upon which the *ruah* is

installed as a result of the awakening of the *nefesh,* which clings to
the body. . . . After these two are arranged, they are disposed
toward acquiring *neshamah,* and the *ruah* becomes a throne for the
neshamah, which is installed upon it.[11]

The *neshamah* is the mystic aspect of the human soul that links
him to the divine world of the *Sefirot.*

The description of the *neshamah* in relation to the other
faculties of man is indistinguishable from descriptions of the
relationship of *Eyn Sof* to the other *Sefirot.* "This *neshamah* is
hidden, above all else, and the most sublime."[12] Man is, therefore, conceived as a structure parallel to and analogous with the
Sefirot. The soul in man is what the essence of *Eyn Sof* is to the
Sefirot. The connection between man and the *Sefirot* is believed to
be even deeper, because the soul originates within the *Sefirot* and
creates an essential connecting link between the divine realm and
man. The important element in this notion is that one who has
the correct insight into this relationship is able to direct the
activities of his *neshamah* toward mystical union with the *Sefirot.*

Man has complete autonomy to direct his spiritual life
toward mystical union. On the other hand this freedom also
entails the choice to accentuate the lower human faculties – body
and *nefesh* – and the possibility of failure to achieve transcendence.

> *Nefesh* and *ruah* are inextricably joined together while *neshamah*
> dwells in the character of man, which place is a sublime and
> unknown abode. If a man seeks fulfillment, he is granted the
> assistance of the holy *neshamah,* through which he is fulfilled and
> made holy and called a 'saint.' And if he does not strive to reach
> fulfillment, he acquires only the two levels of *nefesh* and *ruah.* He
> will not achieve the holy *neshamah.*[13]

The *nefesh,* closely related to the body, is similar in substance and
existence to the material world, whereas the *neshamah* is similar
to the divine world. The Jewish mystics, who accept the concept
of the dualism of body and soul common to most medieval
thinkers, also accept a dualism of *nefesh* and *neshamah.* The
relationship between body and soul can be seen in the following
mythological passage which recasts the creation story in a new
narrative form:

When the Holy One, Blessed be He, created the world, the basis of all was water and from water everything was sown. The Holy One, Blessed be He, made three craftsmen who would carry out His plan in this world. They were: heaven, earth and water. By means of these three, everything in the world was created. God called upon each of these three to fashion the beings necessary for this world. To the water, He said: "Bring forth the earth which is below you; go and gather into one spot." This was done, as it is written: "Let the water be gathered" (Gen. 1:9). To the earth, He called and said: "Bring forth the creatures from within you, animals, beasts and the like." It was done immediately, as it is written: "God said, 'Let the earth bring forth every kind of living (*nefesh*) creature' " (Gen. 1:24). To the heavens, He called and said: Place yourselves between the [upper] and [lower] water. And they did, as it is written: "God made the expanse" (Gen. 1:7). By means of these three, the entire work of creation was completed, each one according to its kind. When the sixth day arrived, they were ready to create as on the previous days. The Holy One, Blessed be He, said to them: "None of you alone is capable of creating this creature [i.e., man] as with the other creatures which came to life so far. All of you, join together with Me, and let us make man! You cannot make him by yourselves. The body will belong to the three of you, but the *neshamah* belongs to Me!" Thus, He called to them and said: " 'Let us make man' (Gen. 1:26), you and Me, I will make the *neshamah* and you will make the body." And so it is, that the body is from these three [elements], craftsmen in the work of creation, while the *neshamah* was given by the Holy One, Blessed be He, who joined with the others in this. " 'In our image, after our likeness' (Gen. 1:26), means that man should be worthy of us. Through the body which is from you, he will know you and resemble you. And with that which is taken from Me, the *neshamah,* he will separate himself from mundane affairs and his cleaving and desire will be for holy and divine matters. Moreover, the body which is taken from you three will not have permanent existence just like you. How is he like you? He is like the other creatures which you brought forth, since he is dust like all the other creatures. But the holy *neshamah,* which I gave him, not the body, will grant him eternal existence and through it he will resemble Me!"[14]

Not only is the relationship of the soul and the body analogous to that of *Eyn Sof* and the *Sefirot*, but the soul itself, especially the *neshamah*, originates in the realm of the *Sefirot*. The *neshamah* is the very essence of God encapsulated in human form. Through the human attainment of the *neshamah* man and God share a common nature. The union of the *Sefirot Tiferet* and *Malkhut*, masculine and feminine potencies respectively, produces the original prototype of the *neshamah*. Other mystics suggest that the *Sefirah Binah* ovulates and gushes forth souls that overflow upon *Malkhut*.[15]

It is a fundamental axiom of Jewish mysticism that whatever exists in the world must first exist, in divine form, in the divine realm. Nothing can exist unless it has its "root" in the *Sefirot*. A human being is defined as the composite of its body and soul. Therefore, if the body is created by its father and mother, the soul must also be produced by a similar union. Since the soul comes from heaven, the "parents" of the soul must also reside in the divine realm. The father and mother of the soul are, therefore, the masculine and feminine aspects of God within the realm of the *Sefirot*.

There is a mother and father to *neshamah* [above] just as there is a mother and father to the body on earth. This means that on all levels, whether earthly or divine, everything is produced by masculine and feminine.[16]

Once the *neshamah* is generated by the union of the masculine and feminine aspects of God, the prototype comes to reside in the realm below the *Sefirot*. The number of *neshamot* (pl. of *neshamah*) rapidly multiplies as the union of *Tiferet* and *Malkhut* produces further offspring. All of these come to reside in a realm of spiritual beings located intermediate between the world of the *Sefirot* and the realm inhabited by human beings. This realm contains the forms produced by the *Sefirot* but none of the matter that characterizes the world in which we live. The *neshamot* reside in a form called the "treasury of souls" (*otzar ha-neshamot*) which is located in the heaven called *Aravot* found in this realm.[17]

The *neshamah* has a rich and colored existence in this realm.

Since it is the progeny of the *Sefirot,* it has something of their nature. The spiritual structure of the *neshamah* at this level is androgynous: it contains elements of the masculine and feminine forces that produced it. It has, at this point, an indeterminate gender because it contains both genders in equal measure and balance. Only later on, when the soul is ready to enter the body, does it separate into its masculine and feminine components. Each half of the soul enters a different body, one half determining that its host will be a man, the other, a woman.[18]

The birth of a human being and the formation of human character are the result of processes that begin in the realm of the "treasury of souls." The mystics believe that the original androgynous nature of the human soul is a harmonious balance between contradictory masculine and feminine forces. The unity is disturbed by the necessary descent of the soul into a human body. On one hand birth represents a loss of the original unity of the soul that is separated from its heavenly abode. On the other hand the soul cannot accomplish its destiny except by living in a human body.

Each soul yearns to reunite with its original mate and to recapture the unity of their existence prior to entering the world. This is the highest form of human love, according to the Jewish mystics, because it is the spiritual attraction of one soul for its mate. Each soul has one specific destined mate, its "other half," with which it was once united. Left to their own devices, men and women wander aimlessly in search of their destined partners. This idea, which is found originally in the Symposium of Plato, is known as 'Platonic love.'[19] 'Platonic love' is not asexual love, but rather the spiritual attraction of one soul for its original mate. This conception was adopted by many medieval writers including the author of the *Zohar.* Only God, the architect who designed the different roads on which these souls travel, can match the destined partners correctly. Truly, these are marriages made in heaven. True love then is the love between two destined "soul mates" and their reunion.

Jewish mystics exhibit a candid and comfortable attitude toward sexuality within the strict parameters of what is permissible under Jewish law. Within these limits the mysteries of human sexuality are seen as reflections of processes and sexuality within God. Since the mystics believe that the lower world is totally a reflection of the divine world, human sexuality is seen as emblematic of divine sexuality.

This attitude is expressed in the following passage, a description of the descent of the soul into the world:

> All the souls (*neshamot*) of the world, the handiwork of the Holy One, Blessed be He, are one in one mystery. When they descend into the world, they separate into masculine and feminine forms after once having been united as masculine and feminine together. Come and see: The arousal of the feminine for the masculine produces a *nefesh* and the desire and arousal of the masculine for the feminine and his cleaving to her also produces a *nefesh*. He encompasses the passion of the feminine and carries it so that the passion of the lower is subsumed under the higher and is made one inseparable desire. Then, the feminine carries it all and becomes impregnated by the masculine; the passion of each is indistinguishable from the other and the whole is included in each.
>
> When the souls exit [the treasury of souls], masculine and feminine exit as one. Then, when they have descended [to the world], they separate, each to their respective place. The Holy One, Blessed be He, rejoins them later on. The ability to join a couple together is reserved for the Holy One, Blessed be He, for He alone knows how to match a couple together properly.
>
> Happy is the man who is pure in his ways and walks the path of truth so that his soul is joined with another soul just as they were joined originally.[20]

The souls possess infinite wisdom having been impregnated with a residue of the *Sefirah Hokhmah* in the course of their passage to this realm. All the souls in the treasury possess perfect knowledge of the Torah that is lost as they are born into the world. This notion is based on a rabbinic legend, also derived from Plato, concerning the birth of a child, which suggests that the soul knows the entire Torah before it comes into the world. At the moment of birth it forgets what it has already learned. "As soon as it comes into the world, an angel arrives and slaps it on its mouth and causes it to forget the whole of the Torah."[21] According to legend, the philtrum, the dimple on the upper lip, is where it was struck by the angel. It also suggests that one never learns, only recalls the Torah.

According to the *Kabbalah*, while all humans have a *nefesh*, only Jews have a *neshamah*. This is because one can only achieve a *neshamah* through following the Torah. The following dialogue in the *Zohar* illustrates this point:

> Said Rabbi Hiyya: If this is true [that *neshamah* is acquired through following the Torah], is it so that gentiles have no *neshamah*, only the living *nefesh*?
>
> Rabbi Yohanan said: That is correct.
>
> Then, Rabbi Elazar asked: What, then, is given to Israel?
>
> Rabbi Hiyya expressed astonishment.
>
> Rabbi Elazar responded: Come and see what was taught: 'One who seeks to become pure, is given assistance.' (Shabbat 104a) What sort of assistance is he given? That very same holy *neshamah* which serves as a pillar and which provides man with assistance in this world and the world to come. Until age thirteen, the human being is occupied with the living *nefesh*. From the age of thirteen [when he accepts the responsibility of the Torah], if he wishes to be righteous, he is given the holy and exalted *neshamah*, hewn from the king's throne of glory.[22]

Man is created as a replica of the realm of the *Sefirot*, which is often referred to as the "throne of glory" or the "heavenly glory." Just as the essence of *Eyn Sof* fills the *Sefirot*, so too do the *Sefirot* fill man. These *Sefirot* are present in man as he acquires each of the respective souls. When the mystics speak of man as being created in the image of God, they literally mean that man is created as a microcosm and embodiment of the *Sefirot*.

Nefesh is associated with God's *Hesed*, a freely given gift of life, a pristine state of animal existence. *Ruah*, identified with *Din*, severity, is the human power and ability to choose good or evil. *Neshamah*, linked with *Tiferet*, not only provides a balance between *Hesed* and *Din*, but also the reconciliation of the animal and spiritual tendencies in man. When man acquires the *neshamah*, he has reached an inner state of equilibrium that represents the state of harmony within the divine realm.

Man was created as a vehicle for God's own self-fulfillment. God is a vibrant being whose masculine and feminine aspects are in a constant state of ebb and flow, now united, now separate. Man, the embodiment of the *Sefirot,* is the result of the union of the masculine and feminine in God. This reunion, however, can only be achieved by human religious acts that influence God. Therefore, the cultivation of the spiritual powers in man and the union of the masculine and feminine souls on earth is indispensable to God. Ultimately, this leads to the view that man was created as the agent for the reunification of God.

Religious actions produce *ascents* of the soul. When the soul acts according to the requirements of Jewish religious law, it triggers forces in the world that influence the various *Sefirot.* The correspondence and influence between the *Sefirot* and man are mutual. Just as the different souls represent the action of different *Sefirot,* the actions of the soul influence various *Sefirot.* Consequently, there is a perpetual and dialectical relationship between God and man through the medium of the soul. When the soul is involved in religious activity, it affects the *Sefirot.* Religious actions are primarily devoted to aligning the *Sefirot* in such a manner as to bring about the union of the masculine and feminine *Sefirot.* When this occurs, the essence of the *Sefirot* continues to flow upon the world.

For example, religious rituals are linked with the *neshamah* which itself is associated with *Tiferet,* the masculine *Sefirah.* When the *neshamah* is activated, it contributes to the alignment of the masculine and feminine aspects of God. This, in turn, rains blessings upon the soul:

> When the *neshamah* ascends, the desire of the feminine for the masculine is aroused and the waters pour from above to below.[23]

One who acquires the *neshamah* achieves immortality. This soul comes from the masculine aspect of God and, therefore, returns to it. In an elaborate parable, the *Zohar* describes the destiny of the *neshamah* in the course of life and after it leaves this world:

> A king has a son whom he sends to a village to be educated until he shall have been initiated into the ways of the palace. When the king is informed that his son is now come to maturity, the king,

out of his love, sends the Matron, his mother, to bring him back
to the palace, and there the king rejoices with him every day. In
this wise, the Holy One, be blessed, possessed a son from the
Matron, that is, the supernal holy soul. He dispatched it to a
village, that is, to this world, to be raised in it, and initiated into
the ways of the King's palace. Informed that his son was now
come to maturity, and should be returned to the palace, the King,
out of love, sent the Matron for him to bring him into the palace.
The soul does not leave this world until such time as the Matron
has arrived to get her and bring her into the King's palace, where
she abides forever. Withal, the village people weep for the depar-
ture of the King's son from among them. But one wise man said
to them: Why do you weep? Was this not the King's son, whose
true place is in his father's palace, and not with you? . . .

If the righteous were only aware of this, they would be filled with
joy when their time comes to leave this world.[24]

Death is not a tragedy in most instances, according to the Jewish
mystics. It is the return of the soul to its source. There is death for
the body but not for the soul, since the soul, not the body, is the
essence of man. In fact, the death of a righteous person is
approached with a certain anticipation:

At the moment when the soul of a righteous man wants to depart
there is happiness. The righteous man is confident in his death
that he will receive his reward.[25]

Changes begin to occur thirty days before a person's death. At
night his soul ascends to heaven while he is sleeping and makes
tentative forays into the afterlife, the world to come. There it is
introduced to its next abode and becomes acquainted with this
realm. Man begins to lose awareness and control of his soul
during this period as the connection between it and the body is
weakened.

During this period before death, his shadow begins to disappear. The shadow is equated in Jewish mysticism, as it is later
in Dante's *Purgatory*, with the astral body (*tzelem*).[26] The astral
body is a nonphysical projection of an individual's physical self.
Just as the soul comes from without, the physical body is said to

have an independent spiritual existence prior to its becoming a real body. Before birth the astral body resides in the heavenly treasury known as "the heavenly Garden of Eden." Man is born with the physical manifestation of this astral body which is sometimes described as the 'image (*tzelem*) of God.' The astral body stays with man during his lifetime and becomes a garment woven from his deeds that accompanies his soul to the grave. The astral body may also hover over man and serve as a protecting angel during his lifetime.[27] The connection between the actual body and the astral body is weakened as death approaches and the latter prepares for its separate journey.

On the day of death the soul and the body together undergo a preliminary reckoning. On that day God judges man according to his actions while he was alive. At that moment man is especially vulnerable to the forces of evil in the world and to great terror and anxiety about his fate. Although modern Judaism has dispensed with much of the mythology of rabbinic and medieval Judaism, the Jewish mystical tradition is replete with descriptions of heaven and hell, consuming fires, vicious snakes, and threatening demons. These mythological images are taken as real phenomena that await the sinner after death:

> Woe to those who are ignorant of and do not pay attention to the ways of Torah. Woe to them when the Holy One, Blessed be He, brings man to judgment for his actions and his body and soul stand in testimony on his account before they separate. That very day is the day of reckoning, the day on which the record books lie open and the forces of judgment stand ready. At that moment, the serpent takes his place ready to strike him and all his limbs tremble. The soul departs from the body and takes flight not knowing where it is heading or where it will land. Woe for that day, a day of anger and contention.[28]

Before a man dies he has a visionary encounter with Adam, the first man. Adam asks him why he is leaving the world and how he will depart. He replies: "Oh, it is because of your sins that I am about to depart this world." Adam then responds: "My son, I violated just one commandment and was punished for it. Look at how many sins you committed and how many commandments of your Master you have violated!"[29]

On the day of death, when the soul departs the body, man is able to experience mystical and ecstatic achievements. Although no man can have a direct vision of the *Shekhinah*, the last *Sefirah*, during his lifetime, it may occur on his dying day.[30]

At the moment of death, man also sees close relatives and friends who have already died. They appear to him lifelike and inviting. If he is destined for the afterlife, they greet him cheerfully. If he is destined for perdition, they do not acknowledge him unless they themselves are condemned. In this case they utter, "Woe, Woe!" In either case, his relatives lead him to view heaven and hell once he has died and leave him at the appropriate destination.[31]

As a person is being laid to rest in the grave, he is confronted by all the deeds that he has committed in his lifetime. All human words and actions have an existence independent of man which may yet return to haunt him. The *Zohar* describes graphically how these appear alongside the coffin at the graveside:

> When he is being carried to his grave, [his words and deeds] appear and walk before him. Three heralds, one before him, one to his right and one to his left, announce: This man – who rebelled against his master and against heaven, earth, the Torah and its commandments – look at his deeds, look at his words! He ought never to have been created!
>
> Then all the dead are stirred up against him from their graves and say: "Woe, Woe – that he should be buried among us!"[32]

During the seven-day mourning period, the soul travels back and forth between the grave and his home and participates as a mourner over his own body.

The soul of the deceased passes through many trials before it reaches the heavens. If the soul is not worthy of the afterlife, it may be "tossed around like a rock in a sling" and transmigrated into another body.

Transmigration of souls (*gilgul nefashot*), the recycling of a soul from one deceased person into another body, was the subject of great concern and disagreement among Jewish mystics.[33] One school of thought maintained that transmigration was a form of punishment; a second school saw it as an opportunity to repair sins committed in a previous life. There is agreement that there can only be transmigration of the *nefesh.*

Transmigration may occur as both opportunity and punishment. For example, sins included in the thirty-six classes of mortal sins[34] are often said to require the complete obliteration of the offending soul without the possibility of any afterlife or ultimate resurrection in messianic times. Transmigration is an act of divine mercy that saves the soul from extinction and provides it with a second chance at perfection.[35]

A righteous individual may undergo transmigration in order to complete commandments that he did not fulfill in the previous life or to correct actions that were not according to Jewish norms. This form of return may also provide the occasion for a saint to contribute to the welfare of humanity a second time or to bring additional divine revelation to the world. It is generally regarded that souls can have no more than three transmigrations, except for the righteous whose returns are not limited.

On the other hand, transmigration is also a form of punishment for offenders, especially those who transgress sexual norms. Even a man or woman who chooses to be childless may suffer transmigration for not having fulfilled the biblical injunction to "be fruitful and multiply." The alternative to transmigration is perdition (*geihinnom*), which is portrayed as a cleansing fire that purges and punishes but does not necessarily destroy the soul. Transmigration is clearly preferable to perdition. Some mystics even suggested that under dire conditions a soul may be resurrected in the body of an animal.[36]

Closely related to the concept of transmigration is 'the mystery of conception' (*ibbur*). According to this teaching, the soul of another person can attach itself to the resident soul of a particular person. The attendant soul of a saint or a relative attaches itself to a soul in order to guide and assist it in accomplishing a particular task or mission. The attendant soul can come or go throughout the life of the host as necessary. It serves as a guardian which ministers to its host and helps it through the course of life.

A sinful soul that has no hope of reward may be condemned to trials of fire and purgatory. Although many Jewish theologians, such as Maimonides, objected to the idea of an inferno or purgatory for souls, and others denied that there are such beliefs in Judaism, many Jewish mystics believed in the fiery extermination of unworthy souls.[37]

Despite the terrors associated with death from natural causes, the Jewish mystics were especially troubled by the premature death of children:

> When we see a young man – a good man who learns Torah and Mishnah – who dies before the age of twenty, [we wonder] what caused him to be taken from this world? If you were to say that [it was due to] his father's sins, I would disagree because he is himself [accountable] from the age of thirteen. If you were to say that [it was due to] his own sins, I would disagree because he is not yet twenty [and liable for his actions.][38]

The mystics explain that the death of children is an anticipation of sins that they would have committed had they lived. Their premature death is an "early gathering" that plucks them while their lives are still in full bloom and before the flower withers on the branch. This is seen as an act of divine mercy that entitles them to reward in the afterlife that they would have been denied had they lived their full life.

The kabbalistic doctrine of the soul explains that the spiritual dimension of the human being can link him to the *Sefirot*. The soul is the part of man that comes from the divine realm and, therefore, leads him back to the *Sefirot*. The mystic faculty in man establishes the possibility that the mystic quest can lead him to God. The mystic path in Judaism begins with the doctrine of the soul.

9

THE MYSTIC DRAMA:

The Religious Life of the Jewish Mystic

T he outward manifestations of religious observance among Jewish mystics were not essentially different from the practices of other Jews who followed the rabbinic tradition. Jewish mystics said the same prayers, prayed in the same synagogues, and observed the same rituals (*mitzvot*) as other Jews. Although they acted like their contemporaries, the Jewish mystics approached the meaning of their religious life differently.

UNITY AND RESTORATION

Jewish mystics believe that the two primary purposes of religious observance are to connect the soul to its source in the *Sefirot* and to restore the intrinsic unity within the *Sefirot* through ritual actions.[1] These two functions, the unitive and restorative, permeate every aspect of Jewish mystical approaches to religious life.

Since the mystics believe that the soul comes, indirectly, from the realm of the *Sefirot,* it naturally yearns to return there. All forms of religious observance are vehicles that transport the human soul upward through the heavens and palaces of the upper world, through the chambers of the spiritual world, to the gate of the realm of the *Sefirot*. Jewish mystics are extremely cautious on the question of how high up the soul can ascend on the chain of divine being. Most mystics agree that the rituals are not directed at, nor does the soul ascend to, *Eyn Sof*. Most mystics agree that ritual cannot affect, and the soul cannot ascend, higher than *Hokhmah*. They disagree, however, on how high the soul can ascend. Some, like Isaac the Blind, believe that the soul could unite with *Hokhmah*.[2] Others, like Nahmanides, believe the highest station it can reach is *Malkhut*.[3] Only one appears to suggest that the soul can ascend to *Eyn Sof* itself. Isaac of Acre, of the fourteenth century, asserts that "the soul can cleave to *Eyn Sof*."[4]

With the exception of some of the modern Hasidic mystics, most Jewish mystics do not believe that the separate existence of the soul is annihilated or that the soul is absorbed into the *Sefirot* at the moment of unity. Because the theistic strictures of Judaism are so fundamental, Jewish mysticism is constrained from pursuing absorptive and annihilative forms of mystical union. The soul may come to stand in the highest domains of the *Sefirot*, but it never becomes a *Sefirah*. Its separate identity remains, and the human never merges into the divine. Mystical union is called *devekut* (cleaving, or adhesion). It does not convey the same degree of oneness as does the Latin derivative *union*. It is a communion of two separate and distinct entities that retain their separateness. *Devekut*, the mystical goal, will be discussed at greater length in the last chapter.

The mystics place special emphasis on attentiveness and directedness to each specific ritual action. Rabbinic Judaism has always stressed the importance of seriousness of purpose and willfulness while performing the *mitzvot*. This is expressed in the famous aphorism: "The commandments require intention (*kavvanah*)."[5] The mystics go further in stressing that all ritual actions must be directed to the proper *Sefirah*. They also maintain that knowledge of the specific effects of these actions is an indispensable feature of mystical consciousness.

Intention (*kavvanah*, also called *re'uta*, willfulness, in the *Zohar*), involves the concentrated effort of the heart and body in the performance of the ritual.

One must direct his heart and will (*re'uta*) in order to bring blessings above and below. . . . One who seeks to unite the holy name (i.e., the *Sefirot*) but does not direct his heart, will and awe, in order to grace above and below with blessings, will have his prayers thrown out and evil will be pronounced upon him. . . . But for one who knows how to unite the Holy Name properly, the walls of darkness are split and the King's countenance is revealed and seen by all. When this occurs, everything above and below is blessed.[6]

Intentional action produces an ascent of the soul through the heavens and through the lower levels of the *Sefirot*. First the soul arrives at the gate of the *Sefirot*, and then it continues up to *Hesed, Binah,* or even *Hokhmah*:

> The person who offers his prayer and unites the holy name properly draws the strand of mercy (*hesed*) upon himself. He looks up to the heavens and the light of enlightenment of divine knowledge shines down upon him and crowns him; all stand in awe of him. Such a man is called a son of the Holy One, Blessed be He, a member of the royal entourage.[7]

Ritual action also causes the ascent of the *Shekhinah,* the last *Sefirah,* which is also called *Malkhut,* to the *Sefirah Tiferet*: "The *Shekhinah* dwells in his prayer and [through it] ascends to the Holy One, Blessed be He."[8] This union is necessary for the continued flow of divine blessing and providence upon the world.

Intentional prayer produces many positive results for the world, which are designated *perfections* (*tikkunim*):

> The first perfection is self-fulfillment; the second is the perfection of this world; the third is the perfection of the upper world and all its heavenly hosts; and the fourth is the perfection of the divine Name.[9]

There is a hierarchy of the levels of human accomplishment. Man must first cultivate and develop the faculties of his soul, especially the *neshamah*. Then he must work for the moral and religious improvement of society through observance of the *mitzvot*. Next he must perform the religious rituals that will bring about the elevation of his soul to the world of pure forms. Finally he should strive to unite *Tiferet* and *Malkhut* and achieve *devekut* with the *Sefirot*.

The restorative approach to ritual is based on the belief in 'theurgy.' 'Theurgy' is the possibility of influencing God through ritual means without an act of will on God's part. Rituals affect the *Sefirot* because there exists a mystical nexus between human action and specific *Sefirot*. It is as if Jewish rituals constitute a special language, a system of signs intelligible only to God that trigger responses in God that are incomprehensible to man. The mystic, however, is able to penetrate the causal connection between the theurgic act and the divine response.

The *Sefirot* are conceived of as a series of dynamic forces that are susceptible to human manipulation. The proper alignment of the *Sefirot* is necessary in order for the divine essence to flow smoothly from *Eyn Sof* to *Malkhut* and on through the lower worlds. In particular, this alignment is conditional upon human rituals that manipulate the *Sefirot* properly or improperly. If the *Sefirot* are aligned properly, it will produce divine goodness. If the *Sefirot* are misaligned, divine grace is withheld from the world. Therefore, ritual has a restorative function because it is the primary means by which the theurgic manipulation of the *Sefirot* occurs.

Jewish mystics attribute great power to religious ritual and took upon themselves the obligation to perform theurgic acts. Yet, Jewish mystics also lived within the norms of Jewish life and accommodated themselves to the routine of daily observance. Jewish mystics prior to the sixteenth century rarely created separate societies to practice special devotions contrary to the custom of the rest of the community. When special practices were introduced, especially in the sixteenth century, they did not replace traditional ritual but rather augmented it. Most Jewish mystics were indistinguishable from other Jews because they too believed in the primacy of Jewish ritual, but they viewed it as the means to union with, and restoration of, the *Sefirot*. They did not dispense with conventional ritual in favor of other more individual and idiosyncratic paths to union and restoration.

PRAYER

The mystics differed from conventional religiously observant Jews in several important ways. They believed that the traditional liturgy of daily, Sabbath, and festival prayers contain hidden mystical meanings and references to dynamic processes within the *Sefirot*. The mystical interpretation of the prayer *Shema Yisrael* as an evocative and theurgic wedding ceremony between *Tiferet* and *Malkhut* is a classic illustration of this approach.

The mystics also believed that the words of the prayers themselves take on a life of their own. The words of prayer, once uttered, become entities unto themselves and ascend upward to the *Sefirot* with which they unite and manipulate:

> All that which man thinks and every meditation of his heart is ineffective until his lips utter them out loud. . . . That very word which he utters splits the air, going, rising and flying through the world, until it becomes a voice. That voice is borne by the winged creatures who raise it up to the King who then hears it.[10]

Daily prayer is understood to bring about the perfection (*tikkun*) of the *Shekhinah*. According to rabbinic law certain prayers can only be said when a prayer quorum is assembled. The minimum number that defines a congregation is set at ten adult males.[11] This is based upon Moses' designation of the ten scouts who explored the land of Israel at his command as a congregation (*edah*).[12] Rabbinic legend maintains that the *Shekhinah* dwells in the midst of a congregation of ten men who pray together.[13] In the same source God is depicted as being angry when he comes to a congregation and does not find a prayer quorum.

The rabbinic prayer quorum (*minyan*) is a precondition for the creation of a 'perfection' among the *Sefirot*. The prayer quorum of ten reflects and invokes the assembly of the ten *Sefirot*. Just as there are ten *Sefirot,* there ought to be a quorum of ten men assembled for each regularly scheduled prayer service:

> How precious is Israel in the sight of the Holy One, Blessed be He! In every place they dwell, the Holy One, Blessed be He, is found among them because He never takes His love from them. . . . Blessed is the man who is among the first ten to arrive at the synagogue. Among them is completed that which ought to be completed [i.e., the quorum and the reenactment of joining the ten *Sefirot* together]. These are sanctified by the *Shekhinah* before any others, as has been explained. Ten should arrive at the synagogue simultaneously rather than separately so as not to

delay the completion of the limbs [of the ten *Sefirot*] just as man
was created by God all at once and all his limbs were perfected
together.[14]

The notion that there is a correspondence between human
religious actions and divine processes is axiomatic in Jewish
mysticism. This is evident in the mystical approach to the
synagogue itself. The earliest synagogues were established
during the Babylonian Exile following the destruction of the first
Temple in Jerusalem in 586 B.C.E. Later, synagogues, called *the
minor sanctuary* in rabbinic parlance (*mikdash me'at*), replaced the
Temple, and formal prayers replaced Temple sacrifices as the
authorized form of worship.[15] In mystical symbolism the destroyed Temple still exists within *Malkhut* as the divine prototype of the earthly Temple. The synagogue, therefore, corresponds to *Malkhut*:

> It is commanded to build a sanctuary below corresponding to the
> [heavenly] sanctuary above. . . . One should build a synagogue
> and should pray within it daily and worship the Holy One,
> Blessed be He, for prayer is called worship (*Sifrei Dev.* 41). The
> synagogue should be constructed with great beauty and adorned
> with all manner of refinements because the synagogue below
> corresponds to the heavenly synagogue.[16]

Because of the correspondence between the earthly synagogue
and *Malkhut*, the *Zohar* prefers conventional prayer said in a
synagogue to prayer offered anywhere else. In fact, the *Zohar*
introduced into the body of Jewish customs several new practices
and rites based on mystical principles. For example, the prefer-
ence for synagogue prayer over prayers said elsewhere is based
on the idea that since the *Shekhinah* can only be reached by a
narrow path, earthly prayers must be concentrated into a narrow
channel in order to ascend. The very structure of a synagogue is
preferable to an open field because the former would concentrate
whereas the latter would diffuse the ascending channel of prayer.
The *Zohar* also introduces as law the notion that a synagogue
must have windows so that the prayers could exit the synagogue
and ascend through the narrow passage of the window.[17] The
Zohar also states that congregational prayer is preferable to indi-

vidual prayer because God scrutinizes critically the worthiness and actions of an individual who prays alone. His prayer can ascend only as far as his actions warrant. Congregational prayer, however, ascends easily because of the aggregate merit of those assembled.[18] If, however, one cannot pray with a congregation, he should at least pray at the same time as the congregation.

THE SABBATH

According to rabbinic tradition there are 613 commandments.[19] The specific number was not originally intended to reflect the actual number of ritual obligations of a Jew as much as it conveyed an ideal. The number originally represented the sum of the days of the year (365) and the supposed number of bodily organs in the human body, which the rabbinic sages somehow calculated to be 248. It conveyed the idea that Jewish law was comprehensive and addressed all the possible actions that a human might actually perform in the course of time. Later scholars took this to be a real number, and many attempted to codify their own listing of the 613 commandments. Since there are many variations and infinite possibilities, no authoritative identification of the specific 613 commandments exists. There is, however, consensus among medieval rabbinic authorities on the specific patterns of Jewish ritual behavior that are to be followed.

Jewish mystics applied their own mystical interpretations to the meaning of individual religious actions just as they did to the general meaning of prayer and observance. The unitive and restorative approach to observance can be seen in the formula that Jewish mystics invoke:

> In every ritual action, let your effort be directed toward uniting the Holy One, Blessed be He, and his *Shekhinah* through all camps above and below.[20]

The most central of all Jewish rituals, perhaps, are those related to Sabbath observance. Not only are the Jewish people called "the people who sanctify the seventh day" (*am mekadeshei shevi'i*), but rabbinic sources clearly attest to the centrality of this day in the religious life of a Jew: "Sabbath [rituals] are balanced against all other observances."[21] The Sabbath rituals constitute the most important of all the Jewish rituals.

The Sabbath symbolism in rabbinic and mystical Jewish lore is dominated by the wedding and bridal motifs. The Talmud invokes the beginning of Sabbath with the injunction, "Let us come and go out to welcome the Sabbath bride."[22] This theme is elaborated by Jewish mystics who reinterpret all of the elements of the Sabbath rituals into a consistent thematic drama of the reunion of the *Shekhinah,* the Sabbath bride, with her mate.

Jewish mystics frequently draw associative connections between traditional elements of Jewish rituals and the *Sefirot.* This is often expressed in a formula that states that a certain ritual, or aspect of a ritual, is "against" (*ke-neged*) a particular *Sefirah.* This means that the ritual either symbolizes, influences, or creates a link with that *Sefirah.* The association is often based on the Hebrew etymology of a term related to the ritual. For example, the association of the Sabbath with *Malkhut* is drawn, in part, because of the relationship between the word *malkah,* the Sabbath bride of rabbinic literature, and the name of the last *Sefirah, Malkhut.* Other associations may be based on what appear to be more tenuous interpretive links such as equivalences between the numerical values of two different Hebrew words (*gematria*). Often biblical words suggest associations. For example, a word that appears in one biblical context may suggest a connection to a different passage that contains a similar word. These links are vital to the associative and imaginative thinking of Jewish mystics who saw the biblical text as being replete with hidden meanings.

The Sabbath itself is usually associated with *Malkhut* or *Yesod.* This ambiguity is rooted in the fact that in each of the two versions of the Decalogue the Sabbath commandment is phrased differently. In Deuteronomy 5:12 it reads: "Keep (*shamor*) the Sabbath day," whereas in Exodus 20:8 it reads: "Remember (*zakhor*) the Sabbath day." *Shamor* is associated with *Malkhut* because it is the *Sefirah* that *preserves* (*shomeret*) the world. *Zakhor* is associated with *Yesod,* the masculine *Sefirah,* because the Hebrew word *zakhor* means both *to remember* and *to be masculine.* Occasionally the Sabbath is linked with the *Sefirah Binah,* which is often portrayed as the source of the fulfillment of the prophesies of a messianic age, the era in which every day is Sabbath. The Sabbath wedding is portrayed as a restorative ritual involving the reunion of *Malkhut* with the masculine *Sefirah Yesod* or with *Tiferet*.[23] The elaborate preparations for the Sabbath are treated as preparations for a wedding. The restoration of harmony between masculine and feminine *Sefirot* changes the prevailing order. The *Sefirah Din,* strict judgment, presides over the weekdays with severity. The Sabbath brings a respite from the dominion of *Din* and cancels out *Din* with *Hesed,* mercy. The Sabbath is described as a "tent of peace" (*sukkat shalom*) that spreads over the Jewish people and makes them immune from the forces of evil that preside during the week.

In many traditional Hasidic prayer books the following passage from the *Zohar* is to be recited on Friday night:

> The mystery of Sabbath: Sabbath is unification through oneness, which causes the mystery of oneness to dwell upon it. Prayer, which the Sabbath raises up, unifies and perfects the holy and precious throne through the mystery of oneness so that the divine and holy King may sit upon it. When the Sabbath begins, she is made one and separates from the other side [i.e., evil] and all the forces of severity pass away. She remains unified with the holy light and is adorned with many crowns by the holy King. All the powers of ire and forces of severity are uprooted and there is no evil dominion upon the worlds. Her face is radiant with divine light and she is adorned below with the holy people.[24]

The idea that a special soul enters the body and resides there during the Sabbath dates back to the rabbinic period.[25] The *Zohar* expands this notion and explains that the Sabbath is "the day of the soul, not the body."[26]

Most modern Sabbath observers are unaware of the extent to which Jewish mystics, particularly the Kabbalists of Safed in the sixteenth century, introduced into Jewish practice new rituals that reflected their mystical view of the Sabbath. For example, it was their custom to go out into the fields to greet the Sabbath. They went out dressed in white ready to join the bride as her entourage in the wedding ceremony. They would face the west from where the *Shekhinah* would rise as the sun set. The order of prayers for the Friday evening service that accompanied this ritual was established by these mystics as a unitive and restorative ritual.[27] Their order, including the mystical hymn *Lekhah Dodi,* which was discussed above, prevails even today. The *Zohar* included certain blessings such as "who extends a tent of peace" (*ha-pores sukkat shalom*) and excluded certain prayers such as "He is merciful and acquits transgression" (*ve-hu rahum yikhapper avvon*) from the Friday evening service, to illustrate the notion that unity prevails and severity is annulled on the Sabbath.

The elaborate Friday evening service is not the only mystical Sabbath rite that entered normative practice. The *Zohar* explains that the head of the household must accomplish ten things at the Sabbath table, corresponding to the ten *Sefirot.*[28] Although many of these are rabbinic practices, the enumeration of ten central customs and the associated symbolism are Zoharic:

1. Light at least two Sabbath candles: The woman head of the household lights at least two Sabbath candles at the table before the onset of the Sabbath, corresponding to the two versions of the Sabbath law in the Decalogue. In the *Zohar* the candles symbolize *Hesed* (mercy), and the table symbolizes *Din* (severity). Symbolically, this act dispels *Din* from the table.

2. Bless the cup of wine: The male recites the *Kiddush,* the Sabbath blessing, over wine at the table. The first part of the *Kiddush,* taken from the biblical description of the first Sabbath,[29] is associated with *Yesod,* a masculine *Sefirah.* The second section is associated with the feminine *Malkhut.* Together, the *Kiddush* symbolizes the unification of masculine and feminine *Sefirot.*

3. Perform the ritual handwashing before breaking bread: This rabbinic law is a requirement before eating bread.[30] The *Zohar* requires that one hold a cup filled with water in the right hand, which symbolizes *Hesed,* pass the cup to the left hand, which symbolizes *Din,* and pour it first upon the right hand then pass the cup again and pour upon the left. This is done so that the priority of *Hesed* over *Din* on the Sabbath is emphasized.[31]

4. Put two loaves of bread on the table: Two loaves are traditionally used to recall the double portion of manna that rained down before the Sabbath.[32] According to the *Zohar* the two loaves placed together symbolize the union of *Malkhut* and *Tiferet*. The *Zohar* requires that the diners eat from the lower of the two loaves, when one is placed on top of the other, to symbolize the lower *Sefirot*, especially *Malkhut*.

5. Eat three festive meals: The major meals of the Sabbath are Friday evening, Saturday lunch, and later on Saturday following the late afternoon service. According to the *Zohar* these meals ceremoniously invoke the power of *Malkhut*, *Keter*, and *Tiferet*, respectively. Special songs (*zemirot*) are sung at each of the meals, many of which were composed as hymns to the *Sefirah* associated with that meal.

6. Discuss Torah at the table: According to the rabbinic tradition, the *Shekhinah* dwells at any table where Torah is discussed.

7. Welcome poor guests to the table: Charitable concern for the poor is a feature of the social consciousness of the *Zohar*. The poor are believed to bring special merit to the table and aid in the achievement of unity.[33]

8. Perform ritual handwashing after the meal: This is a rabbinic custom called *final water* (*mayyim aharonim*).[34] It is done after the meal before saying the blessing after food. The *Zohar* explains that this custom is performed in order to cleanse the hands of evil and to remove the impurities that cling to them.[35] It is also intended to wash away particles of food which are then considered a concession and nourishment to the evil forces.[36]

9. Recite the blessing after food: This rabbinic practice is associated, according to the *Zohar*, with the *Sefirah Hesed*.[37] The *Zohar* explains that one who says this blessing with intention will invoke *Hesed* upon the world.

10. Bless a final cup of wine: According to rabbinic tradition a final cup of wine is blessed following the blessing after food.[38]

These practices illustrate the way Jewish mystics reinterpret traditional practices in light of mystical teachings. The Sabbath is turned into a theurgic drama that unfolds in sequence.

The mystics also introduced completely new customs. For example, the custom of singing *Eshet Hayyil* ("Woman of Valor")[39] as a hymn at the Sabbath table in praise of the wife and alluding to the *Shekhinah* was introduced by the Safed Kabbalists.

Ritual innovation can also be seen in the *Zohar*'s approach to human sexuality. The *Zohar* considers Sabbath the most propitious occasion for unitive and restorative mysticism through human sexual intercourse. Sexual intercourse on Sabbath eve produces the special Sabbath soul.[40] Therefore, this is the time when a righteous man and woman should have sexual contact. The themes of mystical reinterpretation and innovation can be seen in regard to other Jewish rituals.

THE FESTIVALS

The Jewish holidays are unitive and restorative sacraments to devotees of Jewish mysticism. The specific rituals of each holiday serve several functions in Jewish mysticism. They are theurgic sacraments that have the power to realign and reunite the configuration of the *Sefirot*. Since the observance of the festivals brings about perfection in the divine realm, it influences the fate of God and, therefore, of man. Religious practices are always understood to influence God on behalf of man. In Jewish mysticism, however, God does not answer man's prayer or reward him for his actions directly. Rather the actions of man cause involuntary reactions within God. These reactions then produce reverberations that rebound from God to man. These dialectical influences imply a new mode of thinking about the relationship between God and man and a mutual dependence of one upon the other. God is not perfected except by the actions of man, and the unity of the various aspects of God's being depends on human actions. Man does not benefit except through divine grace. Neither God nor man can act or be fulfilled except through the other.

The primary Jewish holidays are the Days of Awe–*Rosh ha-Shanah* and *Yom ha-Kippurim*–and the pilgrimage festivals–

Pesah, Shavuot, and *Sukkot.* The Jewish mystics observed these festivals as do all other observant Jews. Occasionally the mystics introduced new theurgic rituals. Generally, the difference between a mystic and a nonmystic lies in the consciousness of the significance of the festival, not in its practice.

Rosh ha-Shanah is the beginning of the new year in the Jewish calendar. It does not, however, mark the beginning of the first month in the liturgical or religious calendar. That begins with *Nisan,* the month in which *Pesah* occurs. *Rosh ha-Shanah* occurs on the first two days of the seventh month, *Tishrei.* In the time of the prophets Ezra and Nehemiah (c. fifth century B.C.E.), the holiday was observed by the Israelite people with a gathering at the newly restored Temple in Jerusalem where the Torah laws for the day were read and the hollow ram's horn (*shofar*) was blown. It was a day of celebration and feasting. It was a day on which the kingship of God was proclaimed and the supremacy of the divine rule over earthly monarchs was reaffirmed.

By the first and second centuries, new themes for the holiday were introduced. The *Mishnah* states that this holiday marks the anniversary of the date on which man was created. According to Jewish legend man was created and sinned on the same day. Therefore, his birthdate became a day of judgment for him as well as for all his descendants.

The Talmud develops the theme of *Rosh ha-Shanah* as the day of divine judgment upon man. It cites a legend to the effect that three heavenly books are opened on this day – one for those whose actions mark them as unredeemably wicked, one for the completely righteous, and one for those of intermediate status. The wicked are immediately inscribed in the book of death, and their fate is tentatively decreed for the coming year. The righteous are likewise inscribed in the book of life, and their fate is assured. The fate of those who are not in these categories is deferred until *Yom ha-Kippurim* when the books are finally sealed.[41] It is customary to wish "a good inscription" (*gemar ketivah tovah*) before Rosh ha-Shanah and "a good seal" (*gemar hatimah tovah*) from that day until *Yom ha-Kippurim.*

Jewish mystics believe that the aspect of divine judgment is aroused on *Rosh ha-Shanah* through the ascendancy of the *Sefirah Din.* "On *Rosh ha-Shanah,* the power of severity is awakened above. Therefore, every person must arouse himself below to complete repentance. For by this, merciful love is awakened above."[42] The rituals of *Rosh ha-Shanah* are theurgic sacraments that mitigate the power of the *Sefirah Din* by empowering the *Sefirah Hesed*. In Jewish mysticism all of the elements of the holiday are related to this goal.

Without self-reckoning and a genuine decision to change religious and personal behavior, *Rosh ha-Shanah* can be a day when one is exposed to all the forces of evil in existence. Repentance, however, activates the *Sefirah Hesed* and aids it in balancing the *Sefirah Din*. If left unchecked, *Din* would give strength to the destructive powers that stand ready to attack man. With repentance, *Din* is held in check and human vulnerability is protected:

> On the very day of *Rosh ha-Shanah,* when seventy chambers are waiting to pronounce severe judgment upon the world, many armed avengers stand ready above. Some turn to the right in favor, and some turn to the left in contempt, recalling the sins of the world, of each and every one. Therefore, man must confess his sins, every one as they really are.[43]

The ram's horn also symbolizes the predominance of *Hesed* over *Din*. The horn is blown one hundred times during the *Rosh ha-Shanah* service. The ram's horn activates the various *Sefirot* and creates a configuration of the *Sefirot* in which *Hesed* predominates. The horn itself symbolizes *Binah* and emphasizes *Hesed* since it is the *Sefirah* that precedes *Hesed*.

The Torah portions read on the two days of the holiday also symbolize the ritual elevation of *Hesed* over *Din*. In Jewish mystical symbolism certain biblical historical figures are linked to certain *Sefirot* through various word associations. For example, the patriarch Abraham is linked with the *Sefirah Hesed* through the verse, "Deal graciously (*hesed*) with my master Abraham."[44] His son, Isaac, is more loosely associated with *Din,* severity, through the phrase, "the fear (*pahad*) of Isaac."[45] Consequently, the Torah reading for the first day, which details Isaac's assumption of the right of primogeniture over his brother Ishmael, symbolizes the supremacy of *Din* on that day.[46] The Torah portion for the second day narrates Abraham's willingness to sacrifice Isaac at God's command and the sudden intervention that saves Isaac and replaces him on the alter with a ram.[47] It symbolizes the ultimate predominance of *Hesed* (Abraham) over *Din* (Isaac) and explains the significance of the ram's horn in this process.

Confession and repentance on *Rosh ha-Shanah* moderate *Din* with *Hesed* and ultimately bring about the union of *Tiferet* and *Malkhut* on *Yom ha-Kippurim*:

> On *Rosh ha-Shanah*, the left arm [i.e., *Din*] is aroused in order to greet the princess [i.e., *Shekhinah*]. Then the whole world is terrified by *Din*. At the same time, the whole world must be repentant in the presence of the Holy One, Blessed be He. Later, the princess arrives on the eve of *Yom ha-Kippurim* and the whole assembly celebrates and they cleanse themselves in preparation for union with the princess.[48]

Yom ha-Kippurim, the tenth day of *Tishrei*, is described in the Bible as a time for afflicting the soul.[49] Although the Bible says little else about the holiday, it has generally been understood that this is a means of achieving awe and contrition. The Talmud interprets the affliction of the day by identifying five classes of routine activities that are prohibited on *Yom ha-Kippurim*.[50] The prohibitions include abstaining from food and water, washing the body, wearing cosmetics or perfume, wearing leather sandals or shoes, and having sexual relations.

These activities are all forms of physical comfort and pleasure that may be enjoyed at other times. Their denial on *Yom ha-Kippurim* is not intended to punish or afflict the body but rather to promote the transcending of physical pleasures. Despite the nature of these prohibitions, it is the soul, not the body, that is afflicted as a means of spiritual conditioning on *Yom ha-Kippurim*.

The liturgy of the holiday in the rabbinic tradition has its roots in two historical phenomena in Jewish history, each of which has a strong mystical dimension. First, *Yom ha-Kippurim* is a vivid and symbolic recreation of the events leading up to the revelation of the Torah to Moses on Mount Sinai. According to the rabbinic tradition Moses shattered the first set of commandments that God gave to him on the sixth day of *Sivan* [i.e., *Shavuot*] when he saw the Golden Calf. Legend has it that God gave Moses the second set of tablets on *Yom ha-Kippurim*.[51] Each of the five classes of prohibitions represents one or another of the actions that God decreed to Moses and the people in preparation for revelation. For example, Moses was commanded to remove his sandals at the burning bush in one of the key events leading up to Sinai.[52] The people were commanded to remain pure, to be ready, to refrain from sexual contact, and to abstain from food and drink.[53] The contemporary prohibitions, then, are intended to prepare the congregation for reenacting the Sinai revelation by repeating the steps taken by Moses and the Jewish people. The closing *Yom ha-Kippurim* service, *Ne'ilah,* parallels the revelation at Sinai. The Bible recounts that when the laws were given, "all the people witnessed the thunder and lightning, the blare of the horn."[54] The holiday concludes its reenactment of Sinai with one final shofar blast. *Yom ha-Kippurim* is, therefore, a symbolic reenactment of the revelation of Sinai and atonement for the sin of the Golden Calf.

Second, the holy day is a carefully crafted ritual recreation of the preparations of the high priest prior to entering the holy of holies in the Jerusalem Temple on *Yom ha-Kippurim*. These preparations are the subject of the *Avodah* service, which is central to the midday liturgy. The rituals surrounding the high priest are themselves a reenactment of Moses' preparations for Sinai. The high priest alone was permitted to enter the inner sanctum only once a year after completing elaborate preparations including taking off his sandals and other acts that recall Moses at Sinai.[55] When the high priest was ready to enter, the other priests tied a rope around him in order to pull him out in case he should die inside in ecstatic rapture. When the high priest pronounced his benedictions, the people gathered would answer, "Blessed be the name of His glorious majesty forever." Likewise, only on *Yom ha-Kippurim* night is this phrase, which is usually said in a whisper, uttered out loud in response to the *Shema*. On *Yom ha-Kippurim,* the members of the congregation are symbolically Moses and the high priest. The burden of responsibility and the anticipation of redemption are proferred sacramentally to each participant in the holy day liturgy.

Yom ha-Kippurim is the next stage in the process of reuniting *Tiferet* and *Malkhut,* which began on *Rosh ha-Shanah* through softening the power of *Din*. On *Yom ha-Kippurim* the *Sefirah Binah,* the source of *Hesed,* prevails and uplifts the *Shekhinah* in preparation for reunion with *Tiferet.*

> When Israel fasts for her sins, [the *Shekhinah*] atones for them because the heavenly matron [i.e., *Binah*] shines her countenance upon the princess in union with her.[56]

Yom ha-Kippurim is linked symbolically to *Binah,* which is associated with all the rituals of this awesome day. The *Kol Nidrei,* often described as the holiest and most awesome moment in the Jewish liturgy, opens the evening service. It is not really a prayer but a legal formula for the annulment of certain types of vows. Although it was intended to annul past vows, the formula was changed to refer only to vows made during the coming year in order not to abrogate existing contracts. For the mystic the *Kol Nidrei* is an invocation to the highest *Sefirot* to release *Tiferet* and *Malkhut* from the bonds of *Din* in order to facilitate their union. The entire liturgy of the day follows this pattern of invoking *Binah*:

> Today, every joy, every light and all forgiveness in the world depends on the divine matron [i.e., *Binah*]. All the springs start and draw from there. All the lights are illuminated with joy and everything becomes fragrant. Even the forces of *Din* are consumed by light and are extinguished.[57]

The drama of reunification continues throughout the month of *Tishrei. Sukkot,* the feast of booths, begins on the fifteenth of *Tishrei* and lasts for seven days in Israel, eight days in the Diaspora. The holiday of *Simhat Torah,* the celebration beginning the annual cycle of Torah reading, falls on the eighth day, *Shemini Atzeret,* in Israel, and on the ninth day in the Diaspora.

   The holiday is observed in a variety of ways including the construction and use of temporary booths (*sukkot*) reminiscent of the period of wandering in the Sinai desert. In addition the ritual use of four species of vegetation (*arbaah minim*) recalls the agricultural origins of the holiday as the fall harvest festival. The four species that are used in ceremonial ways during the holiday are a palm branch (*lulav*), willows (*aravot*), a citron (*etrog*), and myrtle (*hadas*). The willows and myrtle are bundled together with the palm branch and held in the right hand while the citron is held separately in the left hand in rituals performed at home and in the synagogue.

The construction of the booth is linked symbolically with the seven *Sefirot* from *Hesed* to *Malkhut*, each of which corresponds to one of the seven days of the holiday. The booth itself symbolizes *Binah*, the divine mother, which looks after and protects the seven lower *Sefirot*.

The *Zohar* introduced a *Sukkot* ritual that has gained wide acceptance in traditional circles even today. Because of the association between the seven lower *Sefirot* and the seven days of *Sukkot*, the author of the *Zohar* framed a ritual that symbolically invites the *Sefirah* linked with that day as a guest to the *sukkah* (the booth). Since biblical personages were identified with each *Sefirah*, the custom of welcoming the mystical guests (*ushpizin*) in the *sukkah* emerged. On succeeding days Abraham (*Hesed*), Isaac (*Din*), Jacob (*Tiferet*), Moses (*Netzah*), Aaron (*Hod*), Joseph (*Yesod*), and David (*Malkhut*) are welcomed.[58]

> When you enter the *sukkah*, you ought to openly invite the divine saints to join you because they are your glory. They come in spiritual form to join you on all sides.[59]

Special formulae are recited for each guest, and elaborate wall decorations with fanciful pictures of the guest adorn many *sukkot*.

The *lulav* and *etrog* also have symbolic associations with the *Sefirot*. The seven pieces that make up the *lulav* and *etrog* are also symbolic of the seven lower *Sefirot*. The tall palm branch, which is a phallic symbol, is associated with the masculine *Sefirah Yesod*. The round citron, with feminine connotations, symbolizes *Malkhut*. The three myrtle branches suggest *Hesed, Din,* and *Tiferet,* and the two willow branches denote *Netzah* and *Hod.*[60] With the *lulav* in the right hand and the *etrog* in the left, the branches are waved in the synagogue service in six directions (east, south, west, north, up, and down) each day. Each direction corresponds to another *Sefirah* thus symbolizing the unity of the lower six *Sefirot*.

Finally on the last day, *Simhat Torah,* the final Torah portion of the liturgical year is concluded, and the cycle begins again. But for the Jewish mystic this holiday completes the unification of *Tiferet* and *Malkhut* that began on *Rosh ha-Shanah*.

> On the first day of *Sukkot,* the right side [i.e., *Hesed*] is aroused toward embracing the princess [i.e., *Shekhinah*]. . . . People ought to rejoice in many ways as she is inclined toward celebration. The eighth day, *Simhat Torah,* is the day of union, the day on which all is one, the perfection of all.[61]

If the Days of Awe and *Sukkot* are part of a process of unification, *Pesah* (Passover) is a theurgic drama of vanquishing evil and demonic forces. The *Pesah* festival celebrates the divine deliverance and exodus of the Israelites from Egyptian slavery. It begins on the fifteenth of *Nisan,* the first liturgical month, and lasts for seven days in Israel, eight in the Diaspora.[62] The holiday is observed through strict prohibitions against eating any bread or other leavened products, the injunction to eat *matzah* (unleavened bread), and the telling of the narrative of the Exodus at an elaborate table ritual, the *seder,* on the first night in Israel and on the first two nights in the Diaspora.[63]

Jewish mystics invested the holiday with special significance. For them it symbolizes a victory over the demonic forces that prevail in the world as a result of the separation of *Malkhut* and *Tiferet.* The absence of unity in the divine realm produces an abundance of *Din* and converts the *Sefirah Malkhut* to a source of suffering that is radiated upon the world. Only the reunification of the *Shekhinah* with *Tiferet* can correct this dreadful state of affairs. The enslavement in Egypt and the eventual deliverance is both the result of and symbolic of this process.

According to rabbinic legend wherever the Israelites went into exile, the *Shekhinah* accompanies them to protect them. According to another interpretation, which stresses the idea that exile is a punishment for the religious and moral failures of the people, the *Shekhinah* itself goes into exile along with the Israelites. For Jewish mystics the Exodus from Egypt symbolizes the redemption of the *Shekhinah* from exile and the beginning of her restoration to unity with *Tiferet.*

Egypt is transformed from a historical place to a symbol for all the evil that plagues humanity whenever the *Sefirot* are not aligned harmoniously. Egypt is described as the abode of the "husks," or "shells" (kelipot), that trap the Shekhinah and prevent her from achieving unity.

The many rituals of Pesah are linked to the symbolism of redemption from evil. The paschal lamb was slaughtered in ancient times and eaten on the holiday.[64] A vestige of this practice, which was abandoned after the destruction of the second Temple, can be found in the roasted shankbone that is placed on a special plate at the seder table. Jewish mystics describe this as a theurgic ritual that destroys the power of evil. They explain that the Egyptians worshipped lambs as deities. Thus, the sacrifice or burning of a slaughtered lamb is an act of destruction in which the demonic power of the Egyptian deities is annihilated. It is interesting to note that Jewish mystics acknowledge the reality of other deities. However, they are understood as satanic and evil powers that threaten and attack the holiness of the Sefirot. The slaughter of the lamb is the first ritual performed on the holiday and indicates that the "husks" must be destroyed in order for the Sefirot to escape from their dominion. The lamb is eaten at night, the time when the evil power is ascendant, to vanquish it at the moment of its greatest strength.

Matzah, which is described in the seder ritual as the bread of poverty (lehem oni, usually translated as the bread of affliction), refers to the bread that was prepared hurriedly in the last hours of the Israelites' enslavement as they hastened to depart. In Jewish mysticism the bread of poverty refers to the Shekhinah in exile, which is impoverished due to her separation from Tiferet.

Leavened bread (hametz), which is absolutely forbidden on Pesah, symbolizes the powers of evil. The mystics explain that leavened bread is an allegory for the power of demonic forces over good. Even a small amount of leavening resembles fermentation and causes the food to lose its original flavor.[65] Likewise, even a little evil can cause the total corruption of a good person. Leaven is outlawed because just as it causes the breakdown of the natural essence of food products, it connotes the destruction of divine goodness.

Although leavened foods are prohibited on Pesah, they are permitted throughout the rest of the year. If they connote evil, should not leavened foods be outlawed entirely? The mystics' response is that leaven serves as a reminder of the defeat of the forces of evil. Without such a reminder the consciousness of redemption might fade. Therefore, the use of leaven during the rest of the year is, paradoxically, a reminder of the holiness of the *Sefirot* to which all religious actions are directed. This notion also implies that evil exists as a reminder of goodness, for without it there is no awareness of its opposite.[66]

The mystics find another positive use for leaven in particular and for evil powers in general. They recognize that actions that begin as a result of impure instincts or drives can lead to pure and positive results. For example, they recognize that human sexual urges and lust may derive from evil and demonic impulses. But these instincts, when channeled properly, may lead to pure and holy consequences of sexual union which, in the mystics view, is a theurgic act of divine reunification. As one mystic, the author of the *Lekhah Dodi,* explains: "The evil inclination is vital to the world for the purpose of [proper] sexual union."[67]

The *seder* is a theurgic ritual designed to reunite the *Shekhinah* with *Tiferet.* It is customary to perform the *seder* while leaning to the left. This symbolizes *Binah,* which appears on the left in all diagrams of the *Sefirot,* and which is the *Sefirah* called *freedom.* The entire *seder* is associated with the *Sefirah Binah,* which is ascendant on this holiday. The three *matzot* which are placed on the table symbolize *Tiferet, Malkhut,* and *Yesod.* The middle *matza,* symbolizing *Malkhut,* is broken in half to suggest that *Malkhut* is divided between the two male *Sefirot, Tiferet,* and *Yesod,* until she is finally united with her mate, *Tiferet,* in the ultimate unity. One of the halves is hidden as the *afikomen,* which is recovered after the meal and eaten. Because it is hidden, it is linked with *Binah,* the hidden source of freedom.

The four cups of wine that are consumed during the *seder* are associated with the four *Sefirot, Hokhmah, Binah, Tiferet,* and *Malkhut,* and symbolize the stages in the process of uniting *Tiferet* and *Malkhut.* The bitter herbs (*maror*) suggest the bitterness that plagues *Tiferet* while it is separate from *Malkhut.* The mixture of apples, nuts, and wine (*haroset*) symbolizes the sweetness of the redemption that occurs on this evening. The *seder* ritual culminates in the temporary reunion of *Tiferet* and *Malkhut* and the liberation from the dominion of evil.

The third pilgrimage festival, *Shavuot,* occurs on the sixth day of the month of *Sivan,* and outside of Israel it continues on the following day. It is both the celebration of the anniversary of the revelation of the Torah at Sinai and the festival at the beginning of the spring wheat harvest. Aside from the observances that attend all pilgrimage festivals, there are few rituals associated specifically with this holiday. One of the most common customs is to celebrate the holiday with festive dairy meals. This custom is based on the agricultural origins of the holiday and the affinity between grain and dairy products. It also derives from the designation of Mount Sinai as *har gavnunim,* a ragged mountain with many peaks.[68] Inventive commentators noticed the similarity between the term *gavnunim* and *gevinah,* the Hebrew word for cheese. From this association, the custom of eating dairy products on *Shavuot* gained favor.

The biblical Book of Ruth, a narrative concerning the non-Israelite Ruth and her efforts to join her fate with the Israelite people, is read on *Shavuot* for two reasons. First, the story centers on apparently random agricultural events that had decisive and profound consequences for the destiny of the Israelite people: Following a famine that brought the Israelite Naomi to Moab, she returned to Israel with her widowed daughter-in-law, Ruth, a Moabitess. At the harvest, Naomi's relative Boaz met Ruth, whom he soon married. Boaz and Ruth, explains the genealogical conclusion of the book, were the great-grandparents of King David. Their meeting was consequential for it set in motion a series of events that culminated in the Davidic kingship and, ultimately, in the building of the Temple and the perpetuation of the Jewish religion. Second, the Book of Ruth narrates a tale of betrothal and marriage between Ruth and Boaz. The marriage symbolizes the enduring marriage and covenant between the Jewish people and God that was established at Sinai. The holiday of *Shavuot* and the Book of Ruth are linked together by the theme of marriage.

It is not surprising that Jewish mystics understood this holiday as the grand culmination of the unification of *Tiferet* and *Malkhut.* *Shavuot* is celebrated, according to the Bible, on one day, as opposed to the other pilgrimage festivals, *Sukkot* and *Pesah,* which each last seven days. Jewish mystics explain that this anomaly is due to the fact that on *Shavuot* there is complete unity whereas on the other festivals there is merely anticipation of unity. The result of the divine unity achieved on *Shavuot* is God's revelation of the Torah to Moses and the Jewish people.

According to Jewish theology God revealed to Moses all of the Torah, including details of events that had not yet occurred. All this he then faithfully transcribed in writing. At the same time, according to legend, God revealed to Moses the interpretations and hidden meanings of the Torah. According to tradition these insights, called the *Oral Torah* (*Torah she-be-al peh*), became the basis of the collected wisdom of the ages. They were transmitted faithfully from master to disciple as the authoritative companion to the Written Torah (*Torah she-be-khtav*). Jewish mystics claim that mystical insight is embedded in the Oral Law and can be extracted only by initiation into the teachings of the mystical tradition.

Because *Shavuot* is the paradigm of unity, the Jewish mystics invented special rituals to be practiced on this day. In the guise of ancient custom, the *Zohar,* for example, introduced the practice of "Creating Perfection on the Night of Shavuot" (*tikkun leil Shavuot*), studying selections from the Oral Torah. In mystical symbolism, the Written Torah is associated with *Tiferet* and the Oral Torah is linked with *Malkhut*. The *tikkun* ritual is designed to hasten the divine marriage by joining *Tiferet* and *Malkhut*. The Written Torah is read during the daytime service of *Shavuot*. The Oral Torah is studied intensely the night before as a means to prepare the bride, *Malkhut,* or the Oral Torah, for her wedding in the morning. The ritual of *tikkun leil Shavuot* is conducted from midnight to dawn, the time when *Malkhut* predominates. Thus the marriage ceremony between *Tiferet* and *Malkhut* is considered complete when the Written Torah is read during the morning service:

> Rabbi Shimon used to sit and learn Torah at night when the bride joined with her spouse. It is taught: The members of the bride's entourage are obligated to stay with her throughout the night before her wedding with her spouse to rejoice with her in those perfections (*tikkunim*) by which she is made perfect. [They should] learn Torah, Prophets, and Writings, homilies on the verses and the secrets of wisdom, for these are her perfections and adornments. She enters with her bridesmaids and stands above those

who study, for she is readied by them and rejoices in them all night. On the morrow, she enters the canopy with them and they are her entourage. When she enters the canopy, the Holy One, Blessed be He, asks about them, blesses them, crowns them with the bride's adornments. Blessed is their destiny.[69]

Every ritual aspect of the Jewish liturgical year is related to the unification of *Tiferet* and *Malkhut* and to the restoration of divine harmony. The celebration of the Sabbath and the holidays and the performance of the daily rituals are based on the ritual prescriptions found in the Hebrew Bible and the rabbinic codes. The Jewish mystics believe that each element in Jewish observance is a divinely constructed guide to theurgic action leading to unity and restoration. In his own eyes the Jewish mystic differs from the nonmystic practitioner of Judaism in that he performs the rituals of Judaism with a consciousness of their true purpose. The Jewish mystic thereby transforms all of Judaism into an intricately woven pattern of actions that lead him to the culmination of the mystic quest.

10

UPLIFTING THE SPARKS:

Modern Jewish Mysticism

At the beginning of the eighteenth century, the largest concentration of Jews in Europe was found in Lithuania and the Ukraine, which was then part of Poland. The Jews of Poland numbered about three-quarters of a million people, 3 percent of the total population.[1]

The Jews of Eastern Europe are known as *Ashkenazic* Jews. Actually, *Ashkenaz* is the Hebrew name for Germany. *Ashkenazic* Jews refers to those Jews whose ancestors came from the Rhineland and who moved eastward into Poland following the Black Plague of 1348–1350. The Jews fled Germany in the wake of attacks by Christians who blamed the Jews for causing the epidemic that decimated one-third of the entire population but left the Jews relatively unscathed.

With the decline of the German and Spanish centers of world Jewry by the turn of the sixteenth century, Poland emerged as the preeminent center of Jewish life. Lithuania was annexed to Poland in 1569, and the Ukraine was colonized at about the same time. Poland was a distinct and separate kingdom until 1772, when it was conquered and divided among Russia, Prussia, and Austria.

During this period the Jews enjoyed considerable communal autonomy and flourished as a creative and dynamic civilization. An elaborate system of communal self-taxation supported a vast network of religious, educational, welfare, and publishing enterprises. This period produced some of the great luminaries of Jewish intellectual history including Rabbi Moshe Isserles of Cracow (1520–1572), the author of the important commentary on the *Shulkhan Arukh*, the Code of Jewish Law. The Jews were involved extensively in the many phases of economic life that were granted them by the king. In exchange for high tax revenues, they were granted royal charters that guaranteed them exclusive franchises (*arenda*) on certain occupations such as the distillation, distribution, and sale of alcoholic spirits. Jews dominated the export trade and engaged heavily in many middle-class occupations including shoemaking, furs, carpentry, stonecutting, and goldsmithing. Few Jews were engaged in agriculture.

Jewish residential patterns were concentrated in market towns called *shtetlakh* (sing. *shtetl*, from the Yiddish word *shtot*, *town*), where they were often the majority. These *shtetlakh* ranged in size from small hamlets to large towns with one thousand or more Jewish residents. They were communities united by religion and the Yiddish language, a synthetic language derived from medieval German, Hebrew, and Slavic languages.

Many *shtetlakh* were established as the Jews moved eastward and were instrumental in the colonization and settlement of Lithuania and the Ukraine. Here the Jews came into contact with the local population which viewed them, and the Polish authorities who granted them franchises and the rights of colonization, as foreigners and intruders. In 1648 Bogdan Chmielnicki (pronounced Chmelnitzki), revered today as the father of Ukrainian nationalism, led an organized paramilitary revolt of Ukrainian peasants against the Jews and, indirectly, against Polish interests. It is estimated that one hundred-thousand Jews were murdered, mutilated, or massacred in three hundred towns in the Ukraine.

The Jewish response to this catastrophe was different from previous episodes. There were, of course, religious works and liturgical poetry composed in commemoration of the dead and in defense of God's justice. But the most significant response appeared in the form of a powerful messianic uprising that shook the very foundations of Jewish life.

Even prior to 1648, messianic anticipation had sunk roots among certain segments of Polish Jewry. According to tradition the period of messianic redemption was to be preceded by a period of travail and turmoil in the world. The Talmud suggests that "in the footsteps of the Messiah, audacity (*hutzpah*) would spread."[2] This would usher in a period of chaos, known as the *travails of the Messiah* (*hevlei mashiah*), during which a precursor to the Messiah would be killed. This would be followed by the appearance of the Messiah who would usher in an era of peace. In *gematria,* the system of numerical values assigned to each Hebrew letter, the Hebrew term *hevlei mashiah* has a numerical value of 408, which is equal to the Hebrew calendar year [5,]408, or 1648 according to the Gregorian system.

The messianic upheaval after 1648 had its roots in the kabbalistic mythology of the previous century. Isaac Luria Ashkenazi (1534–1572),[3] the greatest of the luminaries of Safed, wove a fascinating theory concerning the hiddenness of God. His ideas appealed to his contemporaries perhaps because of their intimate familiarity with exile and dislocation. Many of them were the children of the Spanish exiles.

Luria portrayed creation as intrinsically imperfect although man, paradoxically, was invested with the capacity to perfect the world and thus complete the process of creation. The perfection of God, Luria taught, was unique, and the attempt to replicate His own perfection and to embody it in creation could not be accomplished without producing disruption and chaos. In attempting to communicate something of His own essence to the world, God overwhelmed the world's capacity to serve as a vessel for divine perfection. The overload led to a fracture in the process of creation and produced a world in which pain, evil, exile, and disorder predominate. The suffering and moral failures of human life are real features of existence and not primarily the result of human sinfulness.

Luria explained the process of the beginning of all existence as the limitation of the infinite being of *Eyn Sof. Eyn Sof,* portrayed metaphorically as boundless light, is all that exists:

> Know that before the emanated things were emanated and the created things were created, the pure, divine light filled all existence. There was no empty place resembling a void or vacuum.

Everything was permeated by that simple light of *Eyn Sof.* There
was neither beginning nor end. There was just one simple light,
static, in equanimity. It was called the light of *Eyn Sof.*[4]

The only attribute of the infinite being is His will. His will is to
create something other than Himself, to allow something other
than Himself to exist. The purpose of allowing another existence
is to make it possible for His own existence to be known. The
other is created for His own sake. But since His existence is
infinite, it cannot be known except through the *Sefirot.* The *Sefirot*
are the finite actions, names, and attributes of the infinite being.

God's simple will was moved to create worlds, to radiate emana-
tions, to bring to light the perfection of His actions, names and
attributes, for this was the cause of His creating worlds.[5]

Eyn Sof initiated the process of bringing other existences into
being with an act of self-limitation called *contraction (tzimtzum).*
How did *Eyn Sof* restrict His own infinite being? Luria explains
the solution to this great philosophical conundrum with a metaphor drawn from his knowledge of medieval geometry and
physics. The infinite created a void within its boundless existence by contracting itself into a premordial point. It went from
unbounded infinity to unbounded finity. The universe that existed before the contraction was not a physical universe of space
and matter. It was entirely *Eyn Sof.* With the contraction of
infinity, the universe became finite but still unbounded in the
sense that it has no edge or boundary. Physicists today would call
such a phenomenon a *hypersphere.* Within the unbounded hypersphere *Eyn Sof* created a boundary by contracting Himself into a
point. The being of *Eyn Sof* is thus infinitely shrunken into a
point that has an edge and boundary. This is what modern
physics calls a *singularity.*
    After contracting Himself into a singularity, *Eyn Sof* ex-
panded away from the point to the periphery of the hypersphere.
By this He created both space and matter. He created space
within the bounded universe by defining a finite center and an
infinite perimeter. The unbounded perimeter must be spherical
because he withdrew from the center in equal measure in all
directions. The area left within the sphere is His primordial

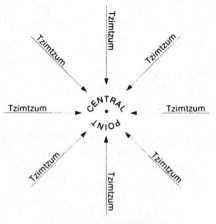

INFINITE UNIVERSE

Figure 10-1 Tzimtzum

space. At the same time, since *Eyn Sof* has traversed from the center to the periphery, the space that He left behind is within Himself and must have a residue of His being. This is the primordial essence of God out of which all existence is formed.

Everything within the world shows traces in its being of the original essence of *Eyn Sof*, which withdrew in order to allow for other beings to exist:

> Then, *Eyn Sof* contracted Himself into a central point with His light in the middle. He contracted this light and then removed Himself to the sides encircling the point at the center. This left an empty place, an ether, and a vacuum around the point at the center.
>
> This contraction, equidistant all around the point at the center, formed a void in such a way that the vacuum was spherical on all sides in equal measure. It did not form a cube with right angles because *Eyn Sof* contracted Himself into a sphere in equal distance on all sides. He intended that the light of *Eyn Sof* should be in absolute equanimity. This necessitated that He contract Himself in equal measure on all sides no more on one side than any other.[6]

According to Luria this act of contraction within and without is

an act of divine self-restriction. Such a limitation gives measure
and definition to the undefined and unbounded. This is described
as "revealing the roots of judgment," the measure of *Din*:

> The purpose of contraction is to reveal the roots of divine judg-
> ment, that is to be able to give the measure of *Din* later on to the
> worlds.[7]

Within this hypersphere existence comes into being. The hypersphere appears to the human imagination as a vacuum, as
empty space. This space, however, is not really a vacuum since it
contains a residue of *Eyn Sof*, the roots of *Din* and the potentiality
of all existence.

> And after this contraction, there was only the vacuum, ether and
> empty space in the midst of the light of *Eyn Sof*. There was now
> place for the emanations, creations, formations and actions.[8]

Eyn Sof then began to create within this primordial space. He
began to act directly within this vacuum to create the ideal
prototypes of existence. First He sought to radiate the ten *Sefirot*
as the ten attributes of the prototype of a human being. *Eyn Sof*
radiated His light in a straight line from one point on the
periphery of the hypersphere through the point in the center to
another point on the periphery.

> Then, one straight line descended from the light of *Eyn Sof* from
> the top to the bottom of the sphere of light. It unfolded down-
> wards through this void.
>
> Into the space of this vacuum, He emanated, created, formed and
> acted upon all the worlds.[9]

A straight line could not penetrate the hypersphere. Since the
hypersphere is unbounded, everything within it is unbounded
and has no edge. A straight line cannot traverse the space without
conforming to its spherical shape. The light of *Eyn Sof* was
refracted from a line into a curve that formed the shape of a
concentric circle within the hypersphere. The straight line, however, before it was refracted, served as a connecting link between

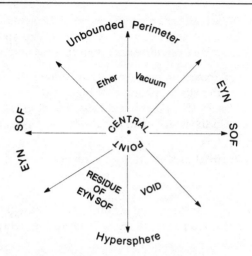

Figure 10-2 The Primordial Void

the boundless hypersphere of *Eyn Sof* and the first bounded sphere within it.

> He spread the straight line bit by bit. At first, the line of light began to spread and, then, it spread out, descended and became a type of sphere round about. This sphere did not cling to the light of *Eyn Sof* which encompassed it. . . . The connection and bond between the emanating sphere of *Eyn Sof* and the emanated sphere is that very same straight line.[10]

This first bounded sphere within the hypersphere is the first *Sefirah, Keter.* It is also the first aspect of the ideal prototype of man and so is called the "*Keter* of primordial man." This same process was repeated within the hypersphere. Each penetration of the straight line of the light of *Eyn Sof* was refracted into another concentric circle within the previous one. Each one represented another stage in the unfolding of the *Sefirot* as ideal prefigurations of the human being:

> This first concentric sphere which adheres closely to *Eyn Sof* is called *Keter* of primordial man. Then, the straight line continues briefly, then retreats and forms another concentric sphere within the other. This sphere is called the *Hokhmah* of primordial man.

That which joins all the spheres together is the subtle thin line which spreads out from *Eyn Sof*, traversing, descending and joining each sphere to another until it reaches the very last.

Next, the line spreads out in a straight way from the top to the bottom, from the highest point of the highest sphere to the very lowest and last of the spheres. It consists of ten *Sefirot* arranged mysteriously in the image of an upright human figure.[11]

Each *Sefirah* formed in this way was a receptacle for the divine light:

Through the contraction and diminution of the light, it was possible for a receptacle to come into being and become apparent.[12]

As each concentric circle formed it became more remote from the original light of *Eyn Sof*. Within this shrinking universe the light remained strong although the vessel became increasingly weaker. Finally, under the impact of the powerful light of *Eyn Sof* the vessels collapsed and exploded, destroying the original prototype:

When the light becomes too strong, the receptacle disintegrates due to its limited capacity to contain the powerful light.[13]

Luria describes this catastrophe as the *breaking of the vessels* (*shevirat ha-kelim*). The light of *Eyn Sof* and the matter of the *Sefirot* were dispersed throughout the universe. On one hand the primordial scene of creation had turned into chaos and disaster. On the other hand the light of *Eyn Sof* was now diffused randomly throughout the hypersphere. Then *Eyn Sof* radiated a second and weaker light that did not overwhelm the structure. This light slowly penetrated the universe and created time, matter, and the world as we know it.

Within this colossal and violent explosion, the birth of the universe took place. The residue of the catastrophe provided the elemental stuff of creation. Luria describes the aftermath of this "big bang" as having produced sufficient "sparks of light" and

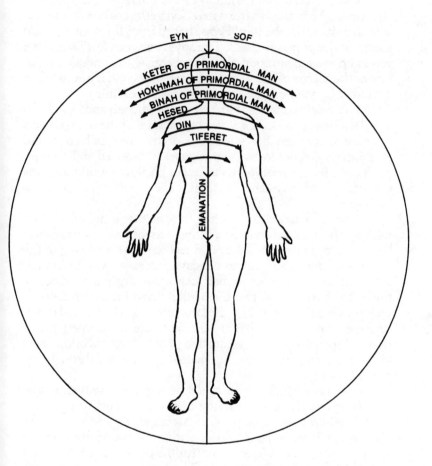

Figure 10-3 Emanation of Primordial Man. Primordial man contains all the attributes of divinity in perfect form. He is also the blueprint for human beings. Therefore, human beings are the embodiment of the *Sefirot* in the world. Every human being is a divine microcosm.

"shards of vessels" to produce a world. The world might have been formed by dross, but it was divine matter.

The outward manifestation of the universe is chaotic and distorted. The explosion frustrated God's effort to create a perfect world. In its wake the world was shaped from the remnants and shards of the primeval chaos. The abyss between *Eyn Sof* and the world appears insurmountable. But because the underlying nature of the matter of the world is divine, the world is not so much devoid of divinity as it is a mask concealing divinity.

The world contains within it deeply hidden and embedded shards of divine light. The very chaotic state of the universe also inherently contains the possibility of its own perfection. All existence is paradoxical in that it appears distorted and corrupt, yet it contains the seeds of holiness. For Luria, the world contains the seeds for its own renewal. This is the possibility of *restoration* (*tikkun*).

Man can choose to repair the fracture that is not of his own making through theurgic rituals and acts of moral repentance. Repentance is transformed from a technique of returning to the correct and prescribed path to an active process in which God and His creation are returned to their status as it was intended before the break. Luria taught that the natural disposition of the soul to seek goodness is affected by the structure of existence. All urges, impulses, failures, and hateful thoughts are the deepest reflections within man of the fracture that permeates the world. These inclinations can themselves be repaired and restored through acts of penitence.

Isaac Luria elevated this moral principle to a universal law. Just as repentance is the striving of the individual to return to harmony and resolution, so all existence struggles to repair the fractures and tears that are visible within the world. Repentance and restoration (*tikkun*) are as vital for the perfection of the world as they are for moral perfection. The tear that permeates existence is the cause of all pain and chaos, and yet, paradoxically, it is a necessary stage in the unfolding of divine perfection. The dichotomies of good and evil, perfection and destruction, are only apparent. In fact all phenomena are extensions and phases of essentially divine matters. In their translation from divine perfection to worldly manifestation, something is tragically, but not hopelessly, lost.

All things proceed from God in a continuous chain of being so that good and evil are necessary and integral stages of existence. The expressions of the religious spirit of Judaism, influenced by these patterns of dislocation and restoration, are subject to oscillations of descent and ascent, growth and decay, and what appears to be destructive may yet prove to be constructive. Those times that appear to be low points in the cycle of a nation's history may also serve a higher purpose.

It struck many in Poland that the catastrophe of 1648 might, in paradoxical fashion, indicate the beginning of redemption. Lurianic mythology and *Kabbalah* were deeply ingrained in Polish Jewish culture prior to 1648. Optimism was generated by the proposition that the pitiful outward appearance of life in the world contradicts the purity of the inner reality. This inspired a movement that was dedicated to spiritual and moral regeneration through penitence and that was spread by the missionizing activities of popular preachers. Poland before and after 1648 was rife with expectation and ready for a popular religious revival.

The revival occurred around 1665 when Jewish missionaries began to reach Poland with the news that the Ottoman Sultan had crowned someone as king of the Jews. Fabulous stories of miracles and other rumors concerning his great military feats were spread. In their wake many believers in Poland stood ready to be transported to the Land of Israel to witness the restoration of the Jewish kingdom. Some went so far as to sell their homes, liquidate their assets, and proselytize aggressively in Christian neighborhoods.

These legends were based on real events. In 1666 Shabbetai Tzvi (1626–1676), a Kabbalist, was arrested and imprisoned in Gallipoli by the Ottoman Sultan.[14] Shabbetai Tzvi had begun to attract a following among Ottoman subjects who viewed him as the Messiah. He preached a version of the Lurianic *Kabbalah,* which stated that the Messiah himself will represent all the contradictions of existence within himself. The soul of the Messiah would reflect the trapped sparks of light among the husks of broken vessels. The Messiah would be able to prescribe ritual acts of penitence that would bring the travails of the world to their final conclusion.

Prior to his arrest Shabbetai Tzvi had attracted followers throughout the Mediterranean basin and Eastern Europe. In

Eastern Europe in particular the combination of latent kabbalistic belief and genuine messianic anticipation provided fertile ground for rumors of redemption. The early movement flourished as a force for moral regeneration and messianic anticipation.

When the Sultan arrested Shabbetai Tzvi, the ruler sought to restore the equilibrium between the regent and his subjects that messianism could disrupt. He challenged Shabbetai Tzvi to prove his claim, or, if he could not, he could choose between accepting Islam or death. Shabbetai Tzvi converted to Islam on September 15, 1666, and went on to justify his apostasy as part of the messianic plan implicit in the Lurianic system. The soul of the Messiah must perform the final act of restoration by uplifting the sparks of light trapped deepest in the mire of the broken vessels. This means that the Messiah must combat evil at its source and must assume the burden of descending into the deepest recesses of the world of darkness. In real terms the final act of ingathering is a temporary descent into sin in order to conquer its power and destroy its vitality. Shabbetai Tzvi and his followers explained his apostasy as a necessary feature of the messianic process.

The followers of Shabbetai Tzvi were a strong force within Eastern European Jewry even after his apostasy. Many expected him to return to Judaism and to shortly usher in the messianic era. Few were prepared for the fact that nothing actually happened over the course of time. Those who continued to believe in him were divided. Some believed that the soul of the Messiah was in eclipse, but that he would soon complete his mission. Their task was to wait patiently with belief in their hearts. Others took an active approach to hastening his final work by assuming personal responsibility as messianic agents. They sought to strengthen him by imitating his descent into darkness. In real terms this meant that they violated certain norms of Jewish law in order to fulfill the messianic requirements. Many Sabbateans lived public lives of probity while committing religious transgressions in private.

The Sabbatean heresy, in both its moderate and extreme forms, swept through Poland in the years after 1666. Many respected Polish rabbis were caught up in this maelstrom, and the movement survived well into the middle of the eighteenth century. It gradually receded as a popular movement, but it left

deep impressions on the Jewish population. It kindled a deep
yearning for messianic redemption on all levels of Jewish society.
It legitimized popular forms of religious devotion especially
penitential rites of devotion, amulets, and other folkloristic customs. It also reinforced the idea that Jews could live with a sense
of inner redemption and fulfillment despite the poverty, oppres-
sion, and other external circumstances of their daily lives. The
world to come could be realized in the present and was not
restricted to the afterlife.

The provinces of Galicia and Podolia, areas in the southern
Ukraine, were deeply affected by the Sabbatean outbreak
through the middle of the eighteenth century. One of the radical
offshoots of Sabbateanism sprouted there in 1756. Jacob Frank
(1726–1791) encouraged his Sabbatean followers to declare their
faith openly. In order to 'fulfill the Torah through its violation,'
he preached a gospel of anarchy and destruction of world order.
In 1757 Frank persuaded the bishop of Kamenetz-Podolsk, a city
on the Dniester River, to convene a debate between the Frankists
and Jewish leaders. The Frankists charged that the Jews were
guilty of murdering Christians and using their blood for ritual
purposes. These charges led to the desecration and burning of the
Talmud later that year. In 1758 Frank led one thousand followers in conversion to Catholicism.

Against this complex background of religious heresy, strife,
and messianism, a popular religious revival of more traditional
proportions emerged. In 1735 Israel ben Eliezer, known as the
Besht (an acronym for *baal shem tov,* master of the good name), a
popular folk preacher and healer, gathered a following of devotees to a new religious discipline. This discipline (Polish), *Hasidism* (*Hasidut,* i.e., Pietism), involved a technique for achieving
liberation from the vicissitudes of this world and achieving union
with the divine. The central teaching of the Besht is that man is
capable of detaching himself from this world through ecstatic
prayer and transcendence of the material world and, thereby,
achieving oneness with the divine.

Hasidism promoted a new human ideal, the *Hasid,* as opposed to the scholar, who is intoxicated with the presence of God
and who becomes illuminated with God's presence through
ecstatic prayer. Hasidic teaching is strongly panentheistic. That
is, it teaches that only God is truly real. All the phenomena of the

world are only vessels that contain the divine light and have no independent reality of their own. This is not the same notion as pantheism, which teaches that God's being infuses all of the phenomena of the world. Hasidic teaching asserts that there is nothing that truly exists except God's being. The world is really a veil that, if removed, leaves only divinity.

Nothing exists in the world independent of God. Everything that exists can be elevated back to its divine source. In fact the Baal Shem Tov suggests that there is no autonomous human will except to the extent that it is implanted in man by God. There is little room in this conception for anything but God.

> One should know that everything in the world is infused with the Creator, may He be blessed. Every product of human thought is the result of His providence.[15]

The beauty of the world lies not in the things of this world but in God, the source of all beauty. The task of the Hasid is to elevate the sparks, to raise everything back to its source, to transcend the partial and seek the absolute. Things in this world do not really matter except as they are the manifestations of God. Beauty does not really exist in the world other than as a concretization of divinity in human form. Everything thus is a vessel for the divine essence:

> If one should notice a beautiful woman, he thinks: What is the cause of her beauty? Is it not true that if she were to die, she would not have this appearance? If so, her beauty comes from the divine power which suffuses her. He gives her the beauty and complexion. Thus, the source of her beauty is the divine power. Why, then, should I be drawn to the partial when I can unite with the source of all the universe?[16]

Every Hasid, and not the Messiah alone, must raise the sparks. He must elevate everything to its source, must transcend the partial for the whole, must see the divine essence in every material thing. Every object that vibrates internally with the Sefirot, must be raised back to its source. True worship of God is the pursuit of the essence within the vessel, the divine within the worldly, the spiritual within the material. For this reason Hasidism even suggests that there is nothing that is essentially evil. Evil is the distorted appearance of that which has not been redeemed:

> What is the meaning of elevating the sparks? When you see something corporeal and do not find it to be evil, heaven forbid, you can worship the Creator, may He be blessed. For in this thing you can find love or awe or the other qualities [i.e., *Sefirot*] by which you can elevate it.[17]

The teachings of the Besht were elaborated by his most prominent disciple, Dov Baer Friedman, the Preacher (*Maggid*) of Mezritch. He taught that all existence is God and that nothing has a separate and autonomous existence. God created man because God is known only in relation to that which is different from Him. If God had not created the world, there would have been no consciousness of God. Man exists in order to know God. In order to know God, however, man must transcend consciousness of his own separate existence. Human self-consciousness is necessary in order to know God but it is also, paradoxically, the obstacle to knowledge of God. Man must eradicate the barrier between himself and God, that is his own self-consciousness, in order to know and worship God:

> It is well known that God created in us a will different than His own in order to subject our will to His. In this He finds satisfaction. This would be impossible unless our will is different from His. When we annihilate our existence, we are connected with the Hidden.[18]

Ultimately, nothing in the world really exists since God is the only reality. The world is really an illusion that must be overcome. Hasidism introduced an 'acosmism,' a world-denying mysticism, that is a far more radical formulation in Judaism than pantheism. Pantheism is the view that God can be found in every aspect of the world. It affirms the reality of the world and the existence of God and explains that God is found in the world. Panentheism is the view that God exists and the world appears to exist. It posits that the world is really a feature and product of God's consciousness and that the world only really exists within

God. This means that only God really exists and He embraces
and encompasses the world within Himself. 'Acosmism' takes
this one step further and denies the reality of the world. It
suggests that the world is really illusory and nothing other than
God exists. The thinking of the Maggid contains strong panentheistic and even acosmistic tendencies:

> Nothing in the world has any existence other than God's exist-
> ence. All things which exist, existed in potentiality before cre-
> ation. Then, God emanated their potentiality and gave them
> spiritual and material coverings. His powers vitalize them. If they
> were to retreat to their former state before creation, the spiritual
> and material coverings would not exist at all.[19]

The Maggid called for a transformation in the consciousness of
the *Hasid*. The world does exist, but the *Hasid* is privy to a
mystical technique that allows him to obliterate consciousness of
the world and to achieve consciousness of God to the exclusion
of all else. He is able to transcend the world of corporeality
(*gashmiyyut*) and dwell in the pure consciousness of spirituality
(*ruhaniyyut*). The *Hasid* is able to disassociate himself from world-
consciousness, since the world is essentially an illusion woven by
God. He is able to look behind the veil because he knows that in
fact the world is only an illusion, an obstacle to knowing God.
Through prayer the *Hasid* can achieve a state of adhesion (*devekut*) in which he transcends consciousness of his own existence
and ultimately achieves consciousness of oneness with God.

> If we achieve this union, we will think about ourselves as well
> that we are nothing other than God who gives us life. He alone
> exists and there is nothing other than Him. . . . And when we
> realize this, that we are like nothingness in truth and nothing else
> exists in the world but God just as before creation, God, as it were,
> takes genuine pleasure.[20]

The Maggid introduced the technique of *annihilating existence,*
(*bittul ha-yesh*) by which man eradicates self-consciousness and
achieves a state of absorption into God. The process begins with
an understanding that the physical aspect of a human being is

merely external. This can occur as one begins to pray. Meditation that precedes prayer is devoted to understanding the relationship between one's physical self and one's consciousness. For example, the power of one's physical existence is so strong that it diverts one's consciousness to physical sensations and considerations. Prayer is made difficult by stimuli that come from one's physical being and assault the consciousness. For example, thoughts of one's business, family, or relationships can intrude upon the mind during prayer. Even more intrusive are thoughts concerning the temptation to sin, especially those of a sexual nature. These thoughts contain within them the sparks of holiness that can be redeemed. This can be seen in the following statement by Jacob Joseph of Polonoye in which he quotes his teacher, the Besht:

> I heard a convincing argument said in the name of my teacher [the Besht]. It concerned the strange thoughts (*mahshavot zarot*) which come to man in the midst of his prayer. They come from the mystery of the broken [vessels] and the 288 sparks which need to be clarified every day. They appear in order to be repaired and elevated. The strange thought which appears one day is different from that of another day. [The Besht] taught that one must pay close attention to this matter. I learned from him how to repair the strange thoughts even if they are thoughts about women. One should elevate them and make them cleave to their source, the [*Sefirah*] *Hesed.*[21]

Prayer is the meditative opportunity for man to come to terms with the range of intrusions upon his consciousness. By recognizing the power and sway over his consciousness that his physical being exercises, he is able to gain conscious control over them. Then he is able to disassociate his consciousness from himself and gradually transcend self-awareness. This requires the total obliteration of self-awareness, which the Maggid characterizes as the *annihilation of [conscious] existence* (*bittul ha-yesh*):

> The desired goal is that one must precede prayer with the act of divestment of corporeality. Man is finite and has limits but he should make himself nothingness, without limit. He can do this by directing all his effort to God alone, not to anything else, or

even to himself. This is impossible unless he makes himself
nothing.[22]

The Maggid introduced a profound awareness of the role of
consciousness in religion. He distinguishes between self-
consciousness, called *smallness* (*katnut*), and mystical consciousness, called *greatness* (*gadlut*). Self-consciousness is an obstacle to
true consciousness since it is illusory. Since only God exists, all
else is illusion. Mystical consciousness is the goal of Hasidism,
and prayer is the technique for its acquisition. Mystical consciousness, of course, is intermittent since the world exerts such a
powerful force in the direction of false consciousness.

The task of the *Hasid* is to achieve a new and enduring
consciousness that God alone is being. The process begins with
his recognizing that his physical self is an obstacle to true consciousness. This is called *hitpashtut ha-gashmiyyut* (divesting his
corporeality). Observing the requirements of Jewish law and the
rituals of the Torah facilitate this process. The process continues
as the *Hasid* becomes aware that everything he sees is really a
manifestation of God. This is the process of *haalat ha-nitzotzot*
(elevating the sparks). Then he thinks less about the world and
only about God. He empties his consciousness of awareness of
the world and thinks himself to be nothingness. This process is
called *laasot atzmo ayyin* (making himself nothing). It is a delicate
moment of transition between two stages of consciousness.
Finally his consciousness is filled with awareness of God and
nothing else. At that moment his consciousness and God's being
are identical. The powerful mystical consciousness that he
achieves induces a powerful and enduring transformation. From
this point the *Hasid* has a new orientation to the world.

He can now worship God effectively in many ways. Since
he now possesses a new and higher level of consciousness, he is
able to live in the world and recognize it for what it is. He can
even worship God in a new way since he sees clearly the divinity
inherent in everything. This new form of worship is called
avodah ba-gashmiyyut (worship through corporeality). In it the
Hasid is indifferent to the seductions of the world because he
knows the goal to which his consciousness is directed. He keeps
consciousness of God before him at all times to such an extent
that he is keenly aware of the divinity in everything around him.

Although Hasidism presented a powerful mystical teaching and discipline, it also presented a uniquely sympathetic approach to the requirements of daily living. Many of these teachings are found in the legends of the Hasidic masters. Some modern scholars discount the significance and authenticity of many of the Hasidic legends about the Baal Shem Tov.[23] The Baal Shem Tov died in 1760, and the first tales were published in 1815, and others were published even later. The sources that are discussed above, however, are taken from homiletic literature (*derashot,* or *droshes*) that date from the lifetime of the Besht and the Maggid and appear to be authentic. The homilies are, in the opinion of scholars, more representative of authentic early Hasidic teaching than the tales. The piquancy and spiritual quality of the tales may have a more immediate attraction to the modern reader than do the homilies.

Nevertheless, the tales represent the popular appeal of early Hasidism. The *Hasidim* tell the story of a simple Jew, Zusha, who appears before heaven on the day of final judgment with fear that he has not lived up to expectations. He is afraid of being asked why was he not as righteous as Abraham, Isaac, or Jacob. But he is asked instead, "Why were you not like Zusha?" In commenting on this, Martin Buber, who first brought the popular teachings of Hasidism to wider recognition, explained that each person's specific task in life is as unique as his specific opportunity to achieve it. Hasidism teaches that each situation in life presents a challenge to man and poses a problem for him to solve:

> Man should not ask what the meaning of his life is, but rather he must recognize that it is he who is asked. Each man is questioned by life and he can only answer to life by answering for his own life.[24]

The *Hasidim* offer the following parable about the nature of communal prayer:

> Once, in a tropical country, a certain splendid bird, more colorful than any that had ever been seen, was sighted at the top of the tallest tree. The bird's plumage contained within it all the colors of the world. But the bird was perched so high that no single person could ever hope to reach it.

When news of the bird reached the ears of the king, he ordered
that a number of men try to bring the bird to him. They were to
stand on one another's shoulders until the highest man could
reach the bird and bring it to the king. The men assembled near
the tree but while they were standing balanced on one another's
shoulders, some of those near the bottom decided to wander off.
As soon as the first man moved, the entire chain collapsed,
injuring several of the men. Still, the bird remained uncaptured.

The men had doubly failed the king. For even greater than his
desire to see the bird was his wish to see his people so closely
joined to one another.[25]

Another parable narrates the Hasidic ideal of personal prayer:

There was once a simple herdsman who did not know how to
pray. But it was his custom to say everyday: "Lord of the world!
You know that if you had cattle and gave them to me to tend,
though I take wages from everyone else, from you I would take
nothing."

Once, a rabbi was passing and heard the man pray in this way. He
said to him: "Fool, do not pray in this way." The herdsman
asked: "How should I pray?" Then, the rabbi taught him the
Shema and other prayers so that he would no longer say what he
was accustomed to.

After the rabbi left, the herdsman forgot all the prayers and did
not pray. And since the rabbi told him not to pray as he once had,
he said nothing. And this was a great catastrophe.[26]

Hasidism may be the most powerful movement of Jewish spirituality in modern times. The Hasidic movement became splin-
tered into different dynasties in the third and fourth generation.
Most of the Eastern European centers of Hasidism were obliter-
ated by the Nazi Holocaust. Several of the Hasidic branches
survived the war and were transplanted to the United States and
Israel. Several small but vital Hasidic communities continue to
thrive in the United States, particularly in New York.[27] The
movement today appears to many outsiders as an archaic and
fundamentalist form of orthodoxy that rejects the modern

world. This may be so, but the mystical core of Hasidism still remains despite external appearances.

Hasidism, however, is not the only modern mystical phenomenon in Judaism. Mysticism has persisted as one of the important strains of modern Jewish religious expression. The enduring vigor of the mystical strain in Judaism is evident in the monumental figure of Rabbi Abraham Isaac Kook, Chief Rabbi of Palestine from 1919 to 1935.[28] Rav Kook, as he is known, was educated in the great Lithuanian rabbinical academy at Volozhin. At once an Orthodox Zionist and a mystic of deep universal vision, he exhibited the complexities of intellect and spirit that characterize those religious masters whose home is Judaism but whose larger domain is human civilization.

Continuing the tradition that began with Luria and the Hasidic masters, Rav Kook offered an explanation of human nature. He teaches that the inner disposition of the soul to seek goodness is affected by the structure of existence. In a variation of the Hasidic notion of *avodah ba-gashmiyyut,* Rav Kook explains a new notion of repentance. Repentance begins with the recognition of the origin, reality, and power of these impulses. Man then proceeds to transfer and transform the passion and force of these urges to the passionate and forceful performance of the penitential act. Holiness is achieved through the freely chosen act of repentance that restores the original impulse to its intended goal.

Rav Kook's great contribution to Jewish thought may be his application of the dialectical theory of existence to the phenomena of Jewish history. Rav Kook suggests that the long periods of exile presented the Jewish people with certain intellectual and spiritual challenges that could stimulate a national process of redefinition and, ultimately, restoration. He stated boldly, much to the chagrin of others, that atheism performed a necessary function when it confronted Judaism and challenged it to examine and redefine some of its more mythic and anthropomorphic expressions of God. In their zeal to preserve the original character of Judaism, the Orthodox assumed a defensive stance in the face of the challenge of the dominant cultural values of the period. According to Rav Kook this only served to isolate the Jewish religion from the healthy winds of challenge while secular culture advanced alone. Moreover, the challenge persisted, and many of the best Jewish minds were alienated from the tradition. The challenge, as Rav Kook sees it, is as necessary as the endurance of the tradition.

The Zionist movement in the twentieth century was the product of a predominantly secular ideology. Many of its adherents had made the break in theory and in practice from the Jewish religious tradition. To Rav Kook the young Zionists represented not so much a threat to traditional Judaism as a necessary challenge to the spiritual condition of Judaism. Their activism meant no less than the revitalization and restoration of Judaism through a new twist in the universal process of exile and return. Political Zionism served the highest purpose in repairing the fracture that had permeated Judaism through the periods of exile by restoring the spirit of the Jewish people to the Land of Israel, the physical base of its existence. Rav Kook elevated the secular activity of Zionism to the level of a religious obligation that performs a restorative function within Judaism.

During his tenure as Chief Rabbi he was often criticized by his Orthodox compatriots for his extreme tolerance of the secular Zionists. In explaining his apparent liberalism, he resorted to a parable regarding the building of the Holy of Holies in the Temple. Although only the high priest was permitted to enter the inner sanctum after its completion, all classes of workmen were needed to construct the edifice. Common laborers, masons, and carpenters were needed to build the sanctuary although, ultimately, when their work was completed and the structure acquired a new character of holiness, they were prohibited from entering it. In a similar fashion, he explained, all types of Jews contributed to the construction of the new homeland and were equally vital in the process of the restoration of Judaism.

Rav Kook sought to define a mode of religious faith that reached beyond the particular and exclusive claims of Orthodox, religious Judaism in pursuit of universal values and ideals. He claimed that the highest sensibility of the Jewish soul is the quest for universality, which has been expressed in many diverse forms in Jewish history. For him the return to Zion was the concrete manifestation of the more subtle process of gathering the dispersed forms of Jewish moral, intellectual, and spiritual expression and the reunification of the Jewish spirit with the source of its inspiration. In this venture all bearers of the spirit, like the workmen in the tabernacle, performed an equally vital role.

Not all modern Jewish mystics follow the path of tradition.

Some have drawn their inspiration from Jewish mysticism without necessarily accepting the religious behavior that had been inseparable from it. The appearance of Jewish mystics who draw their primary inspiration from the *Kabbalah* but do not follow the ritual life of earlier Kabbalists is a modern phenomenon. Is Jewish mysticism separable from the entire culture in which it flourished? Is it possible to speak about modern Kabbalists who do not live according to Jewish law?

Modern Jewish mysticism rarely exists outside of traditional Jewish culture. Today, the only schools in which believers and practitioners of traditional Jewish mysticism are initiated into the tradition are some of the ultra-Orthodox rabbinical seminaries in Israel. Several major research universities in Israel and North America support academic research into the history and literature of Jewish mysticism. These programs, however, produce academic scholars not mystical practitioners or believers. There is one great living personality today whose vision is rooted in the *Kabbalah* and traditional Jewish life. Adin Steinsaltz, the editor in chief of the modern Hebrew translation and commentary on the Babylonian Talmud, has achieved an international reputation for deep spirituality, openness to modernity, an incisive intellect, and genuine mystical vision.[29]

The most significant appearances of modern Jewish mysticism occur in literature. Martin Buber's writings have introduced Hasidism to Jewish and non-Jewish readers. His presentation of Hasidic ideas is highly selective and is filtered through the lens of his own philosophy. Still, Buber has done more than any other writer to popularize Hasidic teachings as ideas with powerful spiritual content and broad human appeal. Despite his own interpretations and interpolations, Buber has successfully opened the closed world of Hasidism to the outside.

The writings of Isaac Bashevis Singer portray a lost world in which mysticism was the spiritual foundation. To Singer the *Kabbalah* appears to teach, as Isaac Luria suggested, that everything is imbued with divinity according to the extent of its proximity or remoteness to God:

> Actually, we were all part of God's light, but through the process of emanation and diminution God's light grew ever darker, ever more specific and accessible, until it turned into matter — earth, rocks, sea, animals, people. According to the Cabala (sic),

Creation was a kind of gradual revelation and popularization of divinity. The Cabala is pantheistic.[30]

From the abstract philosophic understanding of *Kabbalah,* Singer drew imaginative but necessary conclusions. If, as the Kabbalists say, "even in heaven the principle of male and female prevailed,"[31] would not an adolescent infatuation with the mysteries of human sexuality follow? Singer's world view was shaped in some measure by the philosophy of the *Kabbalah* into which he read normal adolescent curiosity about sexuality. After all, if there are couplings and liaisons in heaven, why should humans on earth be any different? His fiction is replete with rich sexual fantasy and supernatural eroticism. Many of the characters in his stories suffer from a confusion about gender identity. This ambiguity may, in part, derive from the androgynous nature of the human soul described amply in the *Kabbalah.* His fanciful interpretation of kabbalistic sexuality is a playful, but not incorrect, reading of the *Kabbalah.*

Singer's fiction is replete with supernatural tales about demons, possessions, transmigrations, dybbuks, and evil spirits. These too, of course, derive from the *Kabbalah.* Much of late kabbalistic and Hasidic demonology is actually an importation of Transylvanian, Ukrainian, and other Eastern European folklore into Jewish popular culture. Still, much of kabbalistic demonology is based on the notion that there is a realm in the creation where God could not reach, a realm of darkness and evil where his light does not shine. In the kabbalistic universe there is no dead matter. Everything is alive with divinity. But since God cannot reach everywhere in his frustrated attempt to create a perfect world, Jewish mystics assume that the dark realm is equally vibrant with the power of evil. This world, for Singer, is the lowest and therefore weakest link in the chain of being.

The occult has always played a role in the *Kabbalah.* The mystical belief in theurgy can easily lead to a belief in magic. If one can influence God through ritual, perhaps one should more easily be able to bring magic to bear upon the world. For example, the legend of the *golem* has persisted for centuries. It goes back to the talmudic legends according to which the sage Rava is said to have created a man whom he sent for some reason to his associate Rav Zira. The same legend also says that Rav Hanina and Rav Ushaya were accustomed to studying cosmology each week before the beginning of the Sabbath. As a result, they were able to create a miniature calf which they would eat.[32]

The *Hasidim* of Germany in the twelfth century probably originated the idea of the *golem* itself.[33] For them the ritual of creating a *golem* involved a materialization of a person's astral body. The instructions for making a *golem* are as follows: First, one begins with mastery of the occult science of cosmology found in the *Sefer Yetzirah*, with ritual purification, with dressing in clean white garments, and with two or three companions. Next, one takes virgin soil from a mountainous area and mixes it with fresh water to form a humanoid. Through invoking various magical combinations of Hebrew letters, one is able to determine the gender and duration of the *golem*'s existence.

The idea of the *golem* as homonculus, that is, a robot that can serve man, developed in the seventeenth century under the influence of these earlier notions that were mixed together with magical and alchemical theories. As the legend grew, the creation of the *golem* was attributed to the great eighteenth-century rabbi, the Maharal of Prague. His *golem* would serve him six days a week but would remain inert on the Sabbath. One Sabbath, however, the *golem* went berserk until Maharal deactivated him permanently.

Jacob Grimm, of the Brothers Grimm, helped to popularize this Jewish legend throughout Europe. In his version,[34] the Jews of Poland were able to construct a homonculus from mud and to give him life by using the power of the divine name. This mute automaton could perform manual tasks for its master. The legend was given special impetus by the publication of Gustav Meyrink's novel, *The Golem,* and by popular legends, many of which appear in the writings of Yiddish authors such as Isaac Bashevis Singer.

While the occult assumes a prominent role in Singer's fiction, there is also a strong tendency to see the *Kabbalah* as a source of eternal truth. The invisible world of the *Sefirot* animates all things, according to Singer's understanding of the *Kabbalah*. Every bug, every book, every person vibrates internally with the power of divinity. The world is composed of the sparks of divine light that shine invisibly within all things.

To Singer, the truth of the *Kabbalah* is identical with the truth of modern science. The science of electricity and atomic theory, in a general sense, and the view that matter is alive and not inert seems to him to be what the *Kabbalah* has been saying all along. Singer was raised in the world of Hasidic piety at a time when urbanization and modernization were beginning to shatter the walls of tradition. As a young boy the bridge between these two worlds was his faith that the *Kabbalah* and modern science agree.

An outstanding example of modern Jewish mysticism that appears outside of a traditional context is the artist, Yaacov Agam. Agam is noted for his three-dimensional graphic artworks that invoke possibilities of the dimension of time. An appreciation of his art requires the viewer to move around his art, to see fluid images change as one's perspective shifts. His art is transformative and involves movement on the part of the viewer as each shifting perspective creates another vision.

Agam, born in 1928 in Rishon le-Tzion in Palestine, was the son of a rabbi. He was raised in the milieu of the *Kabbalah* and religious orthodoxy. According to his own testimony, the *Kabbalah* has been one of the guiding forces behind his artistic enterprises. Agam explains that the basic principle in Judaism is the reality of the infinite that does not exist except in the complete form.[35] In Judaism, God is invisible and unattainable in the abstract. He can be known, however, through His traces in the world. But human vision is too narrow to grasp the totality of God's presence in the world. Human perception is limited to partial awareness, fleeting glimpses, and occasional awareness of divinity in the world. Since all vision is partial, God simply cannot be grasped in the world. God can only be perceived in stages as one becomes increasingly aware that the infinite can be found only in the totality of the universe.

For Agam, art is the medium by which the infinite can be grasped. Art provides the vehicle for transcending the visible world and reaching new modes of perception. Since the infinite can be discovered only in the totality of the universe, art can lead one to the level of sublime awareness of the infinite. God can only be perceived in stages leading to an integrated awareness of the whole.

The principle of Agam's art is that it can only be perceived in stages. His art is a vehicle through which he expresses the reality of the infinite. His art draws the viewer in, requiring that the viewer move around and about his graphic work in shifting perspectives. For Agam, the work of art, like the infinite, can exist only in the totality of fluid stages.

In his credo as an artist, Agam explains the relationship between the *Kabbalah* and art:

> In Judaism, God is invisible, just as in life the essence of power is invisible. In my work I try to capture and suggest the same invisible, endless reality behind things. In any one of my works, always transformable, there are almost infinite ways of seeing it – different angles, different situations, different movements – all suggesting a basic, invisible essence, which is behind it all, and never really totally visible.[36]

Jewish mysticism has not lost its attraction to traditional and contemporary Jews. The spiritual dimension of Jewish mysticism has strong appeal to contemporary Jews who seek transcendent values. For example, the concept of the infinite and invisible God who does not act directly in the world holds a powerful theological attraction today. In a world that has suffered through the Holocaust, it is often difficult to imagine how a good God could allow such horrors. The *Kabbalah,* which posits a distant and transcendent *Eyn Sof,* teaches that it is human action rather than divine action that ultimately directs the course of the world. The idea of a transcendent God whose presence is palpable only in His absence may open doors to new meaning in theology. The simplistic notions of God as a human father or mother figure can be seen as lower orders of divinity. The abstract unknowable God might provide a way of understanding how He can exist yet be absent from the course of human affairs.

Jewish mysticism probably still contains layers of meaning waiting to be peeled away. The tradition of Jewish mysticism will never recur in the traditional forms of the past. It is impossible, however, to predict how it will inspire new and creative religious ideas in the future. What is certain is that two hundred years after the last strong surge of mystical fervor in Judaism, the *Kabbalah* has not lost its appeal.

11

JEWISH MYSTICISM AND THE

MYSTIC QUEST

Jewish mysticism may be unique among other forms of religious mysticism in that its highest goal is not union with God. Although the object of the mystic quest in Judaism is the mystical encounter with God, the Kabbalists do not describe this as union. The term *yihhud* (union) is used to describe the theurgic act in which God's different *Sefirot* are united among themselves. The highest form of human mystical achievement, according to Jewish mystics, is the *communion*, or encounter, with the *Sefirot*, not *Eyn Sof*. This is called *devekut* (cleaving).

In theistic religions, which believe in the existence of a transcendent God, there are often serious strictures against achieving complete mystical union. These strictures are based on the belief that the differences between the human being and the transcendent God cannot be readily overcome. The character of theistic mysticism is predetermined, to a great extent, by the theist's belief that God and man are separated by an unbridgeable abyss. Theistic mysticism, therefore, rarely becomes the kind of absorptive mysticism in which the mystic becomes completely undifferentiated from God.

Jewish mysticism is predominantly theistic and nonabsorptive. Even in the highest stage of *devekut,* the Jewish mystic never becomes united with *Eyn Sof* or identical with the *Sefirot*. He maintains his distinct individuality and separateness from God. The Jewish mystic is more concerned with effecting the unity and restoration of God than with his own personal encounter. His mysticism is indirect in the sense that he brings about the mystical union of God within Himself and benefits from the overflow of divine grace that he has caused. The Jewish mystic is perhaps more concerned with understanding the dynamics by which he can influence and perfect God for his own benefit. He quests for mystical knowledge of the patterns of God's inner life more than for direct encounter with the divine. The mystic quest in Judaism requires a deep knowledge of the mechanics of the divine realm and rigorous training through performance of the prescribed theurgic rituals. The ultimate goal of the mystic quest is the direct and unmediated influence upon the *Sefirot* and the restoration of unity within the realm of the *Sefirot*. The Jewish mystic never loses the awareness that although his actions are for the sake of heaven, the earth and all its glory are man's.

Pantheistic mysticism, in which God *is* nature and is not transcendent, is absent from Jewish mysticism. The Jewish mystic believes, on the contrary, that the world originated within God's essence. While that certainly means that the world is replete with traces of divinity – the divine sparks – nature is not identical with God. The Jewish mystic sees the world as a reminder of the levels and layers of reality that must be traversed in the quest for God. He never mistakes the world for other than what it is – the most remote manifestation of the divine essence. At the same time he recognizes that the world is God's signature. He is concerned not with the letter but with the writer.

Panentheistic mysticism, in which the world exists within God and is not distinct from him, appears only in early Hasidism. Although Eastern European Hasidism called for living in a perpetual state of *devekut,* with one's mind focused only on God, it never denied the reality and significance of functioning in the world. The true panentheist believes the world is illusory and should be overcome. The Hasidic panentheist is more likely to believe that the abyss separating man and God is an illusion and that it may be overcome.

Rarely, if ever, does acosmist mysticism, which denies the reality of anything other than God appear in Judaism. The oceanic feeling appears in Jewish mysticism among those followers of the Maggid who believed in perpetual *devekut*. But the acosmic idea that all being is essentially undifferentiated oneness is foreign to theistic Judaism.

There is little room for spontaneous mystical experience in Judaism. The daily regimen of the Jewish mystic is structured by the requirements of Jewish rituals and Sabbath and festival observances. Jewish mystics transform the routines of traditional Jewish practice into mystical acts of great power and consequence. For the Jewish mystic no ritual is routine since every action has an influence upon the *Sefirot*.

In the *Kabbalah* there are a variety of paths leading to *devekut*. Each of these paths constitutes a legitimate approach to the goal. The precondition necessary for achieving *devekut* is mystical consciousness, the perception and awareness of the structure of the universe. Jewish mystics traditionally share a common understanding about the nature of the divine world and its relation to the human realm. Without a common notion of the topography of the divine world, no journey there is possible. The paradigm of the world of the *Sefirot* provides an implicit framework for traditional Jewish mystics. It defines the parameters within which a Jewish mystic can legitimately function. One major activity associated with *devekut* is the mystical interpretation and study of the Torah.

The perception of the workings of the transcendent world of the *Sefirot* provides the mystic with a vehicle for cleaving to it. The power of theurgic rituals to restore the unity of the *Sefirot* through *kavvanah* (intention) is an indirect means of achieving *devekut*. It is not the mystic himself who achieves *devekut* with God, but rather his actions bring about *devekut* within God. A theurgic ritual, a mystical activity that elevates the routine performance of a ritual to the status of a cosmic action, is called *yihhud* (unity). It is prescribed as a popular form of mysticism.

A higher level of *devekut* is characterized as *zivvug*, sexual union. In this state the mystic sublimates his natural eroticism and transfers it to union with the *Shekhinah*. This type of mystical activity requires special training and is generally reserved for the exceptional saint who is able to fully control his own sexuality. *Zivvug* entails the performance of specific rituals such as waking at midnight to study prescribed sections of the Torah, reciting the *Shema* ("Hear O Israel, the Lord our God, the Lord is One"), or greeting the Sabbath accompanied by an intense consciousness of the possibility of union with the *Shekhinah*. This is often portrayed in erotic terms, whereby the mystic is joined to the *Shekhinah* as a bridegroom is with his bride. This is a special state of transitory transcendence for which one must possess mystical consciousness and training in theurgic rituals. Closely associated with this state is the stage described as *hitorrerut* (awakening). The mystic can experience erotic union with the *Shekhinah* as he simultaneously brings about the union of *Tiferet* and *Malkhut*.

Mystical meditation can lead to a state known as *meshikhah* (drawing down). By following a prescribed meditative technique, the mystic is able to draw vitality upon himself from the particular *Sefirah* to which he directs his actions. The technique involves a form of concentration upon the unique power of a *Sefirah*. An example of this technique can be found in the following instructions:

> One who fixes a matter firmly in his consciousness acquires the thing in its true nature. Therefore, when you pray, offer a blessing, or desire to meditate upon the essence of a thing, imagine in your consciousness that you are light and all about you, in every direction, is light. In the midst of the light is a throne of light and above it, bathed in light, is a radiant splendor. In front of this is another throne and upon it is light. You are standing between the two thrones.

> When it is necessary to carry out an act of *din*, face the radiant splendor. When it is necessary to carry out an act of *hesed*, face the good light. Let the words of your mouth be directed toward the light above them and between them which is the light of Glory.

> Above this light is a crown, the light which crowns the desires of consciousness, which illumines the ways of illumination, which radiates the splendor of visions. This light is infinite and boundless. And from the Glory of its perfection blessing, peace and goodness will come to those who preserve its unity. Those who stray from the path of light, which changes from one hidden thing to another, will receive admonition and correction.

> It is up to the intention of one who knows how to meditate upon the truth to create a union of his mind and will which are emanated in full strength from the Boundless.

According to the power of the meditation one can draw strength to his will, will to his consciousness, imagination to his mind, power to his action, and bravery to his thought when no other thought or desire interferes with his meditation and when he is strengthened by conditioning so that it draws the influx which comes from *Eyn Sof.* Only then is his action, consciousness and will fulfilled.[1]

These instructions for meditation describe a state whereby the mystic can draw upon the *Sefirot of Hesed* and *Din* for himself. The psychological connection between the *Sefirot* and his own attributes expresses the view that man is ultimately an extension of divinity into matter. Therefore, man can also reach a state of connection with the source.

The penultimate stage of mystical achievement is *aliyat ha-neshamah* (ascension of the soul). This requires special training to be able to release the soul from the body, cause it to traverse the heavens and the lower stages of the world of the *Sefirot* until it reaches *Binah.* This is the type of mysticism described in the chapter on the soul. The Baal Shem Tov also claimed to have had several encounters of this type in which his soul ascended to the heavenly realm. He conversed directly with the Messiah whose soul resides there until the end of days and interceded on behalf of the Jewish people.[2]

The highest stage of mystical *devekut* is intellectual. The mystic who acquires a mystical consciousness and masters the theurgic rituals is trained in the topography of the divine world. If the individual has mastered all of the other stages in the mystical discipline, he will have acquired a highly trained mystical consciousness. He will have perfected his *neshamah,* including his mystical intellect. This mystic may be able to ascend the ladder of the *Sefirot* beyond *Shekhinah* and *Binah* to *Hokhmah.* This is the highest level of *devekut.* No Jewish mystic can transcend *Hokhmah* to *Keter* or *Eyn Sof.* The highest mystical achievement is union with *Hokhmah.* At this level the consciousness of the mystic is absorbed into the intellect of God without becoming identical with the hidden God.

The Jewish conception of the mystic quest culminates in the goal of *devekut.* To most contemporary Jews the existence of such mystical practices and theories may be surprising. The

mystic quest has permeated Judaism deeply, yet knowledge of
these elements within Judaism is minimal.

Jewish mysticism is practically extinct as a living part of
Judaism today. It has largely been relegated to the past and
discarded as a meaningless relic of the Jewish cultural legacy. It is
considered by many to belong to the category of old wives tales
(*bubbe mayses,* in Yiddish).[3]

Many historical factors contributed to the demise of the
Jewish mystical tradition. The European Enlightenment of the
eighteenth century changed the character of Judaism in Western
and Central Europe. Until then the Jews had been considered by
their contemporaries as aliens who needed to be excluded from
Christian society and confined to special residential districts
(ghettos). Denied citizenship, frequently prohibited from taking
part in productive economic activity, and subject to capricious
treatment by the political authorities, the status of Western and
Central European Jewry was precarious. The change and improvement in the status of the Jews in the eighteenth century
was due to a series of intellectual, political, and economic factors.

The European Enlightenment brought about a profound
change in the intellectual outlook of many Europeans and led to
a reconsideration of the status of the Jews. The philosophies of
Descartes, Voltaire, Montesquieu, and Hume evoked a reexam-
ination of the meaning of religion. Many intellectuals began to
distinguish between revealed religions and natural religion. Revealed religions are those based on the claim of historical revelation of truths directed toward a specific people. Natural religion,
also called the religion of reason, is the universal truth about the
nature of God and the world that any rational being can realize
by observing the world around him. As Voltaire explained:

> Men are intelligent beings but such beings could not have been
> created by an uncouth, blind and insensible being. There is
> certainly a difference between [a Sir Isaac] Newton and a mule's
> droppings.[4]

He deduced from the order and reasonableness of nature and the
world the existence of a rational deity who established the order
and laws of nature.

As men began to posit order in the world rather than divine

intervention, religion was reexamined in light of this new philosophy. Enlightenment philosophers concluded that religion is the recognition of the order of the world and acknowledgment of the existence and providence of the deity who established nature. This understanding of the world order was not limited to the adherents of any particular religion. It could be acknowledged by any rational being despite the differences of his particular religious allegiance.

The role of religion, according to Hume, is to promote social goodness:

> The proper task of religion is to regulate the heart of man, to humanize his conduct, and to infuse the spirit of temperance, order and obedience.[5]

The new notion of natural religion led some liberal Christians to reconsider the status of the Jews. Perhaps the Jews were not inherently odious but had become so by virtue of their history, environment, and distorted notion of religious truth. Perhaps if the Jews were made to be economically useful in the emerging mercantile economy, if they were to abandon their loyalties to the Jewish people and were to become loyal citizens of the states in which they resided and if they were to dispense with the unenlightened aspects of their religion, Jews could be accepted. The proposition that "all men are created equal and endowed with inalienable rights to life, liberty and the pursuit of happiness" could be extended to the Jews if they changed their ways.

The process of Jewish emancipation was predicated on the expectation that Jews needed to bring about profound changes in their behavior and outlook. Even the Christian defenders of Jewish emancipation saw the Jewish religion as the primary obstacle to progress toward this goal. The price of citizenship in Europe was willingness on the part of the Jews to abandon their religious teachings and supposed superstitions that conflicted with the religion of reason such as their different modes of dress, their restrictions against socializing (especially over food) with gentiles, their use of foreign languages (Yiddish and Hebrew), their belief in the return to Zion, their restrictions against intermarriage, and their belief in the existence of a separate Jewish people. Jews were not admitted to citizenship anywhere in

Europe until 1791, when two years after the French National Assembly adopted the Universal Declaration of the Rights of Man, they were enfranchised in France. Although the process was fraught with setbacks, Western and Central European Jews were gradually emancipated during the nineteenth century. A large segment of Western and Central European Jewry attempted to respond to this challenge of emancipation by instituting changes. Reform Judaism, which began in Germany early in the nineteenth century, attempted to preserve the rational and universal core of Judaism while removing the superstitious, nationalistic, and separatist elements of rabbinic Judaism. The *Kabbalah,* which had been one aspect of the religious legacy of European Jewry, was discarded in the process.

At the same time, in Eastern Europe Lurianic *Kabbalah* and Hasidism continued to sink deep roots in the popular religious consciousness. Although modernism had greatly changed the character of Western and Central European Jewry, Eastern European Jewry was still living in the medieval world. In the early nineteenth century Hasidism was growing as the predominant religious movement among Eastern European Jewry.

The European Enlightenment began to change the character of Eastern European Jewry after 1848. As the czar began to encourage the westernization of Russia, Jewish intellectuals formulated a program for Jewish emancipation. Their program, which they called *Haskalah,* the Hebrew word for *enlightenment,* called for reforms and modernization of Jewish religious behavior and the adoption of an enlightened educational curriculum and the social habits, styles, and language of their societies. Others pursued a similar program but argued for the use of Hebrew as the *lingua franca* of the Jewish people.

Despite the optimism of the Eastern European *Haskalah,* the Jews were not met with a welcome response. Successive czars continued to reinforce the restriction of Jewish residence to the frontier area known as the Pale of Settlement, to limit areas of Jewish economic activity, and to resist efforts to achieve emancipation. Legal emancipation came in Eastern Europe with the Russian Revolution, but even this did not bring about genuine acceptance of the Jews.

In the late nineteenth century the increase in the frequency and brutality of the pogroms led many Jews to despair of emancipation and to explore other solutions including secularization and assimilation, socialist and communist militancy, emigration to America, and Zionism. Although a core of Eastern European Jews continued to live as they always had until the obliteration of the entire society by the Nazi Holocaust, by the late nineteenth century many Jews had already broken with tradition. With the breakdown of the traditional world of the *shtetl,* the *Kabbalah* and Hasidism were discarded as vestiges of an earlier time.

Jewish mysticism flourished in a period when most Jews were devout practitioners of Jewish ritual. Until the time of Shabbetai Tzvi, there was little chance that a mystic would break away from traditional Jewish practice. As a result the initiation into Jewish mysticism was quite explicit and conventional. Initiation into the mysteries of the *Kabbalah* was limited to rabbis and other Jews whose mastery of rabbinic literature and practice was advanced. The *Kabbalah* was simply incomprehensible to those who could not easily comprehend the Bible, Talmud and *midrash.* Since the *Kabbalah* was so richly symbolic, initiation required a master teacher who could guide the novice along. There are no records of independent Jewish mystics, from the time of Ezekiel until the nineteenth century, who practiced their own forms of mysticism. The testimonies of mystics that exist are all expressed in the language of the mystical movements prevailing at that time – *Merkavah,* German Hasidism, *Zohar,* Lurianism, Sabbateanism and Hasidism.

In the last two centuries, as Judaism ceased to hold monolithic control over Jews, independent and autonomous mysticism has appeared. Apart from the examples mentioned – Buber, Singer, and Agam – most forms of contemporary mysticism among Jews exhibit few Jewish elements. There are no significant forms of eclectic Jewish mysticism that successfully combine traditional Jewish mysticism with other forms of human spirituality.

Modern, secular meditational techniques foster relaxational, attentional, and deautomizational states of consciousness. Some Kabbalists throughout history have practiced specific breathing and attentional meditative techniques. These have largely been adapted from other than Jewish systems, particularly yoga. Indigenous forms of kabbalistic meditation center on the intense forms of traditional Hebrew prayer and Torah study rather than on relaxation techniques. The Jewish mystic seeks insight into the workings of the *Sefirot* in order to influence them, not in order to achieve stillness and relaxation for its own sake.

It is unlikely that there will be a revival of Jewish mysticism in its traditional form. The teachings of Jewish mysticism are too rooted in the medieval way of thinking for them to appeal to the modern mind. But mysticism is an enduring feature of human spirituality that continues to hold great interest for many.

What is the possibility of a contemporary Jewish mysticism? The revival of interest in Jewish identity in the last two decades has brought about a corresponding exploration of the Jewish cultural legacy. The popularity of books, lectures, and study groups on Jewish mysticism is strong testimony that the interest in Jewish mysticism endures. Although this interest may simply reflect a search for cultural roots, it may also represent a more profound phenomenon.

Interest in religion is a persistent feature of human nature. As science has become increasingly specialized and theoretical, its theories have become so complex and symbolic that most laymen cannot follow or understand the emerging theories on the origins of the universe, the nature of consciousness, and the elementary structures of being. For many religion is a system of axiomatic beliefs about the nature of the universe and all that is within it. Religion fills the intellectual void created by the increasing inability of science to articulate its understanding of life in lay terms. Although religion then may become a pseudoscience, it is a genuine effort to address the question of the meaning of life in a contemporary context.[6]

The resurgent interest in religion may also be attributed to cultural factors. Humanity inherently searches for a basis of meaning outside of itself. The mechanistic view of the world and the individual as nothing more than the results of blind biochemical forces, natural processes, and random astronomical events hardly begins to answer the questions of why the world is this way and not another. The deep human impulse to search for meaning, order, and cause has left many humanists with a deep sense that the human mind is limited in its ability to provide explanations for the mysteries of existence. Human beings yearn for explanations that transcend the state of human knowledge. Each of us strives in some way for a transcendent experience, an oceanic feeling, the sense of undifferentiatedness. The vehicle for these forms of human expression is religion and, often, mysticism.

Religion is one avenue within today's society to attain a sense of community. Prayer services can provide an important form of public expression, of belonging to a community, and of affirming one's Jewishness in a social context. For many, the social aspect of formal worship in a synagogue is much more important than the meaning of the liturgy itself. The synagogue is the only institution in Jewish life where entire families can be together with other families. Although many secular contexts for expressing one's Jewishness are available through social welfare and voluntary associations, the nature of the religious community in Judaism is unique.

In a subtle way, religious rituals frequently change the psychological structures that organize, limit, select, and interpret one's normal consciousness. Traditional Jewish prayer involves a surrender to a mode of consciousness quite different from routine consciousness. To the involved worshipper, attention to the service itself necessitates a receptivity to stimuli not encountered anywhere else. The physical sensation of singing, the presence of unusual ritual objects, the use of the Hebrew language, the codes, signals, and rituals of the service, and the invocation of religious concepts all contribute to the transformation of routine consciousness. If this involvement is sustained over time, it can produce a feeling of awe and oneness. It is hardly surprising that many Jews report that *Yom ha-Kippurim* produces a great religious exhilaration.

Psychologists refer to this change in normal consciousness as *deautomatization*[7] and theologians call it *transcendence*. The religious experience of the synagogue worshipper often leads to the sense of oneness and being uplifted that is characteristic of mystical experiences. The oceanic feeling that accompanies some religious experiences is evaluated in vastly different ways by modern psychology. Strict Freudians view this type of religious experience as a form of regression to a relatively undifferentiated ego state.[8] Others see it as a necessary stage of integration of human consciousness. Erich Neumann, a Jungian thinker, viewed mysticism as an essential stage in human development. In his view the ego develops from undifferentiatedness into distinct self-consciousness. He posits a further integrative stage in which the differentiated ego can experience individuality and undifferentiatedness.[9] This may in fact provide an important insight into the psychological value of communal prayer. Communal prayer provides the occasion for simultaneous individuality and undifferentiatedness as an advanced form of human consciousness.

The religious experiences of involved worshippers are diverse. The common element, however, is the production of an unusual state of consciousness that is accompanied by a sense of the reality and ineffability of the experience. A synagogue worshipper cannot easily explain what it is that he experiences in prayer. He may try to describe it in terms of "a good feeling" or "being a part of community." But underlying the experience is usually a change in consciousness.

Prayer can also provide the primary vehicle for an individual religious experience within a religious context that otherwise emphasizes the communal dimension. The constant reiteration in Judaism of the centrality of revelation can reinforce the notion that the mystical experience is at the heart of Judaism. Yet it is striking that the central theological theme in Jewish liturgy – revelation – is regarded as a past event and not as an invitation for every contemporary Jew to have a mystical encounter with God. As long as the central theme of Judaism is the direct and unmediated relationship between God and man, individual Jews will pursue their own individual religious experiences. As long as there are persons who take Judaism seriously, there will be Jews who take mysticism seriously.

The renewed interest in Jewish mysticism may also arise, paradoxically, out of alienation from the formal liturgical structures in Judaism. The strangeness of Hebrew and conceptual difficulty with Jewish theology make Judaism inaccessible or alien to many. Yet these same individuals who do not find a home in the traditions or the formal institutions of Judaism often yearn for a spiritual way to express their Jewishness. Many today are caught between their alienation from formal Jewish religion and a deep desire to be Jewish. They see the secular and social opportunities for Jewish communal activity without a religious or spiritual dimension as petty and trivial. For these individuals who do not find a place for themselves in the community, Jewish mysticism provides an attractive alternative. It offers the possibility of a highly individualistic spirituality that is not regulated by any external authority. Jewish mysticism may have its greatest appeal to the most alienated of modern Jews. It is impossible, however, to predict what specific forms Jewish mysticism might assume in the future. It is unlikely that the doctrine of the *Sefirot* will be construed today as anything more than a powerful mythology. Is it possible that the underlying philosophic content of Jewish mysticism might be convertible into a form useful to contemporary men and women?

Modern science has demonstrated that the underlying structures of existence are alive. Advances in atomic theory have caused us to rethink our notion of matter as inert. Nothing in the universe is unchanging. Everything vibrates with a myriad of divisible particles that are so infinitesimal they are hidden from our senses. There is no discontinuity in the structure of existence. The universe is composed of energy and mass, and mass is the extension of energy. All of existence is unified.

Such a construction of reality is evocative of the kabbalistic theory of the *Sefirot*. The difference between infinity and the humblest person on earth is simply a matter of degree. Human life is the extension of the infinity of *Eyn Sof* in the world. The *Kabbalah* can serve as a metaphor for evoking a religious response to the miraculous discoveries of modern physics and astronomy. Perhaps the *Kabbalah* can serve as a paradigm for how we can integrate the abstract hypotheses of science into a conscious organization of our understanding of the world.

The kabbalistic doctrine of the soul is perhaps its most distinctive element. Contemporary philosophy and psychology have developed a coherent paradigm that does not assume the separate existence of a soul that comes from without. The psyche is a feature of the biological existence of a human being. It is assumed to have neither preexistence to the body nor duration after death. However, recent studies by Elisabeth Kubler-Ross and others have challenged some of the notions about death, dying, and the afterlife. The demonstrable truths of psychology are still being formulated. The doctrine of the human soul may still be expanded.

Finally, the kabbalistic conception of God may provide a fertile basis for contemporary Jewish theology. Many people assume that if there is a God, He is a personal god. If He is not a responsive, caring, personal God, He does not exist. These popular ideas have led to very simplistic theological ideas about God's existence and nature. The notion of God's essential hiddenness may accord better with human experience. According to Jewish mysticism, God is essentially hidden yet becomes manifest in different ways according to the actions of humanity. What we call God is not God but His manifestations. What appears as divine cruelty or indifference, then, is not a reflection of God's actions but of man's.

The kabbalistic theology provides a new possibility for Jewish theology. God did not permit Auschwitz or the death of a child. Humanity lives in a world in which God does not relate directly to individuals. Human destiny rests entirely in the hands of humanity. God assumes whatever form or manifestation our actions dictate. Yet, at the same time, we are bound to God by a common being that challenges us to act according to His moral attributes. Our failure to do so results in a catastrophe of our own making.

Jewish mysticism, despite its powerful theology, is deeply humanistic. It confers a noble and coherent stature upon man who is bound by his nature to God. At the same time, only man has control over his own destiny. The power to raise himself to the heights or sink to the depths of the broken vessels is vested entirely in man.

NOTES

ABBREVIATIONS

B.T. Babylonian Talmud   **ARN** Avot de-Rabbi Nathan

J. T. Jerusalem Talmud   **M** Mishnah

CHAPTER ONE

1. Geoffrey Parrinder, *Mysticism in the World's Religions* (New York: Oxford University Press, 1976), 8f. Parrinder presents an important survey of mystical topologies and expressions in various traditions. His discussion on Cabbalah (*sic*) is erroneous both from a historical and conceptual point of view.

2. Joseph Campbell, *The Masks of God: Occidental Mythology* (New York: Penguin, 1976), 14, 268.

3. William James, *The Varieties of Religious Experience* (London and Glasgow: The Fontana Library, 1960), 366.

4. James, p. 371 quoting H. F. Brown, *J. A. Symonds: A Biography* (London, 1895), 29–31. James is unaware of the existence of Jewish mysticism and, therefore, does not draw on Jewish mystical testimonies in his study.

5. James, p. 385 and note, quoting (with variations) R. M. Bucke, *Cosmic Consciousness* (Philadelphia, 1901), 7f.

6. New Testament, II Cor. 12:1–4.

7. Parrinder, 185, quoting J. N. Findlay, *Ascent to the Absolute* (London: Allen and Unwin, 1970), 164.

8. W. R. Inge, *Mysticism in Religion* (London: 1947), appendix.

9. Sigmund Freud, Civilization and its discontents, *The Standard Edition of the Complete Psychological Works of Sigmund Freud* (London: Hogarth Press, 1961) 21:64,65.

10. James, 404 (with variations).

11. Inge, appendix.

12. Inge, appendix.

13. Gershom Scholem, *Major Trends in Jewish Mysticism* (New York: Schocken, 1941), 4, quoting Rufus Jones.

14. Inge, appendix.

15. Inge, appendix.

16. Bertrand Russell, *Mysticism and Logic* (London: Longmans, Green and Co., 1921), 3. Quoted in W. T. Stace, *Mysticism and Philosophy* (Philadelphia: Lippincott, 1960), 15.

17. Steven T. Katz, Language, epistemolgy and mysticism, in *Mysticism and Philosophical Analysis* (New York: Oxford University Press, 1978), 22–74. Katz argues against cross-cultural phenomenological accounts of mystical experience as reductive and inflexible, "forcing multifarious and extremely variegated forms of mystical experience into improper interpretative categories which lose sight of the fundamentally important differences between the data studies" (p. 25). He offers a thorough critique of the various methodological approaches to the study of mysticism using examples of Jewish mysticism as illustrations and, at times, counterevidence to commonly accepted notions about mysticism.

18. Katz, 24.

19. Katz, 25.

20. Katz, 25.

21. Katz, 27.

22. William Wordsworth, "Tintern Abbey." See the various interpretations offered by R. C. Zaehner, *Mysticism Sacred and Profane* (London: Clarendon Press, 1957), 33; and Parrinder, 23.

23. Rudolf Otto, *Mysticism East and West* (New York: Macmillan, 1932), 61.

24. W. T. Stace, *Mysticism and Philosophy* (Philadelphia: Lippincott, 1960), 88.

25. Scholem, G., Devekut, or communion with God, *The Messianic Idea in Judaism* (New York: Schocken Books, 1971), 224. For further discussion of the character of Jewish mysticism, see Gershom Scholem, Mysticism and religious authority, in *On the Kabbalah and Its Symbolism* (New York: Schocken, 1965), 5–31. Scholem, the leading scholar of Jewish mysticism, has recently been the subject of several critical studies including Eliezer Schweid, *Judaism and Mysticism According to Gershom Scholem* (Atlanta: Scholars Press, 1985). Schweid's criticism centers on Scholem's underlying assumptions about Judaism and Jewish philosophy; Moshe Idel, *Kabbalah: New Perspectives* (New Haven: Yale University Press, 1988); for an intellectual biography of Scholem, see David Biale, *Gershom Scholem: Kabbalah and Counter-History* (Cambridge: Harvard University Press, 1978). For a complete bibliography of recent research in Kabbalah, see Joseph Dan, *Gershom Scholem and the Mystical Dimension of Jewish History* (New York: New York University Press, 1987).

26. Meshullam Feibusch Heller me-Zborocz, *Sefer Derekh Emet* (Jerusalem, 1952), 14.

27. Stace, 228.

28. Abraham J. Heschel, The mystical element in Judaism, *The Jews: Their History, Culture and Religion,* ed. Louis Finkelstein, 2:932–951.

29. Isaac Bashevis Singer and Ira Moskowitz, *A Little Boy in Search of God: Mysticism in a Personal Light* (New York: Doubleday, 1976), vii–viii.

CHAPTER TWO

1. II Kings 24:8–20.

2. Ezek. 1.

3. Ezek. 1. The history of Jewish mysticism between the biblical and rabbinic periods is the subject of considerable recent research. For an overview of the period, see Isaiah Gafni, "The Historical Background," in *Jewish Writings of the Second Temple Period,* ed. Michael Stone (Philadelphia: Fortress Press, 1984), 1–31. Recent studies in Jewish apocalypticism and gnosticism, and research on the Essenes and Qumran communities are included in that volume.

4. Gershom Scholem, *Major Trends in Jewish Mysticism* (New York: Schocken, 1941), 40–79. For more recent studies, see Joseph Dan, *Gershom Scholem and the Mystical Dimension of Jewish History* (New York: New York University, 1987), 38–76.

5. *ARN* 6:15.

6. B. T. *Hagigah* 14b; see also *Tosefta Hagigah* 2:1.

7. J. T. *Hagigah* 2:1.

8. See the thorough analysis on this material in David J. Halperin, *The Merkabah in Rabbinic Literature* (New Haven: American Oriental Society, 1980), 88f. Halperin doubts the existence of *Merkavah* mysticism and believes the pattern was *Heikhalot* mysticism. Halperin, 184. For further studies in Merkavah mysticism, see Gershom Scholem, *Jewish Gnosticism, Merkabah Mysticism and Talmudic Tradition* (New York: Jewish Theological Seminary, 1960); Ithamar Gruenwald, *Apocalyptic and Merkavah Mysticism* (Leiden: E. J. Brill, 1980).

9. M. *Hagigah* 2:1.

10. M. *Megillah* 4:10; *Tosefta Megillah* 4:34.

11. *Midrash Tanhuma, Parashah Tzav* 13.

12. Benjamin Lewin, *Otzar ha-Geonim* (Haifa, 1931), vol. 4, 13–15. Quoted in Louis Jacobs, *Jewish Mystical Testimonies* (New York: Schocken Books, 1977), 23.

13. David S. Ariel, The eastern dawn of wisdom: the problem of the relations between Islamic and Jewish mysticism, *Approaches to Judaism in Medieval Times,* ed. David Blumenthal (Chico, CA: Scholars Press, 1985), 149–167.

14. *Koran,* Sura 2:40,57,64,122; 3:64; 4:23; 5:3,26,32; 29:41.

15. *Koran,* Sura 2:86; 5:70,82; 9:29; 59:2.

16. E. Strauss (Ashtor), *Toledot ha-Yehudim ba-Mitzrayim ve-Suriah Tahat Shilton ha-Mamelukim* (Jerusalem: 1944), 1:47.

17. Ariel, 154.

18. Strauss, vol. 1, 352f.

19. Joseph Dan, *Torat ha-Sod shel Hasidei Ashkenaz* (Jerusalem, 1968), 124f.

20. Ariel, 159.

21. Ariel, 156.

22. German Hasidism should not be confused with Polish-Lithuanian Hasidism, which originated in the eighteenth century.

23. Scholem, *Major Trends,* 80–118; Dan, *Scholem,* 92–126. See also Ivan Marcus, *Piety and Society: The Jewish Pietists of Medieval Germany* (Leiden: E. J. Brill, 1981).

24. Isadore Twersky, Aspects of the social and cultural history of Provencal Jewry, *Jewish Society Through the Ages,* ed. H. H. Ben-Sasson and S. Ettinger (New York: Schocken, 1969), 191.

25. Gershom Scholem, *Ursprung und Anfange der Kabbala* (Berlin: Walter de Gruyter, 1962), 30, 216. This book has recently appeared in English translation. See Gershom Scholem, *Origins of the Kabbalah* (Philadelphia: Jewish Publication Society, 1987). See also Joseph Dan and Ronald Kiener, *The Early Kabbalah* (Ramsey, NJ: Paulist Press, 1986).

26. I Kings 18:19.

27. I Kings 19.

28. II Kings 2:1–11.

29. Malachi 3:23f.

30. *Tanna de-Vei Eliyahu,* ed. M. Friedmann (Vienna: 1902, 1904), 27ff.

31. Scholem, *Ursprung,* 219–273.

32. Scholem, *Ursprung,* 47–54.

33. Scholem, *Ursprung,* 59–159; Dan, *Scholem,* 127–146.

34. See H. H. Ben Sasson, Rabbi Mosheh ben Nahman: Ish be-Sivkhei

Tequfato, *Molad* (n.s.), no. 1 (1967), 360–366; Scholem. *Ursprung,* 360–365, 396–401.

35. M. H. Levine, *Falaquera's Book of the Seeker* (New York: Yeshiva University, 1976), 8.

36. On the Barcelona Disputation, see O. S. Rankin, *Jewish Religious Polemic* (Edinburgh: Edinburgh University Press, 1956), 157–176; M. A. Cohen, Reflections on the text and context of the disputation of Barcelona, *Hebrew Union College Annual* 35(1964), 157–192.

37. Scholem, *Major Trends,* 156–204; J. Dan, *Scholem,* 203–229.

38. Isaiah Tishby, *Mishnat ha-Zohar* (Jerusalem: Bialik Institute, 1957), 1:29ff.

CHAPTER THREE

1. Rudolf Otto, *The Idea of the Holy* (London: Oxford University Press, 1923), 25ff.

2. Gershom Scholem, *Major Trends in Jewish Mysticism* (New York: Schocken, 1941), 7. For a critique of Scholem's philosophy of Jewish history, see Schweid, *Judaism and Mysticism,* 25–27, 61–68.

3. Gen. 3:8.

4. Gen. 18:24–33.

5. Exod. 3:5.

6. Exod. 3:13.

7. Exod. 20:16–25.

8. *Pesikta de-Rav Kahana,* ed. Mandelbaum (New York, 1962), 3. Quoted in E. Urbach, *The Sages* (Jerusalem: Magnes Press, 1975), 1:52.

9. Found in standard editions of the *Musaf Amidah* for festivals.

10. *Eykhah Rabba,* ed. S. Buber, proem 24, 13a. Quoted in Urbach, 55.

11. *Targum* on Exod. 12:11; 33:14–15, 20; Num. 14:14,42. For a history of the concept, see Scholem, *Pirkei Yesod be-Havanat ha-Kabbalah u-Semaleha* (Jerusalem: Bialik Institute, 1976), 259–307.

12. *Midrash Tehillim,* ed. S. Buber, 14:1, 121. Quoted in Urbach, 29.

13. B. T. *Baba Metzia* 59b.

14. B. T. *Sota* 14a.

15. *M. Avot* 3:2.

16. Urbach, 38–39.

CHAPTER FOUR

1. See Jacob Neusner, *First Century Judaism in Crisis* (Nashville: Abingdon Press, 1975), 34ff. For a more complete analysis of the Pharisees and Sadducees, see M. Stone, Jewish Writings . . . 23–24, 27–31.

2. Neusner, *Understanding Rabbinic Judaism* (New York: Ktav, 1974), 13ff.

3. Neusner, *Rabbinic Judaism,* 165ff.

4. Daniel Jeremy Silver, *Maimonidean Criticism and the Maimonidean Controversy* (Leiden: E. J. Brill, 1965); A Shohat, Beirurim be-Parashat ha-Pulmus ha-Rishon al Sifrei ha-Rambam, *Zion* 36 (1971), 27–60; Y. Shatzmiller, Le-Temunat ha-Mahloqet ha-Rishonah al Kitbhei ha-Rambam, *Zion* 34 (1969), 126–144.

5. Moses Maimonides, *Guide of the Perplexed,* trans. S. Pines (Chicago: University of Chicago, 1963), II:13–31, III:17–7.

6. Maimonides, I:71ff.

7. Maimonides, I:50–61.

8. Maimonides, *Hilkhot Teshuvah* 3:7.

9. RABaD on *Hilkhot Teshuva* 3:7.

10. B. T. *Yevamot* 71a. Quoted in Maimonides, I:26.

11. The passage appears in A. Habermann's *Shirei ha-Yihud ve-ha-Kavod* (Jerusalem, 1948), 173. See also my unpublished diss., *Shem Tob ibn Shem Tob's kabbalistic critique of Jewish philosophy in the commentary on the Sefirot* (Waltham: Brandeis University, 1981), 58f.

12. *Sefer Maarekhet ha-Elohut* (Mantua, 1558), 82b.

13. Exod. 19:18.

14. *Sefer ha-Zohar* II:239a. Tishby, *Mishnat ha-Zohar* (Jerusalem: Bialik Institute, 1957).

15. *Sefer ha-Zohar* I:22b. Tishby, 1:119–120.

16. Azriel of Gerona, *Shaar ha-Shoel* (known as *Perush Eser Sefirot*). Printed in Meir ibn Gabbai, *Sefer Derekh Emunah* (Warsaw, 1890), 3.

CHAPTER FIVE

1. *Sefer Maarekhet ha-Elohut,* 5a–6a.

2. This view was introduced by Menahem Rekanati, a fourteenth-century Italian Kabbalist. See R. J. Zvi Werblowsky, *Karo: Lawyer and Mystic* (Philadelphia: Jewish Publication Society, 1977), 200ff.

3. *Zohar* II:42b–43a; Tishby, *Mishnat ha-Zohar* 1:126–127.

4. I Chron. 29:11.

5. Quoted in Shlomo (Mordechai) Elishov, *Sefer Hakdamot u-Shearim* (Pietra-kov, 1904), 3a–4b.

6. *Zohar* I:65a; Tishby, 1:176–177.

7. A. Jellinek, *Beiträge zur Geshichte der Kabbala II* (Leipsig, 1852), 12–13.

8. Quoted in David S. Ariel, *Shem Tob ibn Shem Tob's kabbalistic critique of Jewish philosophy . . . 49, lines 7–11 (Hebrew section)*.

9. Nahmanides, *Commentary on Sefer Yetzirah, in* Gershom Scholem, Perakim me-toledot sifrut ha-Kabbalah, *Kiryat Sefer* 6 (1929–1930), 402–403.

10. Prov. 8:22.

11. *Bereshit Rabba* 1:1.

12. *Zohar* I:15a–b; Tishby, 1:163f. The translation is by Daniel C. Matt, *Zohar, The Book of Enlightenment,* (Ramsey, NJ: Paulist Press, 1983), 49–50.

13. *Tikkunei Zohar,* introduction.

CHAPTER SIX

1. Exod. 25:8. For many of the sources in this chapter, see E. Urbach, *The Sages,* 37–65; Gershom Scholem, *Pirkei Yesod be-Havanat ha-Kabbalah u-Semaleha* (Jerusalem: Bialik Institute, 1976), 259–307; and Isaiah Tishby, *Mishnat ha-Zohar* 1:219–265.

2. B. T. *Sota* 14a.

3. *M. Avot* 3:2.

4. *Mekhilta de-Rabbi Yishmael,* ed. Horowitz (Frankfurt, 1931), *Massekhta de-Pisha* 14, 51–52. Quoted in Urbach, 43.

5. *Mekhilta, Massekhta de-ba-Hodesh* 6, 238. Quoted in Urbach, 43.

6. *Pesikta de-Rav Kahana,* ed. Mandelbaum (New York, 1962), *Vayehi,* 4. Quoted in Urbach, 51.

7. B. T. *Sanhedrin* 39a. Quoted in Urbach, p. 48.

8. *Das Buch Bahir,* ed. G. Scholem (Leipsig: W. Drugulin, 1923); no. 36.

9. *Bahir,* no. 43.

10. *Bahir,* no. 90.

11. *Bahir,* no. 90.

12. *Zohar* III:290a; Tishby, 1:191.

13. *Zohar* III:17a; Tishby, 1:252.

14. *Zohar* III:290a; Tishby, 1:191.

15. *Zohar* III:81a. Quoted in G. Scholem, *Zohar, The Book of Splendor* (New York: Schocken Books, 1963), 115–116.

16. Deut. 6:4.

17. *Zohar* II:133b–134a; Tishby, 2:312–315.

18. *Zohar* III:6a. Quoted in Scholem, 110.

19. B. T. *Shabbat* 119a.

CHAPTER SEVEN

1. Nahmanides, *Commentary on Sefer Yetzirah*. In Gershom Scholem, Perakim me-toledot sifrut ha-Kabbalah, *Kiryat Sefer* 6 (1929–1930), 402–403.

2. Ps. 19:2.

3. *Sefer Yetzirah* (Jerusalem, 1965), ch. 1, 2.

4. *Bereshit Rabbah* 1:4.

5. Prov. 8:22.

6. *Bereshit Rabbah* 1:1.

7. Gershom Scholem, The name of God and the linguistic theory of the Kabbala, *Diogenes* 79 (1972): 59–80; 80 (1972): 164–194.

8. Nahmanides, *Perush al ha-Torah*, ed. C. D. Chavel (Jerusalem: Mossad Kook, 1959), introduction.

9. See H. A. Wolfson, *Religious Philosophy* (Cambridge: Harvard, 1961), 217–245.

10. Maimonides, *Guide*, II:30.

11. Scholem, *Kitvei Yad ba-Kabbalah* (Jerusalem, 1930), 208–213.

12. Gen. 24:12.

13. *Zohar* III:152a. Translation by Daniel Matt, *Zohar: The Book of Enlightenment* (New York: Paulist Press, 1983), 43–45. For other translations of Zohar, see Gershom Scholem, *Zohar, The Book of Splendor: Basic Readings from the Kabbalah* (New York: Schocken, 1963); Harry Sperling, and Maurice Simon, trans., *The Zohar*, 5 vols. (London: Soncino Press, 1931–1934).

CHAPTER EIGHT

1. E. Urbach, *The Sages* (Jerusalem: Magnes Press, 1975), 1: 214.

2. Gen. 2:7. Quoted in Urbach, 214.

3. I Kings 19:10. Quoted in Urbach, 215.

4. Exod. 23:9. Quoted in Urbach, 215.

5. Urbach, 214.

6. Job 12:10. Quoted in Urbach, 215.

7. *Sifre (A Tannaitic Commentary on the Book of Deuteronomy)*, ed. Reuven Hammer (New Haven: Yale, 1986), no. 306, 307; Quoted in Urbach, 220–221.

8. Aristotle, *On the Soul* 2:2.

9. *Zohar Hadash*, Bereshit 18b.

10. *Zohar Hadash*, Midrash Ruth 38c; Tishby, *Mishnat ha-Zohar* 2:50–51.

11. *Sefer ha-Zohar* I:83a–b; Tishby, 2:51–52.

12. *Zohar* I:83a–b.

13. *Zohar* I:62a.

14. *Zohar Hadash*, Bereshit, 27b–28a; Tishby, 2:96–98.

15. *Zohar* I:205b; Tishby, 2:53.

16. *Zohar* III:174b.

17. B. T. *Hagigah* 12b. On differences between this view and rabbinic views see Urbach, 1:237–239.

18. *Zohar* I:85b; Tishby, 2:627.

19. See Plato's *Symposium* f. 189, in *The Dialogues of Plato*, trans. B. Jowett, (New York: Random House, 1937), 2:315–316.

20. *Zohar* I:85b.

21. B. T. *Niddah* 30b. See Urbach, 1:246.

22. *Zohar Hadash*, *Bereshit* 18b; Tishby, 2:44–45.

23. *Zohar* I:235a.

24. *Zohar* I:224b; Quoted in Gershom Scholem *Zohar: The Book of Splendor* (New York: Schocken, 1963), 72–73.

25. *Zohar* I:99b.

26. Gershom Scholem, *Pirkei Yesod be-Havanat ha-Kabbalah u-Semaleha* (Jerusalem: Bialik Institute, 1976), 370–373.

27. Scholem, *Pirkei Yesod,* 375.

28. *Zohar* I:201a; Tishby, 2:154.

29. *Zohar* I:57b; Tishby, 2:159.

30. *Zohar* I:78b; Tishby, 2:160.

31. *Zohar* I:218b.

32. *Zohar* III:1 26a–b; Tishby, 2:162–163.

33. See Scholem, *Pirkei Yesod*, 308–357.

34. *M. Keritot* 1:1.

35. Scholem, *Pirkei Yesod*, 319–320.

36. Scholem, *Pirkei Yesod*, 334.

37. See C. D. Chavel, *Kitvei Ramban*, 2:281.

38. *Zohar Hadash*, Bereshit 33b; Tishby, 2:170.

CHAPTER NINE

1. Efraim Gottlieb, *Studies in Kabbalistic Literature* (Tel Aviv: Tel Aviv University Press, 1976), 38ff.

2. Gershom Scholem, *Ha-Kabbalah be-Provence* (Jerusalem: Hebrew University, 1970), appendix.

3. Tishby, *Mishnat ha-Zohar* 2:292.

4. Gottlieb, 45.

5. B. T. *Berakhot* 13a.

6. *Zohar* II:57a; Tishby, 2:340–341.

7. *Zohar* II:57a.

8. *Tikkunei Zohar* 21; Tishby, 2:342.

9. *Zohar* II:215b.

10. *Zohar* III:294a–b.

11. B. T. *Berakhot* 21b.

12. Num. 14:27.

13. B. T. *Berakhot* 6a.

14. *Zohar* III:126a; Tishby, 2:308–309.

15. B. T. *Berakhot* 26a.

16. *Zohar* II:59b; Tishby, 2:307–308.

17. *Zohar* II:59b–60a; II:237b.

18. *Zohar* I:234; Yissakhar Baer of Prague, *Sefer Yesh Sakhar* (Warsaw, 1901), 13a.

19. B. T. *Makkot* 24a.

20. *Zohar* II:119a.

21. *Midrash Shemot Rabbah*, ed. A. Halevy (Tel Aviv: Mahbarot la-Sifrut, 1959), 25:12.

22. B. T. *Shabbat* 119a.

23. *Tikkunei Zohar* 6.
24. *Zohar* II:135a–b; Tishby, 2:335.
25. B. T. *Betzah* 16a.
26. *Zohar* II:205a.
27. Scholem, *Pirkei Yesod,* 135ff.
28. *Zohar* III:272b; See also *Yesh Sakhar,* 50.
29. Gen. 2:1–3.
30. B. T. *Hullin* 105a.
31. *Zohar* I:53b; See Jacob Katz, *Halakhah ve-Kabbalah* (Jerusalem: Magnes, 1984), 44.
32. Exod. 16:22–26.
33. *Zohar* II:168b, 153b; *Yesh Sakhar* 21a.
34. B. T. *Berakhot* 53b.
35. *Zohar* III:272b.
36. *Zohar* II:154b; *Yesh Sakhar* 22a.
37. *Zohar* II:168b.
38. B. T. *Sota* 38b.
39. Prov. 31:10–31.
40. *Zohar* I:257a.
41. B. T. *Rosh ha-Shanah* 16b.
42. *Yesh Sakhar* 34a.
43. *Zohar* III:231a; Tishby, 2:550.
44. Gen. 24:12.
45. Gen. 31:42.
46. Gen. 21.
47. Gen. 22.
48. *Zohar* III:214b.
49. Lev. 16:30–31.
50. *M. Yoma* 8:1.
51. *Seder Olam Rabbah* 6.
52. Exod. 3:5.
53. Exod. 19:14–15.
54. Exod. 20:18.
55. *M. Yoma* 1–7.
56. *Zohar* III:214b.

57. *Zohar* III:69a.

58. *Zohar* III:103b.

59. *Yesh Sakhar* 39b.

60. *Zohar* I:220a–221a.

61. *Zohar* III:214b.

62. Exod. 34:25.

63. Exod. 12:15.

64. Exod. 12:1–28.

65. Nahmanides on Exod. 23:17.

66. Shlomo ha-Levi Alkabetz, *Brit ha-Levi* (Jerusalem, 1970), 20a.

67. *Brit ha-Levi,* 19a; based on *Bereshit Rabba* 9:7.

68. *Shemot Rabba* 2:4.

69. *Zohar* I:8a.

CHAPTER TEN

1. Simon Dubnow. *History of the Jews of Russia and Poland* (New York: Ktav, 1975).

2. *M. Sota* 9:15.

3. See G. Scholem, *Major Trends,* 244–286. For further studies on the mysticism of Safed, see Lawrence Fine, *Safed Spirituality: Rules of Mystical Piety, The Beginning of Wisdom* (Ramsey, NJ: Paulist Press, 1984); Solomon Schechter, Safed in the sixteenth century, in *Studies in Judaism* (Philadelphia: Jewish Publication Society, 1908).

4. Hayyim Vitale, *Sefer Etz Hayyim* (Jerusalem, 1910), 11b.

5. Vitale, 11b.

6. Vitale, 11b.

7. Vitale, 11b.

8. Vitale, 11b.

9. Vitale, 11b.

10. Vitale, 11b.

11. Vitale, 12a.

12. Vitale, 13a.

13. Vitale, 13a.

14. For a complete biography of this figure, see Gershom Scholem, *Sabbatai Sevi* (Princeton: Bollingen, 1973).

15. *Sefer Tzevaat ha-Rivash* (Jerusalem, 1973), 21. For a full discussion of this issue, see Rivka Schatz, *Ha-Hasidut ke-Mistikah* (Jerusalem: Magnes, 1968), 21–40.

16. *Tzevaat ha-Ribash,* 23–25.

17. Levi Isaac of Berditchev, *Sefer Kedushat Levi* (Jerusalem, 1958), Parashat Pekudei.

18. Hayyim Hayke of Amdur, *Sefer Hayyim va-Hesed* (Jerusalem: 1953), 155. Schatz, 24–25.

19. Meshullam Feibush Heller, *Sefer Derekh Emet* (Jerusalem, 1952), 14.

20. *Derekh Emet,* 14.

21. Yaakov Yosef of Polnoye, *Toledot Yaakov Yosef* (Warsaw: 1841), va-Yakhel.

22. *Sefer Shemuah Tovah* (Warsaw, 1938), 79b. Quoted in Schatz, 29.

23. Gershom Scholem, *The Messianic Idea in Judaism* (New York: Schocken, 1971), 227–250.

24. Martin Buber, *Hasidism and Modern Man* (New York: Harper, 1958), 140.

25. Arthur Green and Barry Holtz, *Your Word is Fire* (Ramsey, NJ: Paulist Press, 1977), 25. For further studies on Hasidism, see Arthur Green, *Tormented Master: A Life of Rabbi Nahman of Bratslav* (New York: Schocken, 1981); Rachel Elior, *Torat ha-Elohut ba-Dor ha-Sheni shel Hasidut HaBaD* (Jerusalem: Magnes Press, 1982).

26. This tale is told in many versions including Martin Buber's *Tales of the Hasidim: The Early Masters* (New York: Schocken, 1947), 69–70.

27. For a contemporary appraisal, see Lis Harris, *Holy Days: The World of a Hasidic Family* (New York: Summit, 1985).

28. See *Abraham Isaac Kook,* trans. Ben Zion Bokser (Ramsey, NJ: Paulist Press, 1978).

29. See Adin Steinsaltz, *The Thirteen Petalled Rose* (New York: Basic Books, 1980).

30. Isaac Bashevis Singer and Ira Moscowitz, *A Little Boy in Search of God* (Garden City, NY: Doubleday, 1976), 43.

31. Ibid., 27.

32. B. T. *Sanhedrin* 65b; Scholem, *Pirkei Yesod,* 388.

33. Scholem, *Pirkei Yesod,* 395.

34. Scholem, *Pirkei Yesod,* 382.

35. Jack Solomon, Jr., *Agam* (New York: Circle Fine Art, 1981), 3.

36. Solomon, *Agam,* 16.

CHAPTER ELEVEN

1. See G. Scholem, *Ursprung,* 369–371; Gershom Scholem, *Monatsschrift fur Geschichte und Wissenschaft des Judentums* 78 (1934), 511–512.

2. Yaakov Yosef of Polnoye, *Ben Porat Yosef* (1781), appendix.

3. The first known Yiddish book is the *Bovo Buch* of Elija Levita of Nürenberg (sixteenth century), which retells an earlier romantic epic concerning Sir Bevis (Bovo) and Druzane. This rhymed poem became known as the "Bovo Mayse" (the Bevis legend). It was corrupted as "bubbe mayse" (grandmother's tale) even though it had a different primary meaning.

4. Norman Hampson, *The Enlightenment* (London: Penguin, 1968), 103.

5. Hampson, *Enlightenment,* 105.

6. See Paul Davies, *God and the New Physics* (New York: Simon & Schuster, 1983), 1–8.

7. Arthur Deikman, Deautomatization and the mystic experience, in *The Nature of Human Consciousness,* ed. Robert E. Ornstein (San Francisco: W. H. Freeman, 1973), 216–233.

8. Freud, *Standard Edition,* 21:64–73.

9. Erich Neumann, Mystical man, in *The Mystic Vision: Papers from the Eranos Yearbooks,* ed. Joseph Campbell (Princeton: Princeton University Press, 1968).

GLOSSARY

Absorptive mysticism: Type of mysticism in which the mystic becomes undifferentiated and absorbed in the object of his quest.

Acosmic mysticism: World-denying mysticism.

Aliyat ha-neshamah: Ascension of the soul to heaven.

Anthropomorphisms: Descriptions of God in bodily terms.

Anthropopathisms: Descriptions of God as having human feelings and emotions.

Attentional Meditation: Restful visualization of and attention to the sequence of ideas and images that enter consciousness.

Atzilut (emanation): Hypertrophy or overflow of divine essence from *Eyn Sof.*

Binah (understanding): Third *Sefirah.*

Bittul ha-yesh: Annihilation of conscious existence.

Deautomatization: Purposely contrived effort to ensure hypnotic and other trance-like stances.

Devekut: Mystical union with the *Sefirot.*

Din (judgment): Fifth *Sefirah.*

Essentialists: Kabbalists who believe that the *Sefirot* are God's essence.

Eyn Sof: Infinite aspect of God.

Gashmiyyut: Corporeality.

Gedulah (greatness); also *Hesed* (mercy):   Fourth *Sefirah*.

Gematria: System of numerical value assigned to each Hebrew letter.

Gilgul: Transmigration of souls, reincarnation.

Gevurah (might); also *Din* (judgment):   Fifth *Sefirah*.

Golem: Homonculus, robot made from soil.

Hesed (mercy):   Fourth *Sefirah*.

Hod (majesty):   Eighth *Sefirah*.

Hokhmah (wisdom):   Second *Sefirah*.

Ibbur: The state in which a guardian or attendant soul of one person attaches to another person.

Kavvanah: Intention or mystical concentration.

Instrumentalists: Kabbalists who believe that the *Sefirot* are the vessels through which God acts.

Kabbalah: Medieval Jewish mystical movement.

Keter (crown):   First *Sefirah*.

Malkhut (kingship); also *Shekhinah*:   Tenth *Sefirah*.

Meshikhah (drawing down):   Concentration of the power of a *Sefirah* upon the soul.

Mishnah: Earliest code of Jewish law (c. 200 C.E.).

Mitzvot: Jewish rituals and commandments.

Nefesh: Life, the lowest grade of soul.

Neshamah: Soul, highest grade of soul.

Netzah (triumph):   Seventh *Sefirah*.

Noetic: An element of insight, knowledge, intuition, or revelation.

Nonabsorptive mysticism: Type of mysticism in which the mystic remains differentiated from the object of this quest.

Oceanic feeling: A sense that the mystic is undifferentiated from the rest of reality.

Pantheism: Type of mysticism in which God is perceived to be indistinguishable from nature (nature mysticism).

Penetration mysticism: Inner voyage centered within the consciousness of the mystic.

Ruah: Breath, middle grade of soul.

Ruhaniyyut: Spirituality.

Sefirot ("Calculi"): Ten aspects of God's unknowable being (sing. *Sefirah*).

Shekhinah: Literally "presence of God;" in Kabbalah, the feminine aspect of God.

Shevirah: The destruction of the harmony of the divine world.

Talmud: Body of Jewish law, lore, philosophy, and ethics compiled between 200 and 500 C.E. in Palestine and Babylonia.

Theism: God as a being, separate and distinct from world.

Tiferet (splendor): Sixth *Sefirah*.

Tikkun: The repair of the shattered world of God.

Tikkunim: Purposeful ritual actions or restorative acts.

Torah: The Five Books of Moses (Genesis, Exodus, Leviticus, Numbers, Deuteronomy). Also Torah she-be-khtav.

Torah she-be-al peh: The orally transmitted body of Jewish religious precepts.

Transportation mysticism: The subject experiences his whole being traveling on a celestial journey.

Tzelem: Astral body.

Tzimtzum: Self-contraction of God.

Yesod (foundation): Ninth *Sefirah*.

YHVH: The Tetragrammaton, traditional four-letter name of God pronounced *Adonai*.

Yihhud (unity): Unification among the *Sefirot*.

Zivvug (union): Union of human soul and *Shekhinah*.

BIBLIOGRAPHY

Aboth de-Rabbi Nathan (1887). Ed. S. Schechter, Vienna.

Abraham Isaac Kook (1978). *The Lights of Penitence, The Moral Principles, Lights of Holiness, Essays, Letters and Poems* (1978). Trans. and ed. B. Z. Bokser New York: Paulist Press.

Alkabetz, Shlomo ha-Levi (1970). *Brit ha-Levi.* Jerusalem.

Ariel, D. (1981). *Shem Tob ibn Shem Tob's Kabbalistic Critique of Jewish Philosophy in the Commentary on the Sefirot.* Ph.D. dissertation, Waltham: Brandeis University.

——— (1985). The Eastern dawn of wisdom: the problem of the relation between Islamic and Jewish mysticism. In *Approaches to Judaism in Medieval Times,* ed. D. Blumenthal, pp. 149–167. Chico, CA: Scholars Press.

Aristotle (1975). *On the Soul. Parva naturalia. On Breath.* Trans. W. S. Hett, Cambridge: Harvard University Press.

Babylonian Talmud (1886). Vilna: Romm.

Ben-Sasson, H. H. (1967). Rabbi Mosheh ben Nahman: Ish be-Sivkhei Tekufato. *Molad* (N.S.) 1:360–368.

Biale, D. (1978). *Gershom Scholem: Kabbalah and Counter-History.* Cambridge: Harvard University Press.

Buber, M. (1947). *Tales of the Hasidim: The Early Masters.* New York: Schocken.

——— (1958). *Hasidism and Modern Man.* New York: Harper.

Bucke, R. M. (1901). *Cosmic Consciousness.* Philadelphia.

Campbell, J. (1976). *The Masks of God: Occidental Mythology.* New York: Penguin.

Cohen, M. A. (1964). Reflections on the text and context of the disputation of Barcelona. *Hebrew Union College Annual* 35: 157–192.

Dan, J. (1968). *Torat ha-Sod shel Hasidei Ashkenaz.* Jerusalem: Bialik Institute.

——— (1987). *Gershom Scholem and the Mystical Dimension of Jewish History.* New York: New York University Press.

Dan, J., and Kiener, R. (1986). *The Early Kabbalah.* Ramsey, NJ: Paulist Press.

Davies, P. (1983). *God and the New Physics.* New York: Simon & Schuster.

Deikman, A. (1973). Deautomatization and the mystic experience. In *The Nature of Human Consciousness,* ed. R. E. Ornstein, pp. 216–233. San Francisco: W. H. Freeman.

Dubnow, S. (1975). *History of the Jews of Russia and Poland.* New York: Ktav.

Elior, R. (1982). *Torat ha-Elohut ba-Dor ha-Sheni shel Hasidut HaBaD.* Jerusalem: Magnes Press.

Elishov, S. (1904). *Sefer Hakdamot u-Shearim.* Pietrakov.

Fine, L. (1984). *Safed Spirituality: Rules of Mystical Piety, The Beginning of Wisdom.* Ramsey, NJ: Paulist Press.

Freud, S. (1961). Civilization and its discontents. *Standard Edition 21.*

Gafni, I. (1984). The historical background. In *Jewish Writings of the Second Temple Period,* ed. M. Stone, Philadelphia: Fortress Press.

Gottlieb, E. (1976). *Studies in Kabbalistic Literature.* Tel Aviv: Tel Aviv University Press.

Green, A. (1981). *Tormented Master: A Life of Rabbi Nahman of Bratslav.* New York: Schocken.

Green, A., and Holtz, B. (1977). *Your Word is Fire.* Ramsey, NJ: Leiden: E. J. Brill.

Gruenwald, I. (1980). *Apocalyptic and Merkavah Mysticism.* Leiden: E. J. Brill.

Habermann, A. (1948). *Shirei ha-Yihud ve-ha-Kavod.* Jerusalem: Mossad Harav Kook.

Halperin, D. J. (1980). *The Merkabah in Rabbinic Literature.* New Haven: American Oriental Society.

Hammer, R. (1986). *Sifre: A Tannaitic Commentary on the Book of Deuteronomy.* New Haven: Yale University Press.

Hampson, N. (1968). *The Enlightenment.* New York: Penguin.

Harris, L. (1985). *Holy Days: The World of a Hasidic Family.* New York: Summit.

Hayyim Hayke of Amdur (1953). *Sefer Hayyim va-Hesed.* Jerusalem.

Heller, Meshullam Feibusch me-Zborocz (1952). *Sefer Derekh Emet.* Jerusalem.

Heschel, A. J. (1966). The mystical element in Judaism. In *The Jews: Their History, Culture and Religion,* vol. 2, ed. L. Finkelstein, 3rd ed., pp. 932–951. Philadelphia: Jewish Publication Society.

Idel, M. (1988). *Kabbalah: New Perspectives.* New Haven: Yale University Press.

Ibn Gabbai, Meir (1890). *Sefer Derekh Emunah.* Warsaw.

Inge, W. R. (1947). *Mysticism in Religion.* London.

Jacobs, L. (1977). *Jewish Mystical Testimonies.* New York: Schocken.

James, W. (1960). *The Varieties of Religious Experience.* London: Fontana Library.

Jellinek, A. (1852). *Beiträge zur Geschichte der Kabbala.* 2 vols. Leipsig: C. L. Firtzche.

Jerusalem Talmud (1948). New York: Shulsinger.

Katz, J. (1984). *Halakhah ve-Kabbalah.* Jerusalem: Magnes Press.

Katz, S. T. (1978). Language, epistemology and mysticism. In *Mysticism and Philosophical Analysis,* ed. S. T. Katz. New York: Oxford University Press, pp. 22–74.

Levi Isaac of Berditchev (1958). *Sefer Kedushat Levi.* Jerusalem.

Levine, M. H. (1976). *Falaquera's Book of the Seeker.* New York: Yeshiva University Press.

Lewin, B. (1928–1962). *Otzar ha-Geonim.* 13 vols. Haifa.

Maimonides (1958). *Mishneh Torah,* 14 vols. Jerusalem: Mossad Harav Kook.

——— (1963). *Guide of the Perplexed.* Trans. S. Pines. Chicago: University of Chicago Press.

Marcus, I. (1981). *Piety and Society: The Jewish Pietists of Medieval Germany.* Leiden: E. J. Brill.

Mekhilta de-Rabbi Yishmael (1931). Ed. Horowitz. Frankfurt.

Midrash Bereshit Rabba (1965). Ed. J. Theodor and H. Albeck. 3 vols. Jerusalem: Wahrmann.

Midrash Shemot Rabbah (1959). Ed. A. Halevy. Tel Aviv: Mahbarot la-Sifrut.

Midrash Tanhuma (1885). Ed. S. Buber, Vilna.

Mikraot Gedolot: Torah (1958–1959). 2 vols. Jerusalem: Schocken.

Nahmanides (1959). *Perush al ha-Torah.* Ed. C. D. Chavel. 2 vols. Jerusalem: Mossad Harav Kook.

——— (1963–1964). *Kitvei Ramban.* Ed. C. D. Chavel. 2 vols. Jerusalem: Mossad Harav Kook.

Neumann, Erich (1968). The mystic man. In *The Mystic Vision: Papers from the Eranos Yearbook.* ed. Joseph Cambell. Princeton: Princeton University Press

Neusner, J. (1974). *Understanding Rabbinic Judaism.* New York: Ktav.

——— (1975). *First Century Judaism in Crisis.* Nashville: Abingdon Press.

The New Testament: an American Translation (1948). Ed. E. J. Goodspeed. Chicago: University of Chicago Press.

Otto, R. (1923). *The Idea of the Holy.* London: Oxford University Press.

——— (1932). *Mysticism East and West.* New York: Macmillan.

Parrinder, G. (1976). *Mysticism in the World's Religions,* New York: Oxford University Press.

Pesikta de-Rav Kahana (1962). Ed. B. Mandelbaum. 2 vols. New York.

Plato (1937). Symposium. In *The Dialogues of Plato*, vol. 2, trans. B. Jowett, pp. 315–316. New York: Random House.

Rankin, O. S. (1956). *Jewish Religious Polemic*. Edinburgh: Edinburgh University Press.

Schatz, R. (1968). *Ha-Hasidut ke-Mistikah*. Jerusalem: Magnes Press.

Schechter, S. (1908). Safed in the sixteenth century. In *Studies in Judaism*. Philadelphia: Jewish Publication Society.

Scholem, G. (1923). *Das Buch Bahir*. Leipsig: W. Drugulin.

_____ (1929–1930) Perakim me-toledot sifrut ha-Kabbalah. *Kiryat Sefer* 6:402–403.

_____ (1930). *Kitvei Yad ba-Kabbalah*. Jerusalem: Hebrew University Press.

_____ (1941). Major Trends in Jewish Mysticism. New York: Schocken.

_____ (1960). *Jewish Gnosticism, Merkabah Mysticism and Talmudic Tradition*. New York: Jewish Theological Seminary.

_____ (1962). *Ursprung und Anfange der Kabbala*. Berlin: Walter de Gruyter.

_____ (1963). *Zohar: The Book of Splendor*. New York: Schocken.

_____ (1965). *On the Kabbalah and Its Symbolism*. New York: Schocken.

_____ (1970). *Ha-Kabbalah be-Provence*. Jerusalem: Hebrew University.

_____ (1971). *The Messianic Idea in Judaism*. New York: Schocken.

_____ (1972). The name of God and the linguistic theory of the Kabbalah. In *Diogenes* 79: 59–80; 80:164–194.

_____ (1973). *Sabbatai Sevi*. Princeton: Bollingen.

_____ (1976). *Pirkei Yesod be-Havanat ha-Kabbah u-Semaleha*. Jerusalem: Bialik Institute.

_____ (1987). *Origins of the Kabbalah*. Philadelphia: Jewish Publication Society.

Schweid, E. (1985). *Judaism and Mysticism According to Gershom Scholem*. Atlanta: Scholars Press.

Seder Olam Rabbah (1897). Ed. Ratner, Vilna.

Sefer Maarekhet ha-Elohut (1558). Mantua.

Sefer Tzevaat ha-Ribash (1973). Jerusalem.

Sefer Shemuah Tovah (1938). Warsaw.

Sefer Yetzirah (1965). Jerusalem.

Sefer ha-Zohar (1970). Jerusalem: Mossad Harav Kook.

Shatzmiller, Y. (1969). Le-Temunat ha-Mahloqet ha-Rishonah al Kitvei ha-Rambam. *Zion* 34:126–144.

Shishah Sidrei Mishnah (1952–1956). Ed. H. Albeck and H. Yalon. 6 vols. Jerusalem: Bialik Institute.

Shohat, A. (1971). Beirurim be-Parashat ha-Pulmus ha-Rishon al Sifrei ha-Rambam. *Zion* 36:27–60.

Silver, D. J. (1965). *Maimonidean Criticism and the Maimonidean Controversy.* Leiden: E. J. Brill.

Singer, I. B., and Moskowitz, I. (1976). *A Little Boy in Search of God: Mysticism in a Personal Light.* Garden City, NY: Doubleday.

Solomon, J. (1981). *Agam.* New York: Circle Fine Art Books.

Sperling, H., and Simon, M. (1931–1934). *The Zohar.* London: Soncino Press.

Stace, W. T. (1960). *Mysticism and Philosophy.* Philadelphia: Lippincott.

Steinsaltz, A. (1980). *The Thirteen-Petalled Rose.* New York: Basic Books.

Strauss (Ashtor), E. (1944). *Toledot ha-Yehudim ba-Mitzrayim ve-Suriah Tahat Shilton ha-Mamelukim.* 2 vols. Jerusalem.

Tanakh: A New Translation of the Holy Scriptures According to the Traditional Hebrew Text (1985). Philadelphia: Jewish Publication Society.

Tanna de-Vei Eliyahu (Seder Eliahu Rabba and Seder Eliahu Zuta and *Pseudo-Seder Eliahu Zuta)* (1902, 1904). Ed. M. Friedmann, Vienna.

Tikkunei Zohar (1558). Mantua.

Tishby, I. (1957–1961). *Mishnat ha-Zohar.* 2 vols. Jerusalem: Bialik Institute.

Twersky, I. (1969). Aspects of the social and cultural history of Provencal Jewry. In *Jewish Society Through the Ages,* ed. H. H. Ben-Sasson and S. Ettinger, pp. 185–207. New York: Schocken.

Urbach, E. E. (1975). *The Sages.* 2 vols. Jerusalem: Magnes Press.

Vitale, H. (1910). *Sefer Etz Hayyim.* Jerusalem.

Werblowsky, R. J. Z. (1977). *Karo: Lawyer and Mystic.* Philadelphia: Jewish Publication Society.

Wolfson, H. A. (1961). *Religious Philosophy.* Cambridge, MA: Harvard University Press.

Yaakov Yosef of Polnoye (1781). *Ben Porat Yosef.*

——— (1841). *Toledot Yaakov Yosef.* Warsaw.

Yissakhar Baer of Prague (1901). *Sefer Yesh Sakhar.* Warsaw.

Zaehner, R. C. (1957). *Mysticism Sacred and Profane.* London: Clarendon Press.

Zohar: The Book of Enlightenment (1983). Trans. D. Matt. Ramsey, NJ: Paulist Press.

Zohar Hadash (1658). Venice.

INDEX